Grover Cleveland
A BIBLIOGRAPHY

Meckler's Bibliographies of the Presidents of the United States

Series Editor: Carol Bondhus Fitzgerald

1. George Washington
2. John Adams
3. Thomas Jefferson
4. James Madison
5. James Monroe
6. John Quincy Adams
7. Andrew Jackson
8. Martin Van Buren
9. William Henry Harrison
10. John Tyler
11. James Knox Polk
12. Zachary Taylor
13. Millard Fillmore
14. Franklin Pierce
15. James Buchanan
16. Abraham Lincoln
17. Andrew Johnson
18. Ulysses S. Grant
19. Rutherford B. Hayes
20. James A. Garfield

21. Chester A. Arthur
22. Grover Cleveland
23. Benjamin Harrison
24. William McKinley
25. Theodore Roosevelt
26. William Howard Taft
27. Woodrow Wilson
28. Warren G. Harding
29. Calvin Coolidge
30. Herbert C. Hoover
31. Franklin D. Roosevelt
32. Harry S. Truman
33. Dwight D. Eisenhower
34. John F. Kennedy
35. Lyndon B. Johnson
36. Richard M. Nixon
37. Gerald R. Ford
38. Jimmy Carter
39. Ronald Reagan
40. President Elected 1988

Grover Cleveland
A BIBLIOGRAPHY

John F. Marszalek

Library of Congress Cataloging-in-Publication Data

Marszalek, John F., 1939-
  Grover Cleveland : a bibliography / by John F. Marszalek.
    p. cm. -- (Meckler's bibliographies of the presidents of the
  United States ; no. 22)
    Bibliography: p.
    Includes index.
    ISBN 0-88736-136-6 (alk. paper)
    1. Cleveland, Grover, 1837-1908--Bibliography. 2. United States --
  Politics and government--1885-1889--Bibliography. 3. United States--
  Politics and government--1893-1897--Bibliography.
  I. Title. II. Series.
  Z8176.45.M37 1988
  [E697]
  016.9738'7'0924   88-9096
                                                                    CIP

British Library Cataloguing in Publication Data

Marszalek, John
  Grover Cleveland : a bibliography. —
  (Meckler's bibliographies of the Presidents
  of the United States, 1789-1989; no. 22).
  1. United States. Cleveland, Grover -
  Bibliographies
  I. Title
  016.9738'5'0924

  ISBN 0-88736-136-6

Meckler Corporation, 11 Ferry Lane West, Westport, CT 06880.
Meckler Ltd., Grosvenor Gardens House, Grosvenor Gardens,
    London SW1W 0BS.

Printed on acid free paper.
Manufactured in the United States of America.

Contents

Foreword

Nothing in the American constitutional order continues to excite so much scholarly interest, debate, and controversy as the role of the presidency. This remains the case in spite of the complaint, so common in the historical profession a generation ago, about the tyranny of "the presidential synthesis" in the writing of American history.

This complaint had its point. It is true enough that the deep currents in social, economic, and intellectual history, in demography, family structure, collective mentalities, flow on without regard to presidential administrations. To deal with these underlying trends, the "new history" began in the 1950s and 1960s to reach out beyond traditional history to anthropology, sociology, psychology, and statistics. For a season social-science history pushed politics and personalities off the historical stage.

But in time social-science history displayed its limitations. It did not turn out to be, as its apostles had promised, a philosopher's—or historian's—stone. "Most of the great problems of history," wrote Lawrence Stone, himself a distinguished practitioner of the new history, "remain as insoluble as ever, if not more so." In particular, the new history had no interest in public policy—the decisions a nation makes through the political process—and proved impotent to explain it. Yet one can reasonably argue that, at least in a democracy, public policy reveals the true meaning of the past, the moods, preoccupations, values, and dreams of a nation, more clearly and trenchantly than almost anything else.

The tide of historical interest is now turning again—from deep currents to events, from underlying trends to decisions. While the history of public policy requires an accounting of the total culture from which national decisions emerge, such history must center in the end on the decisions themselves and on the people who make (and resist) them. Historians today are returning to the insights of classical history—to the recognition that the state, political authority, military power, elections, statutes, wars, the ideas, ambitions, delusions and wills of individuals, make a difference to history.

This is far from a reversion to "great man" theories. But it is a valuable corrective to the assumption, nourished by social-science history, that public policy is merely a passive reflection of underlying historical forces. For the ultimate fascination of history lies precisely in the interplay between the individual and his environment. "It is true," wrote Tocqueville, "that around every man a fatal circle is traced beyond which he cannot pass; but within the wide verge of that circle he is powerful and free; as it is with man, so with communities."

The *Bibliographies of the Presidents* series therefore needs no apology. Public policy is a powerful key to an understanding of the past; and in the United States the presidency is the battleground where issues of public policy are fought out and resolved. The history of American presidents is far from the total history of America. But American history without the presidents would leave the essential part of the story untold.

Recent years have seen a great expansion in the resources available for students of the presidency. The National Historical Publications Commission has done superb work in stimulating and sponsoring editions, both letterpress and microform, of hitherto inaccessible materials. "Documents," as President Kennedy said in 1963, "are the primary sources of history; they are the means by which later generations draw close to historical events and enter into the thoughts, fears and hopes of the past." He saluted the NHPC program as "this great effort to enable the American people to repossess its historical heritage."

At the same time, there has been a rich outpouring of scholarly monographs on presidents, their associates, their problems, and their times. And the social-science challenge to narrative history has had its impact on presidential scholarship. The interdisciplinary approach has raised new questions, developed new methods and uncovered new sources. It has notably extended the historian's methodological arsenal.

This profuse presidential literature has heretofore lacked a guide. The *Bibliographies of the Presidents* series thus fills a great lacuna in American scholarship. It provides comprehensive annotated bibliographies, president by president, covering manuscripts and archives, biographies and monographs, articles and dissertations, government documents and oral histories, libraries, museums, and iconographic resources. The editors are all scholars who have mastered their presidents. The series places the study of American presidents on a solid bibliographical foundation.

In so doing, it will demonstrate the wide sweep of approaches to our presidents, from analysis to anecdotage, from hagiography to vilification. It will illustrate the rise and fall of presidential reputations—fluctuations that often throw as much light on historians as on presidents. It will provide evidence for and against Bryce's famous proposition "Why Great Men Are Not Chosen Presidents." It will remind us that superior men have somehow made it to the White House but also that, as the Supreme Court said in *ex parte Milligan*, the republic has "no right to expect that it will always have wise and humane rulers, sincerely attached to the principles of the Constitution. Wicked men, ambitious of power, with hatred of liberty and contempt of law, may fill the place once occupied by Washington and Lincoln."

Above all, it will show how, and to what degree, the American presidency has been the focus of the concerns, apprehensions and aspirations of the people and the times. The history of the presidency is a history of nobility and of pettiness, of courage and of cunning, of forthrightness and of trickery, of quarrel and of consensus. The turmoil perennially swirling around the White House illuminates the heart of American democracy. The literature reflects the turmoil, and the *Bibliographies of the Presidents* supply at last the light that will enable scholars and citizens to find their way through the literature.

Arthur Schlesinger, Jr.

Editor's Preface

As a central force in government, the presidents of the United States have been both the authors and the subjects of an enormous quantity of literature. However, accessing presidential materials has been a haphazard exercise. Few of the presidents have been the subject of comprehensive monographic bibliographies, and scholars have had to piece together their own bibliographies from catalogs, indexes, and elsewhere.

This bibliographic series seeks to serve contemporary research by organizing the widest possible range of materials. Each president is the subject of a comprehensive, booklength bibliography, compiled by an eminent scholar. The bibliographies itemize and annotate primary resources such as government documents and manuscript collections, monographs, articles, chapters and essays, dissertations and theses, and oral history if available. Each volume follows a uniform format, including a detailed subject index. The study of the individual presidents will be facilitated, and it will also be possible to systematically search topics across presidential administrations. Closer scrutiny of the life and times of each president, whether he is rated a greater or a lesser one, will benefit all presidential scholarship.

Carol Bondhus Fitzgerald

Grover Cleveland. (From the collections of the Library of Congress)

Introduction
and Acknowledgments

The preparation of a bibliography such as this is, at once, an exciting, a tedious, and a fearful task. The excitement comes from the discovery and organization of information and material that, hopefully, will allow later researchers to shed new light on the subject under study. The tedium results from the host of mundane tasks that the preparation of such a work entails. Hanging over all, however, is the dread that, despite all the effort, some old work of importance will be left out or some new classic will be published just when this volume is put to press. Fortunately, Grover Cleveland's dying words have provided some solace: "I have tried so hard to do right."

Grover Cleveland was president during the so-called "Gilded Age," a time often ignored or insulted by historians of United States history. In fact, this era was a time of rapid transformation when American citizens tried to come to grips with the industrialization and urbanization of their society and the resulting changes to their old ways of life. Grover Cleveland's presidency, consisting of two separate terms, filled four years each in two decades: the 1880s and the 1890s. He inhabited the White House longer than any other Gilded Age president and was the nation's chief executive in both of this era's major decades.

Though Cleveland is neither one of the most famous nor was he one of the most effective American presidents, his reputation as the best of the Gilded Age's chief executives has resulted in much historical interest. Many books and articles have been written about him. So have chapters, pages, and sometimes only paragraphs in books and articles on other Gilded Age issues. Information on him is found not only in memoirs and biographies about him and his close associates but also in books, articles, pamphlets, and graduate student dissertations about other Gilded Age topics and the American presidency.

In preparing this bibliography, I attempted to include

material on Grover Cleveland from this wide variety of
sources. I tried to include any sources which in any way
threw some light on this president: an entire book or
article centered on him or only one pertinent line in a book
or article on another Gilded Age topic.
      Anyone undertaking a task such as this is the
beneficiary of a host of historians and librarians who have
come before him. Without the work of such bibliographers as
Grace Gardiner Griffin and such historians as Allan Nevins,
the task of preparing this volume would have been nearly
impossible. The chronological outline of Cleveland's life
in Tim Taylor, The Book of Presidents (1972) was helpful in
preparing the chronology for this bibliography. There are
many more such individuals who helped me without ever
realizing it. Rather than risk leaving someone out, I hope
this mention of just these three people will serve as a
"thank you" to all.
      I tried to make this volume's organization as
straightforward as I could. The Table of Contents lists the
eighteen section headings and the many more sub-headings I
have utilized to organize this material. Most entries do
not fit perfectly under any one heading because they contain
information useful for several aspects of Cleveland's
career. Readers, therefore, should be flexible and
imaginative in their search of the Table of Contents and the
Index.
      Rather than organizing each section or sub-section
strictly alphabetically, I have attempted, instead, to
present the material in order of importance: the most
recent, most significant, most inclusive material first;
the older, less important, less-inclusive material last. A
researcher might, of course, find an article or book listed
last in a section to be the most important source for
his/her needs, but generally such material is not as
comprehensive as that which appears ahead of it. Such a
hierarchical method of listing material allows all
researchers, from the serious to the more casual, to readily
find material which provides the best overall information on
the matter in question.
      An example might be helpful. In Section 1, "Manuscript
and Archival Resources," there is a sub-section entitled
"Published Compilations of Cleveland Manuscripts" which is
further subdivided into "Public" and "Private." In the
"Public" sub-section, the first entry is the major published
compilation of Cleveland's official presidential documents.
This is followed by other published collections of
presidential documents. Next come sources containing
Cleveland's annual messages, then his inaugural addresses,
executive orders, vetoes, messages on particular topics,
and, finally, the published collection of his official
papers as governor of New York. Researchers can scan this
list from the general to the particular to find what they

need more efficiently than if the material were organized
strictly alphabetically.

Some sections are arranged alphabetically, however,
because the hierarchical arrangement is not appropriate.
See, for example, the manuscript collections sub-sections of
Section 1. In a few cases, a section is organized
alphabetically after the most significant work is cited
first. The various sub-sections on campaign biographies are
a good example of this arrangement. Finally, Section 2,
Grover Cleveland's Writings, is organized chronologically.

Many individuals and institutions provided invaluable
help in the preparation of this volume. The libraries that
were combed for pertinent material included: Mitchell
Memorial Library, Mississippi State University; the
libraries of the State Historical Society of Wisconsin and
the University of Wisconsin, Madison; The Buffalo and Erie
County (NY) Public Library and the Buffalo and Erie County
Historical Society; The Library of Congress; The Theodore
M. Hesburgh Library, University of Notre Dame; The
University of Alabama Library; and The Eudora Welty Public
Library, Jackson, Mississippi.

In addition, numerous libraries provided information
through the mail and through inter-library loan. The
Princeton University Library was particularly helpful in
this category. Librarians at all these various libraries,
unfortunately too numerous to mention, were uniformly
helpful, and I owe a great deal to each of them and their
institutions.

Several individuals provided especial support. Jim and
Beverly Sefcik not only provided accommodations and
camaraderie during a research trip, but Jim, at the time
Assistant Director of the State Historical Society of
Wisconsin, now Director of the Louisiana State Museum, New
Orleans, provided professional assistance that was without
peer. Vincent P. DeSantis, Professor-Emeritus, University
of Notre Dame, not only encouraged me to take on this
project but also provided expert advice along the way,
including an evaluation of a final draft. Similarly,
Geoffrey Blodgett, Professor of History, Oberlin College,
like Professor DeSantis a noted Grover Cleveland scholar,
kindly read and extensively commented on the entire
manuscript. Carol Fitzgerald, Series Editor, Anthony
Abbott, Vice President, and Brenda Mitchell-Powell,
Production Manager of Meckler Publishing, skillfully guided
the manuscript to publication. Marcie Rarick, old friend
and Notre Dame librarian, provided important help at key
times when it seemed that the project's time was running
out. Larry and Wendy Held of Herndon, Virginia, provided
their usual fine bed and board during a Washington research
trip, and Sister Rosalie Marie Marszalek, G.N.S.H., helped
search through a Buffalo card catalog. Jamie Marszalek
helped with numbering the entries. J. Gipson Wells,

Professor of Sociology, Mississippi State University, and long-time neighbor and friend, provided access to his printer and advice on how best to format this volume. Charles D. Lowery, Head, History Department and Director of the Institute for the Humanities, Mississippi State University, provided financial support at a crucial time and encouragement all along. Mississippi State University History Department lunch-time colleagues, Elizabeth Nybakken and Clifford G. Ryan, heard more about Grover Cleveland than I'm sure they cared to. I appreciate their patient unflagging interest both in "Grover" and in my William T. Sherman biography project and their many years of friendship and support.

It is customary to thank one's spouse in a book's acknowledgements, but my thanks are hardly proforma. Jeanne Kozmer Marszalek played a major role in the preparation of this volume. She accompanied me on every research trip, labored over card catalogues, searched through countless reference works and guides, and walked up and down innumerable library staircases carrying armfuls of books. She also kept telling me that "it" would indeed get done. Without her research help, love, and encouragement, this volume would not now be completed.

Chronology

<u>March 18, 1837</u>   Stephen Grover Cleveland was born in the manse of the First Presbyterian Church, Caldwell, New Jersey, the third of nine children of the Rev. Richard Falley Cleveland and his wife, Anne Neal Cleveland.

<u>1841</u>   moved with family to Fayetteville, New York.

<u>1851</u>   moved with family to Clinton, New York.

<u>1853</u>   moved with family to Holland Patent, New York.

<u>October 1, 1853</u>   Richard Falley Cleveland died.

<u>1853-1854</u>   was a teacher in the New York Institute for the Blind, New York City.

<u>1855</u>   moved to Black Rock, New York (now part of Buffalo) where his uncle, Lewis F. Allen, hired him as an assistant for the <u>American Shorthorn Handbook.</u>

<u>1855</u>   worked for the firm of Rogers, Bowen, and Rogers where he also began his study of the law.

<u>1859</u>   admitted to the Buffalo Bar.

<u>1859</u>   became managing clerk, Rogers, Bowen, and Rogers.

1863   appointed assistant district attorney of Erie
County.

1865   Lyman K. Bass, a friend and later law partner,
defeated him in the election for district attorney.

1865   formed a law firm with Isaac K. Vanderpoel.

1869   the law firm became Lanning, Cleveland, and Folsom,
when Vanderpoel resigned.

1870   won the election for sheriff of Erie County.

1871   began his three year term as sheriff.

1874   returned to the practice of law in the firm of Bass,
Cleveland, and Bissell.

1881   elected mayor of Buffalo.

January 1, 1882   began his two year term, becoming the
"veto mayor" as he battled corruption in Buffalo public
life.

July 19, 1882   his mother, Anna Neal Cleveland, died.

September 22, 1882   captured the Democratic nomination for
governor of New York.

November 7, 1882   won the gubernatorial election.

January 1, 1883   began his two year term, increasing his
reputation as a no-nonsense opponent of corruption in public
life.

July 11, 1884   gained the Democratic nomination for
president; Thomas A. Hendricks of Indiana was his running
mate.

November 4, 1884   defeated Republican James G. Blaine and
several minor candidates, 219-182 in electoral votes, though
he did not gain a majority of the popular vote.

March 4, 1885   inaugurated as 22nd president of the United
States, the first Democrat since before the Civil War.

March 5, 1885   announced his cabinet: Thomas F. Bayard,
Secretary of State; Daniel Manning, Secretary of the
Treasury; William C. Endicott, Secretary of War; Augustus
H. Garland, Attorney General; William C. Whitney, Secretary
of the Navy; William F. Vilas, Postmaster General; L. Q.
C. Lamar, Secretary of the Interior.

March 13, 1885   withdrew the December 1, 1884
Zavala-Frelinghuysen Nicaraguan canal treaty from the
Senate.

March 13, 1885   issued a presidential proclamation warning
settlers to stay off Oklahoma lands.

April 17, 1885   nullified former president Chester A.
Arthur's executive order opening some Dakota territory
Indian lands to white settlement.

July 23, 1885   issued a presidential proclamation
mandating that cattlemen leave Cheyenne and Arapaho
reservation lands.

November 25, 1885   Vice President Thomas A. Hendricks
died.

December 7, 1885   First session of the 49th Congress met.
The Senate consisted of 41 Republicans, 34 Democrats, and
one vacancy. The House consisted of 182 Democrats, 140
Republicans, two from other political parties, and one
vacancy.

December 8, 1885   his first annual message to Congress
recommended more money for the foreign service; an end to
mandatory silver coinage; more civil service reform;
modernization of the navy; and a presidential succession
law.

January 19, 1886   signed Presidential Succession Law
establishing the order of cabinet succession to the
presidency in case of death or removal of the president and
vice president.

January 25, 1886   The Senate, in executive session,
challenged Cleveland's refusal to provide reasons for his
removal and appointment of government officials, by chosing
a case to test Senatorial power under the Tenure of Office
Act.

February 18, 1886   The Senate Judiciary Committee issued a
report stating its position in the appointment-removal
conflict with the president.

March 1, 1886   sent a special message to Congress refusing
to produce the desired papers, using the expression
"innocuous desuetude" to describe the previous twenty year
history of the Tenure of Office Act.

March 2, 1886   sent a special message to Congress
recommending indemnity for those killed or hurt in the
September 2, 1885, Rock Springs, Wyoming massacre of 400
Chinese railroad laborers.

March 10, 1886   vetoed a bill for the relief of one J.H.
McBlair, the first of his 414 first term vetoes.

May 8, 1886   vetoed the bill providing for a pension for
one Andrew J. Hill, the first of his 282 first term pension
bill vetoes.

May 10, 1886   in Santa Clara Co. v. Southern Pacific R.R.
Co. (118 U.S. 394), the Supreme Court accepted the concept
that the protection granted to "persons" in the 14th
amendment applied to legal persons, i.e. corporations.

June 2, 1886   married Francis Folsom, the daughter of his
former Buffalo law partner and a woman 27 years his junior.

June 29, 1886   signed a bill allowing the incorporation of
national labor unions.

August 5, 1886   first session, 49th Congress adjourned.

October, 1886   made a tour of the West and the South,
speaking in cities along the way.

October 25, 1886   in Wabash, St. Louis & Pacific R.R. Co.
v. Illinois (118 U.S. 557), the Supreme Court invalidated an
Illinois law prohibiting long-in-short-haul contract clauses
as a violation of Congress's constitutional control over
interstate commerce.

October 28, 1886   participated in the ceremonies
dedicating the Statue of Liberty.

December 6, 1886   second session, 49th Congress convened,
and, in his second annual message, Cleveland asked for
treasury surplus reduction; a modern navy; coastal
defenses; and public land disposition reform.

February 3, 1887   signed Electoral Count Act which was an
attempt to prevent another disputed national election, like
that of 1876, by giving the states the power to judge
returns and electors.

February 4, 1887   signed Interstate Commerce Act
establishing the Interstate Commerce Commission to try to
insure railroad fair practices.

February 8, 1887   signed Dawes Severalty Act which
dissolved Indian tribes as legal entities and granted Indian
families 160 acres apiece from tribal lands.

February 11, 1887   vetoed Dependent Pension Bill which
would have allowed a pension for any veteran of 90 days
service, whether or not he had incurred a disability while
in military service.

February 16, 1887   vetoed Texas Seed Bill to benefit
several drought-ridden Texas counties, commenting that
"though the people support the government, the government
should not support the people."

February 23, 1887   signed a law prohibiting the
importation of opium from China.

March 2, 1887   signed Hatch Act providing Federal
subsidies for the establishiment of state agricultural
experiment stations.

March 3, 1887   Tenure of Office Act repealed.

March 3, 1887   Second Session, 49th Congress adjourned.

March 22, 1887   appointed first commissioners to
Interstate Commerce Commission.

April 1, 1887   appointed Charles S. Fairchild to be
Secretary of the Treasury to replace Daniel Manning who
resigned.

June 7, 1887   signed a War Department order authorizing
the return of captured Confederate battle flags to the
states.

June 16, 1887   revoked the battle flag order because of
protests.

December 5, 1887   first session, 50th Congress convened.
There were 39 Republicans and 37 Democrats in the Senate;
170 Democrats, 151 Republicans, and 4 Alliance in the House
of Representatives.

December 6, 1887   third annual message was devoted completely to a call for downward revision of the tariff.

December 6, 1887   appointed his Secretary of the Interior L.Q.C. Lamar to the Supreme Court to replace William B. Woods who had died.

January 16, 1888   appointed Postmaster General William F. Vilas to be Secretary of the Interior to replace Lamar, and appointed Donald M. Dickinson to be the new Postmaster General.

February 15, 1888   Bayard-Chamberlain treaty calling for a reciprocal tariff and a fishing agreement with Canada was rejected by the Senate.

April 30, 1888   appointed Melville W. Fuller as chief justice to replace Morrison R. Waite who had died.

June 1, 1888   appointed Philip Sheridan to the rank of general of the army.

June 6, 1888   renominated for the presidency by the Democratic party.

June 13, 1888   signed the act establishing the Department of Labor.

July 26, 1888   vetoed bill providing railroad right-of-way through Indian lands.

August 23, 1888   sent a special message to Congress indicating retaliation plan against Canada over fishing dispute.

October 20, 1888   first session, 50th Congress adjourned.

November 6, 1888   lost his bid for re-election to Republican Benjamin Harrison 233-168 in electoral votes. (He received almost 100,000 more popular votes.)

December 3, 1888   second session, 50th Congress convened
and heard Cleveland's 4th annual message

January 14, 1889   signed an act elevating the Department
of Agriculture to cabinet rank.

January 15, 1889   special message to Congress calling the
Samoan disagreement with Germany and Great Britain serious
and recommending Samoan autonomy and independence.

February 12, 1889   named Commissioner of Agriculture
Norman J. Colman to be the first Secretary of Agriculture.

March 4, 1889   attended inauguration of Benjamin Harrison
and moved to New York to practice law.

February 10, 1891   opposed a pending congressional bill
calling for the free and unlimited coinage of silver in his
so-called "Silver Letter" read at a New York City meeting.

October 3, 1891   his first child, Ruth, was born.

June 23, 1892   received Democratic nomination for the
presidency; Adlai E. Stevenson was his running mate.

November 8, 1892   defeated Harrison, the Republican, and
James B. Weaver, the Populist Party candidate, 277-145-22,
but he did not gain a popular vote majority.

March 4, 1893   inaugurated as 24th president of the United
States.

March 5, 1893   announced his cabinet: Walter Q. Gresham,
Secretary of State; John G. Carlisle, Secretary of the
Treasury; Daniel S. Lamont, Secretary of War; Richard
Olney, Attorney General; Hilary A. Herbert, Secretary of
the Navy; Wilson S. Bissell, Postmaster General; Hoke
Smith, Secretary of the Interior; J. Sterling Morton,
Secretary of Agriculture.

March 9, 1893   withdrew annexation of Hawaii treaty from the Senate and appointed James H. Blount as special commissioner to investigate the American role in the revolt there.

March 30, 1893   appointed Thomas F. Bayard ambassador to Great Britain, the first ambassador in U.S. history.

April 27, 1893   attended ten nation International Columbian Naval Review in New York City.

May 1, 1893   presided at official opening of the Columbian Exposition in Chicago.

June 27, 1893   the Stock Market crash precipitated the Panic of 1893.

June 30, 1893   issued call for a special session of Congress to begin on August 7.

July 1, 1893   secret cancer operation on his jaw took place on board a ship in Long Island Sound; additional surgery performed on July 17.

August 7, 1893   first session, 53rd Congress convened; the Senate consisted of 44 Democrats, 38 Republicans, 3 others, and 3 vacancies; the House consisted of 220 Democrats, 126 Republicans, and 11 Populists.

August 8, 1893   special message to Congress calling for repeal of the Sherman Silver Purchase Act.

August 15, 1893   An international tribunal ruled on the pelagic sealing dispute with Canada that the United States had no rights beyond the 3 mile limit and could not kill seals within 60 miles of the Pribilof Islands.

August 23, 1893   issued presidential proclamation opening Cherokee Strip, Oklahoma to settlement on September 16, the most spectacular of the famous Oklahoma "runs."

September 9, 1893   second child, Esther, was born, the
only child of a president born in the White House

September 19, 1893   appointed William B. Hornblower to the
Supreme Court to replace the deceased Samuel Blatchford.
The Senate refused to confirm him on January 15, 1894.

November 1, 1893   signed repeal of the Sherman Silver
Purchase Act.

November 3, 1893   signed amended version of Chinese
Exclusion Act.

November 3, 1893   1st session, 53rd Congress adjourned.

December 4, 1893   second session, 53rd Congress convened
and listened to 1st annual message of the second term.

December 18, 1893   sent special message to Congress
explaining his determination to prevent Hawaiian annexation.

January 17, 1894   vetoed a bill to provide relief for
timber and stone lands purchasers, the first of 170 vetoes
of his second term.

January 22, 1894   nominated Wheeler H. Peckham a justice
of the Supreme Court, but the Senate rejected this
nomination on February 16.

February 19, 1894   nominated Edward D. White a justice of
the Supreme Court, and he was immediately confirmed.

March 29, 1894   vetoed a bill calling for coinage of
silver bullion.

April 30, 1894   Coxey's Army reached Washington, D.C. only
to have its leaders arrested for trespassing on the Capitol
grounds.

May 26, 1894   in Reagan v. Farmers' Loan and Trust Co.
(154 U.S. 362), the Supreme Court upheld the right of courts
to review rates established by a state commission acting
under state law.

June 28, 1894   instituted the first Monday in September as
a legal holiday, Labor Day.

July 3, 1894   ordered U.S. Army troops to Chicago to
enforce a federal injunction against Pullman Strikers,
arguing that such action was necessary to protect mail
delivery and interstate commerce.

July 19, 1894   a letter he wrote to Representative William
L. Wilson protesting a Senate tariff proposal was read in
the House.

August 8, 1894   recognized the recently created Republic
of Hawaii.

August 18, 1894   signed act providing one million acre
grants to states, the funds accrued by the states to be used
for land reclamation.

August 27, 1894   Wilson-Gorman Tariff became law without
Cleveland's signature. It provided for lower rates and the
first graduated income tax.

August 28, 1894   second session, 53rd Congress adjourned.

December 3, 1894   third session, 53rd Congress convened
and heard Cleveland's second annual message of his second
term.

December 8, 1894   promulgated the treaty regulating
Chinese immigration.

December 12, 1894   issued executive order placing internal
revenue workers under civil service.

January 21, 1895   in U.S. v. E.C. Knight Co. (156 U.S. 1),
the Supreme Court held that the Sherman Anti-Trust Act did
not extend to intrastate corporations.

February 1, 1895   vetoed act allowing a railroad
right-of-way through the San Carlos Indian reservation in
Arizona.

February 6, 1895   ruled in favor of Brazil in her boundary
dispute with Argentina.

February 7, 1895   gold conference with J. P. Morgan which
resulted in banker loans to the U.S. government.

February 23, 1895   vetoed Eunice Putnam pension bill, the
first of 54 pension bill vetoes of the second term.

March 1, 1895   appointed William L. Wilson Postmaster
General to replace Wilson S. Bissell who resigned.

March 4, 1895   third session, 53rd Congress adjourned.

March 5, 1895   "Appeal of the Silver Democrats" in the
House called for the restoration of free and unlimited
coinage of silver at the rate of 16 to 1.

April 8, May 20, 1895   in Pollock v. Farmers' Loan and
Trust Co. (157 U.S. 429, 158 U.S. 601), the Supreme Court
ruled that the income tax provision of the Wilson-Gorman
Tariff was unconstitutional.

May 27, 1895   In Re Debs (158 U.S. 564), the Supreme
Court ruled that the government action against Pullman
strikers had been constitutional.

June 7, 1895   appointed Attorney General Richard Olney to
replace the deceased Walter Q. Gresham as Secretary of
State.   Judson Harmon became the new Attorney General.

June 12, 1895   issued warning to all Americans against
participating in Cuban insurrection through filibustering
expeditions.

July 7, 1895   third daughter, Marion, was born.

July 20, 1895   Secretary of State Richard Olney invoked
the Monroe Doctrine to insist on the American right to
arbitrate a boundary dispute between Great Britain and
Venezuela in South America (Olney Corollary).

December 2, 1895   first session, 54th Congress convened.
The Senate consisted of 44 Republicans, 39 Democrats, and 5
others.   The House held 246 Republicans, 104 Democrats, and
7 Populists.   Cleveland sent the third annual message of his
second term.

December 3, 1895   appointed Rufus W. Peckham Supreme Court
justice to replace the deceased Howell E. Jackson.

December 17, 1895   sent diplomatic correspondence
concerning Great Britain-Venezuela boundary dispute to
Congress, urging the creation of an independent commission.

January 1, 1896   appointed Venezuelan Boundary Commission.

January 4, 1896   Utah became 45th state in the Union.

February 2, 1896   Great Britain and Venezuela agreed to
submit their boundary dispute to arbitration.

February 28, 1896   the House of Representatives passed a
resolution adhered to by the Senate on April 6 granting
Cuban revolutionaries belligerent rights and telling
Cleveland to use his good offices with Spain for the
recognition of an independent Cuba.   Spain declined the
offer on May 22.

May 18, 1896   in Plessy v. Ferguson (163 U.S. 537), the
Supreme Court ruled that "separate but equal" facilities for
black people were constitutional.

June 3, 1896   vetoed Rivers and Harbors act, which
Congress immediately passed, the first of five of
Cleveland's vetoes that were overridden during his second
term.

June 11, 1896   first session, 54th Congress adjourned.

July 30, 1896   issued second proclamation against Cuban
filibusters.

August 22, 1896   appointed David R. Francis Secretary of
the Interior to replace Hoke Smith who resigned.

November 3, 1896   Republican William McKinley elected
president of the United States.

December 7, 1896   second session, 54th Congress convened
and heard Cleveland's last annual message.

February 6, 1897   issued executive order cutting the
number of pension agencies in half.

February 22, 1897   issued presidential proclamation,
setting aside 20 million acres of forest reserves in six
western states.

March 2, 1897   vetoed immigration act containing
amendments calling for a literacy test and no employment of
aliens on public works projects.

March 4, 1897   second session, 54th Congress adjourned.

March 4, 1897   attended the inauguration of William
McKinley

March 18, 1897   after a hunting and fishing trip, joined
his wife at "Westland," their new home in Princeton, New
Jersey, named after Professor, later Dean, Andrew F. West of
Princeton University.

October 28, 1897   fourth child (first boy), Richard
Folsom, was born.

1899   accepted Henry Stafford Little Lectureship in Public
Affairs, Princeton University.

May 26, 1900   his first of numerous magazine articles
appeared.

1901   named to the Board of Trustees, Princeton University

July 18, 1903   fifth child (second son), Francis Grover,
was born

1904   published Presidential Problems, containing earlier
lectures presenting his views on the Tenure of Office
controversy;   the Pullman Strike; the Panic of 1893 bond
sale, and the Venezuelan Boundary dispute.

1906   reorganized the Equitable Life Assurance Company of
America.

1906   published Fishing and Shooting Sketches.

1907   elected president of the Association of Presidents
of Life Insurance Companies.

1907   elected to Phi Beta Kappa, though he never attended
college.

1908   published Good Citizenship.

June 24, 1908   died of a heart attack in Princeton, New
Jersey.

1
Manuscript and Archival Resources

GROVER CLEVELAND MANUSCRIPT COLLECTIONS

1. Cleveland, Grover. Papers. Buffalo and Erie County
Historical Society. Letters of GC and his wife; scrapbook
and clippings covering GC's legal and political careers
(Sheriff of Erie County, Mayor of Buffalo, and Governor of
New York); also letters from post-presidential years and a
vertical file covering national and local data on him.

2. ___. Papers. Detroit Public Library. Five boxes, mostly
letters received by GC, though there are some GC letters to
Donald M. Dickinson.

3. ___. Papers. Library of Congress. The major GC
manuscript collection consisting of around 100,000 items,
mostly covering the 1885-1908 period including thirty
letterpress books on his first presidential term. This
collection has been microfilmed and is readily available on
inter-library loan.

4. Library of Congress. Index to the Grover Cleveland
Papers. Washington: Government Printing Office, 1965.
Detailed index organized according to senders and recipients
of letters in the collection and its 164 reel microfilm
edition.

5. ___. Papers. Princeton University Library. Two boxes holding 200 photographs and 400 original shorthand letters and typed transcriptions (1902-1906) and numerous GC letters from other collections (1883-1904).

GROVER CLEVELAND MANUSCRIPTS IN OTHER COLLECTIONS
(Including letters to and from Cleveland)

6. American Federation of Labor. Papers. Library of Congress. Letterpress copy books of Samuel Gompers and William Green.

7. Appleton (D.)-Century Company. Records. Lilly Library, Indiana University.

8. Asher, Louis E. Autograph Collection. Library of Congress.

9. Bayard, Thomas F. Bayard-Emory Correspondence. Maryland Historical Society Library, Baltimore.

10. ___. Papers. Library of Congress.

11. Bushyhead, Dennis W. Papers. Texas Archives, University of Texas Library.

12. Camden, Gideon D. Papers. West Virginia University Library.

13. Camden, Johnson Newlon. Papers. West Virginia University Library.

14. Carnegie, Andrew. Papers. Library of Congress.

15. Choate, Joseph H. Papers. Library of Congress.

16. Cockran, Bourke. Papers. New York Public Library.

17. Contemporary Club, Philadelphia, PA. Thornton Oakley Collection. Historical Society of Pennsylvania, Philadelphia.

18. Cooley, Thomas M. Papers. William L. Clements Library, University of Michigan.

19. Davis, David B. Papers. Chicago Historical Society.

20. Davis, Richard H. Papers. University of Virginia Library.

21. DeCoppet, Andre. Papers. Princeton University Library.

22. Dickinson, Donald M. Papers. William L. Clements Library, University of Michigan.

23. Dickinson, Jacob M. Papers. Tennessee State Archives, Nashville.

24. Douglass, Frederick. Papers. Library of Congress.

25. Elkins, Stephen B. Papers. West Virginia Library.

26. Executive Committee on the Celebration of the 250th Anniversary of the Settlement of the Jews in the United States. Records. American Jewish Historical Society.

27. Finley, John Huston. Papers. New York Public Library.

28. Frederic, Harold. Papers. New York Public Library.

29. Fuller, Melville W. Papers. Library of Congress.

30. ___. Papers. Chicago Historical Society.

31. General Collection. Clay County (Minnesota) Historical Society.

32. Gilder, Richard W. Papers. New York Public Library.

33. ___. Papers. Henry E. Huntington Library, San Marino, California.

34. Goodyear, Anson Conger. Papers. Buffalo and Erie County Historical Society.

35. Gordon Family. Papers. Georgia Historical Society, Savannah.

36. Gorman, Arthur Poe. Papers. Maryland Historical Society Library, Baltimore.

37. Gresham, Walter Q. Papers. Library of Congress.

38. Hamlin, Charles E. Papers. Library of Congress.

39. Harrison, Burton Norvell. Papers. Library of Congress.

40. Harrison, Zoe. Scrapbook. Atlanta Historical Society.

41. Hemphill Family. Papers. Duke University Library.

42. Hendrix, Eugene R. Papers. Duke University Library.

43. Herbert, Hilary A. Papers. Southern Historical Collection, University of North Carolina Library.

44. Historical Manuscript Collection. Franklin D. Roosevelt Library, Hyde Park, New York.

45. Irish, John P. Papers. Stanford University Library.

46. Johnson, Martha Waller. Papers. Virginia Historical Society, Richmond.

47. Kishinev Protest Meeting Committee. Papers. American Jewish Historical Society.

48. Knopf, Sigard Adolphus. Papers. National Library of Medicine, Bethesda, Maryland.

49. Lamar, L. Q. C. Papers. Mississippi Department of Archives and History, Jackson.

50. Lamont, Daniel S. Papers. Library of Congress.

51. Lamoreaux, Silas W. Scrapbook. State Historical Society of Wisconsin, Madison.

52. Lanman, Charles. Papers. Library of Congress.

53. McClellan, George B. Papers. Library of Congress.

54. McCook Family. Papers. Library of Congress.

55. McElroy, Robert M. Papers. Library of Congress.

56. McKelway, Alexander J. Papers. Historical Foundation of the Presbyterian and Reformed Churches, Montreat, North Carolina.

57. McKinley, William. Papers. Library of Congress.

58. MacVeagh, Wayne. Papers. Historical Society of Pennsylvania, Philadelphia.

59. Manning, Daniel. Papers. Library of Congress.

60. Marble, Manton. Papers. Library of Congress.

61. Miscellaneous Manuscript Collection. University of
Chicago Library.

62. Moore, Charles. Papers. Library of Congress.

63. Morton, Levi P. Papers. New York Public Library.

64. Noble, Alfred. Papers. Bentley Historical Library,
University of Michigan.

65. Olney, Richard. Papers. Library of Congress.

66. Page, Thomas Nelson. Papers. Duke University Library.

67. Palmer, John M. Papers. Illinois State Historical
Library, Springfield.

68. Parsons, William B. Papers. Columbia University
Libraries.

69. Pepper, William. Papers. University of Pennsylvania
Libraries.

70. Presidential Papers. Washington State Historical
Society Library, Tacoma.

71. Presidents and Vice Presidents of the United States,
1766-1924. Papers. Albany Institute of Art and History,
New York.

72. Reed, Fayette Hildreth. Papers. Oregon Historical
Society Library, Portland.

73. Reich, Jacques. Papers. New York Historical Society.

74. Reich, Lorenz. Papers. New York Historical Society.

75. Rice, William Gorham. Papers. New York State Library, Albany.

76. Riggs, Family. Papers. Library of Congress.

77. Rogers, Henry Wade. Papers. University of Michigan.

78. Schurz, Carl. Papers. Library of Congress.

79. Shepard, Edward M. Papers. Columbia University Libraries.

80. Sherman, John. Papers. Library of Congress.

81. Sloan, Benjamin. Papers. South Caroliniana Library, University of South Carolina.

82. Spaulding, Oliver L. Papers. University of Michigan.

83. Springer, William M. Papers. Chicago Historical Society.

84. Stovall, Pleasant Alexander. Papers. Georgia Historical Society, Savannah.

85. Strauss, Oscar S. Papers. Library of Congress.

86. Stillman, James. Papers. Columbia University Libraries.

87. Stone, Edward C. Papers. Boston University Library.

88. Thomas, Charles Spaulding. Papers. State Historical Society of Colorado, Denver.

89. Thompson, Hugh Smith. Papers. South Caroliniana Library, University of South Carolina.

90. Thompson, Richard W.   Papers.   Rutherford B. Hayes
Presidential Center, Fremont, Ohio.

91. Thurber, Henry Thomas.   Papers.   Detroit Public Library.

92. Trumbull, Lyman.   Papers.   Illinois State Historical
Library, Springfield.

93. Uhl, Edwin F.   Papers.   University of Michigan.

94. United States Presidential Papers, 1753-1935.   Duke
University Library.

95. Vilas, William Freeman.   Papers.   State Historical
Society of Wisconsin, Madison.

96. Weil, Gertrude.   Papers.   North Carolina State Office of
Archives and History, Raleigh.

97. White, Andrew D.   Papers.   University of Michigan.

98. Whitman, Walt.   Papers.   Library of Congress.

99. Wilder, Marshall P.   Papers.   Library of Congress.

100. Williams, Thomas John Chew.   Papers.   Maryland
Historical Society Library, Baltimore.

101. Wright, Carroll Davidson.   Papers.   Clark University
Library, Worcester, Massachusetts.

PUBLISHED COMPILATIONS OF CLEVELAND'S PAPERS

PUBLIC

102. Richardson, James D. (ed.) A Compilation of the
Messages and Papers of the Presidents. New York: Bureau of
National Literature, 1897. Volumes 12-14 contain GC
material and volume 19 contains GC quotations on major
issues, factual data on his administrations, and an index.

103. ___. (comp.) Messages and Papers of the Presidents.
Washington: Government Printing Office, 1897, 1909. Volume
8 contains GC material.

104. The Public Papers of Grover Cleveland, Twenty Second,
Twenty Fourth President of the United States, March 4, 1885
to March 4, 1889, March 4, 1893 to March 4, 1897.
Washington: Government Printing Office, 1889, 1897.
Includes acceptances of nominations, special messages, veto
messages, pardons, and so forth.

105. Cleveland, Grover. Principles and Purposes of Our Form
of Government As Set Forth in Public Papers of Grover
Cleveland. Compiled by Francis Gottsberger. New York: G.
G. Peck, 1892. A collection of GC's first term presidential
messages, including veto messages and letters on the silver
issue.

106. Coletta, Paolo. "The Democratic Party, 1884-1910." in
History of U.S. Political Parties. Edited by Arthur M.
Schlesinger, Jr. 4 vols. New York: Chelsea House in
association with R. R. Bowker, 1973. Vol. 2: 1860-1910:
The Gilded Age of Politics. Excerpts from a variety of GC's
messages to Congress.

107. Israel, Fred L. (ed.) The State of the Union Messages
of the Presidents, 1790-1966. 3 vols. New York: Chelsea
House, 1966. GC's 8 annual messages are found in volume II,
pp. 1514-1625 and 1736-1855.

108. U. S. President. Inaugural Addresses of the Presidents
of the United States From George Washington, 1789, to
Richard Milhous Nixon, 1973. Washington: Government
Printing Office, 1974.

109. Lott, Davis Newton. (ed.) The Inaugural Addresses of
the American Presidents from Washington to Kennedy. New
York: Holt, Rinehart, and Winston, 1961.

110. Lord, Clifford L. (ed.) Presidential Executive Orders,
Numbered 1 - 8030. New York: Books for Historical Records
Survey, 1944. GC's executive orders. (vol. I, pp. 3-10)

111. U.S. President. Presidential Executive Orders. Dobbs
Ferry, New York: Transmedia Publishing Company, 1980. GC's
included.

112. ___. Presidential Vetoes: List of Bills, Vetoes, and
Action Taken Thereon by the Senate and House of
Representatives, 1789-1976. Washington: Government
Printing Office, 1978. Chronological lists, including GC's.

113. Orations of American Orators . . . . Rev. ed. 2 vols.
New York: Colonial Press, 1900. GC's first inaugural
address. (vol. I, pp. 449-55)

114. Morris, Richard B. Great Presidential Decisions. New
York: Harper and Row, 1973. GC's 1893 message calling for
a special session of Congress and his 1895 Venezuelan
Boundary dispute message.

115. Cleveland, Grover. "Messages, 1893 and 1896 -
Excerpts." Current History n.s. 8 (January 1945): 39-40.
Excerpts from GC's 1893 and 1896 annual messages opposing
American expansion into Hawaii and Cuba.

116. ___. "President Cleveland's Message." Public Opinion
15 (August 19, 1893): 469-75. Text of GC's special session
message and the press reaction to it.

117. Goldsmith, William M. The Growth of Presidential
Power, A Documented History. 3 vols. New York: Chelsea
House, 1974. GC's Tenure of Office Act statement, Pullman
Strike documents, and reprints of GC's December 18, 1893,
message to Congress on Hawaii.

118. Udall, David King. Arizona Pioneer Morman, David King
Udall: His Story and His Family, 1851-1938. Tucson:
Silhouettes, 1959. See pp. 142-3 for GC's pardon of this
man after he had served three years for perjury.

119. Cleveland, Grover. Public Papers of Grover Cleveland,
Governor, 1883 [-1884]. Albany: Albany Argus, 1883-1884.
Annual messages, proclamations, veto messages, pardons, and
so forth.

PRIVATE

120. Cleveland, Grover. Letters of Grover Cleveland:
1850-1908. Edited by Allan Nevins. 1933. Reprint. New
York: DaCapo Press, 1970. This is the most extensive
printed edition of GC letters.

121. ___. The Writings and Speeches of Grover Cleveland.
Edited by George F. Parker. New York: Cassell, 1892.
Letters and speeches up to 1892.

122. ___. Grover Cleveland, Addresses, State Papers, and
Letters. Edited by Albert Ellery Bergh. New York: Sun
Dial, 1909. GC letters and speeches (1875 to
post-presidential years) and excerpts from some public
papers.

123. Thorp, Willard. (ed.) "The Cleveland-West
Correspondence: Record of a Friendship." Princeton
University Library Chronicle 31 (Winter 1970): 69-102.
Twenty two letters and two telegrams from GC to Dean Andrew
F. West (1896-1906).

124. Cleveland, Grover. "Cleveland and the Civil Service
Reformers; His Attitude as Shown in Letters to a Friend."
Century 84 (August 1912): 625-30. GC letters to S. W.
Burt, later president of the New York Civil Service Reform
Association (1885-1888, 1892).

125. ___. "Correspondence of President Cleveland and
Melville W. Fuller, Chief Justice After 1888." American
Scholar 3 (1934): 245-9. Six GC letters on a variety of

judicial and political matters (1886, 1890, 1891, 1893, 1900).

126. ___. "Letters to a Friend; Letters to H. M. Robbins of Buffalo, 1876-1890." Niagara Frontier 2 (Summer 1955): 49-52. Personal letters to a tobacco merchant, frequently thanking him for sending tobacco.

127. Knoles, George H. (ed.) "Grover Cleveland on Imperialism." Mississippi Valley Historical Review 37 (September 1950): 303-4. GC's November 9, 1898, letter to California Democrat John P. Irish opposing imperialism.

128. Taylor, John M. (ed.) "Presidential Letters: Grover Cleveland on Shakespeare." Manuscripts 24 (Summer 1972): 214-5. A March 30, 1896, letter written during the Venezuelan Boundary controversy praising Shakespeare and Anglo-American friendship.

129. Cleveland, Grover. "President Cleveland's Letter." Public Opinion 16 (October 5, 1893): 17-19. Text of GC's September 25, 1893, letter to Georgia Governor W. J. Norther opposing free silver and the press reaction to the letter.

130. ___. "President's Financial Position: Text of Letter to W. J. Norther." Outlook 48 (October 7, 1893): 645. Text of September 25, 1893, silver letter cited above.

131. ___. "President Cleveland's Letter to W. L. Wilson on the Tariff Question." ibid 50 (July 28, 1894): 151. GC's July 2, 1894, letter calling on Democrats to rally behind the proposed party tariff bill.

132. Hornsberger, Caroline T. (ed.) Treasury of Presidential Quotations. Chicago: Follett, 1964. GC on a wide variety of subjects from "Achievement" and "Citizenship" to "Voters" and "Wealth."

133. Tourtellot, Arthur B. The Presidents on the Presidency. New York: Russell and Russell, 1970. GC's comments on such matters as appointments and removals, civil service, congressional relations, national leadership, presidential oath, foreign policy, and so forth.

MANUSCRIPTS OF CLEVELAND ASSOCIATES

JOHN PETER ALTGELD, ILLINOIS GOVERNOR

134. Altgeld, John P.   Papers.   Illinois State Historical
Library, Springfield.   Only 100 pieces.

135. Alschuler, Samuel.   Papers.   Illinois State Historical
Library, Springfield.

136. Cleveland, Grover.   Papers.   Library of Congress.

137. Harrison, Carter Henry.   Papers.   Newberry Library,
Chicago.

138. Lloyd, Henry Demarest.   Papers.   State Historical
Society of Wisconsin, Madison.

139. Palmer, John M.   Papers.   Illinois State Historical
Library, Springfield.

140. Parsons, Lewis B.   Papers.   Illinois State Historical
Library, Springfield.

141. Schilling, George A.   Papers.   University of Chicago
Library.

142. Sulzer, William.   Papers.   State Historical Society of
Wisconsin, Madison.

THOMAS F. BAYARD, SECRETARY OF STATE

143. Bayard, Thomas F.   Papers.   Maryland Historical
Society, Baltimore.   Only 13 letters.

144. ___. Papers. Library of Congress. 60,000 items.

145. Black, Jeremiah S. Papers. Library of Congress.

146. Capek, Thomas. Papers. Library of Congress.

147. Cleveland, Grover. Papers. Library of Congress.

148. Curry, Jabez L. M. Papers. Library of Congress.

149. Dawson, Francis W. Papers. South Caroliniana Library, University of South Carolina.

150. Gilpin, Henry D. Papers. Historical Society of Pennsylvania, Philadelphia.

151. Gresham, Walter Q. Papers. Library of Congress.

152. Holliday, Frederick W. Papers. Duke University Library.

153. Manning, Daniel. Papers. Library of Congress.

154. Marble, Manton. Papers. Library of Congress.

155. Moore, John Bassett. Papers. Library of Congress.

156. New Jerseyana. Papers. New Jersey Historical Society.

157. Olney, Richard. Papers. Library of Congress.

158. Risley, Hanson A. Papers. Duke University Library.

159. Rogers, Henry Wade. Papers. University of Michigan.

160. Schurz, Carl. Papers. Library of Congress.

161. Straus, Oscar S. Papers. Library of Congress.

162. Vilas, William F. Papers. State Historical Society of Wisconsin, Madison.

163. Ward, Samuel. Papers. New York Public Library.

164. Ward, Samuel, and Anna Hayard (Barker). Papers. Houghton Library, Harvard University.

JOHN G. CARLISLE, SECRETARY OF TREASURY

165. Camden, Johnson Newlon. Papers. West Virginia University Library.

166. Cleveland, Grover. Papers. Library of Congress.

167. Conrad, Holmes. Papers. Virginia Historical Society, Richmond.

168. Davis, Richard H. Papers. University of Virginia Library.

169. Green, Norvin. Papers. Filson Club, Louisville, Kentucky.

170. Holmes, Conrad. Papers. Virginia Historical Society, Richmond.

GEORGE B. CORTELYOU, PRIVATE SECRETARY

171. Cortelyou, George B. Papers. Library of Congress. Around 12,000 items mostly from McKinley and Theodore Roosevelt years.

172. Appleton, Nathan. Papers. Library of Congress.

173. Bonaparte Family. Papers. Maryland Historical Society Library, Baltimore.

174. Corbin, Henry C. Papers. Library of Congress.

175. Day, William Rufus Papers. Library of Congress.

176. Dewey, George. Papers. Library of Congress.

177. Fairbanks, Charles W. Papers. Indiana University.

178. Gage, Lyman J. Papers. Library of Congress.

179. Hill, Samuel. Papers. Minnesota Historical Society.

180. Logan Family. Papers. Library of Congress.

181. MacVeagh, Franklin. Papers. Library of Congress.

182. Mellen, Charles S. Papers. New Hampshire Historical Society, Concord.

183. Platt, Thomas C. Papers. Yale University Library.

184. Pulitzer, Joseph. Papers. Library of Congress.

185. Roosevelt, Theodore. Papers. Library of Congress.

186. Root, Elihu. Papers. Library of Congress.

187. Taft, William Howard. Papers. Library of Congress.

188. Wellslager, Anna (Belkman). Papers. Iowa State Department of History and Archives.

GEORGE WILLIAM CURTIS, REFORMER

189. Curtis, George William. Papers. Boston Public Library. 125 items.

190. ___. Papers. Brown University Library. 100 items.

191. ___. Papers. Houghton Library, Harvard University. 16 boxes and 372 items.

192. ___. Papers. Rutherford B. Hayes Presidential Center. 2 boxes.

193. ___. Papers. Staten Island Institute of Arts and Sciences Library. 553 items and 27 bundles.

194. Abbott, Edward. Papers. Bowdoin College.

195. Akerman, Amos T. Papers. University of Virginia Library.

196. American Writers Papers. Duke University Library.

197. Buchanan, A. W. Papers. Texas Archives, University of Texas Library.

198. Child, Lydia Maria (Francis). Papers. Columbia University Library.

199. Cleveland, Grover. Papers. Library of Congress.

200. Cornell, Alonzo B. Papers. Cornell University
Library.

201. Corson, Hiram. Papers. Cornell University Library.

202. Cranch Family Papers. Massachusetts Historical Society
Library.

203. Davis, Richard H. Papers. University of Virginia
Library.

204. Holmes, Oliver Wendall. Papers. Library of Congress.

205. Ingersoll, Henrietta (Crosby). Papers. Library of
Congress.

206. Jones, George. Papers. New York Public Library.

207. Melville, Herman. Papers. University of Virginia
Library.

208. Olmstead, Frederick Law. Papers. Library of Congress.

209. Rossiter, Thomas P. Papers. Archives of American Art.

210. Schurz, Carl. Papers. Library of Congress.

211. Smith, Goldwin. Papers. Cornell University Library.

212. Thurston, Robert H. Papers. Cornell University
Library.

213. Tracy, Gilbert A. Papers. New Jersey Historical
Society.

214. Wilder, Burt G.   Papers.   Cornell University Library.

215. Williams, George F.   Papers.   Duke University Library.

DONALD M. DICKINSON, POSTMASTER GENERAL

216. Dickinson, Donald M.   Papers.   Library of Congress.
Only about 350 items.

217. ___ .   Papers.   University of Michigan.   Two feet of
manuscripts but also contains microfilm editions of Grover
Cleveland Papers and Daniel S. Lamont Papers, Library of
Congress.

218. Bayard, Thomas F.   Papers.   Library of Congress.

219. Brown, Everett S.   Papers.   University of Michigan.

220. Cleveland, Grover.   Papers.   Detroit Public Library and
Library of Congress.

221. Cooley, Thomas M.   Papers.   University of Michigan.

222. Heald, Joseph.   Papers.   Detroit Public Library.

223. Lamont, Daniel S.   Papers.   Library of Congress.

224. Norris, Mark.   Papers.   University of Michigan.

225. Packhurst, John G.   Papers.   University of Michigan.

226. Shetterly, Seth K.   Papers.   University of Michigan.

227. Spaulding, Oliver L.   Papers.   University of Michigan.

228. Villard, Henry. Papers. Houghton Library, Harvard University.

229. White, Peter. Papers. University of Michigan.

WILLIAM C. ENDICOTT, SECRETARY OF WAR

230. Endicott, William C. Papers. Massachusetts Historical Society, Boston. 55 vols. and 17 boxes of material.

231. Bayard, Thomas F. Papers. Library of Congress.

232. Cleveland, Grover. Papers. Library of Congress.

233. Hawley, Joseph R. Papers. Library of Congress.

234. Williams, George Frederick. Papers. Duke University Library.

CHARLES S. FAIRCHILD, SECRETARY OF THE TREASURY

235. Fairchild, Charles S. Papers. New York Historical Society. Seven boxes of material.

236. Bayard, Thomas F. Papers. Library of Congress.

237. Hambleton, James Pinkney. Papers. Emory University Library.

238. Higginson, Henry L. Papers. Baker Library, Harvard University Business School.

239. Hill, David. B. Papers. Syracuse University Library.

DAVID R. FRANCIS, SECRETARY OF THE INTERIOR

240. Francis, David R. Papers. Missouri Historical Society, St. Louis. 50,000 items.

MELVILLE W. FULLER, CHIEF JUSTICE OF THE UNITED STATES

241. Fuller, Melville W. Papers. Chicago Historical Society. Around 7,000 items.

242. ___. Papers. Library of Congress. 5000 items.

243. Caton, John D. Papers. Library of Congress.

244. Curry, Jabez L. M. Papers. Library of Congress.

AUGUSTUS H. GARLAND, ATTORNEY GENERAL

245. Bayard, Thomas F. Papers. Library of Congress.

246. Bliss, Calvin C. Papers. Arkansas History Commission, Little Rock.

247. Camden, Johnson Newlon. Papers. West Virginia University Library.

248. Fuller, Melville W. Papers. Chicago Historical Society.

249. Reynolds, Daniel Harris. Papers. University of Arkansas, Fayetteville.

250. Stephens, Alexander H. Papers. Library of Congress.

251. Walker, David. Papers. University of Arkansas, Fayetteville.

RICHARD WATSON GILDER, FRIEND

252. Barbe, Waitman. Papers. West Virginia Library.

253. Carnegie, Andrew. Papers. Library of Congress.

254. Cleveland, Grover. Papers. Library of Congress.

255. Lamont, Daniel S. Papers. Library of Congress.

256. Rockhill, William W. Papers. Houghton Library, Harvard University.

257. Roosevelt, Theodore. Papers. Library of Congress.

WALTER Q. GRESHAM, SECRETARY OF STATE

258. Gresham, Walter Q. Papers. Fort Worth Public Library. 41 vols. and 190 pieces.

259. ___. Papers. Library of Congress. 12,000 items.

260. Allen, William V. Papers. Nebraska State Historical Society.

261. Bayard, Thomas F. Papers. Library of Congress.

262. Chandler, William E. Papers. Library of Congress.

263. Cleveland, Grover. Papers. Library of Congress.

264. Dow, Earle Wilbur. Papers. Bentley Historical
Library, University of Michigan.

265. Fairbanks, Charles W. Papers. Indiana University.

266. Foster, John W. Papers. Library of Congress.

267. Fuller, Melville, W. Papers. Chicago Historical
Society.

268. Harlan, John Marshall. Papers. Library of Congress.

269. Michener, Louis Theodore. Papers. Library of
Congress.

270. Moore, John Bassett. Papers. Library of Congress.

271. Morgan, John T. Papers. Library of Congress.

272. Olney, Richard. Papers. Library of Congress.

JUDSON HARMON, ATTORNEY GENERAL

273. Harmon, Judson. Papers. Historical and Philosophical
Society of Ohio, Cincinnati. 32 boxes of material.

274. ___. Papers. Ohio Historical Society, Columbus.
Approximately 20 feet of material.

275. Bradford, Gamaliel. Papers. Massachusetts Historical
Society Library, Boston.

276. Cleveland, Grover. Papers. Library of Congress.

277. Dickinson, Jacob M. Papers. Tennessee State Archives, Nashville.

278. Holmes, Conrad. Papers. Virginia Historical Society, Richmond.

279. Johnson, James G. Papers. Ohio Historical Society, Columbus.

280. Lochren, William. Papers. Minnesota Historical Society, St. Paul.

THOMAS A. HENDRICKS, VICE PRESIDENT

281. Asher, Louis E. Autograph Collection. Library of Congress.

282. Gordon, George W. Papers. Tennessee State Library and Archives, Nashville.

HILARY A. HERBERT, SECRETARY OF THE NAVY

283. Herbert, Hilary A. Papers. Southern Historical Collection, University of North Carolina Library. 2 feet of material.

284. Kirkland, William A. Papers. East Carolina University Library.

285. Morton, Levi P. Papers. Syracuse University Library.

286. Moses, Montrose J. Papers. Duke University Library.

287. Smith, Washington M. Papers. Duke University Library.

DAVID B. HILL, U. S. SENATOR FROM NEW YORK

288. Hill, David B. Papers. New York State Library, Albany. 16 vols. and 9 boxes.

289. ___. Papers. Syracuse University Library. Only around 125 items.

290. Bixby, George S. Papers. New York State Library, Albany.

291. Bonesteel, Floyd J. Papers. University of Oklahoma Library.

292. Cleveland, Grover. Papers. Library of Congress.

293. Prince, LeBaron Bradford. Papers. University of California at Los Angeles Library.

294. Rice, William Gorham. Papers. New York State Library, Albany.

JOSEPH JEFFERSON, FRIEND

295. Carson, William G. B. Papers. Washington University Library, St. Louis.

296. Cleveland, Grover. Papers. Library of Congress.

297. Davis, Richard H. Papers. University of Virginia Library.

298. Deneale, George. Papers. Virginia Historical Society.

299. Field, Eugene.   Papers.   University of Virginia
Library.

300. Hill, Joel E.   Papers.   Duke University Library.

301. Lander, Frederick W.   Papers.   Library of Congress.

302. Seymour, William.   Papers.   Princeton University
Library.

303. Smith, Isaac S.   Papers.   Detroit Public Library.

L. Q. C. LAMAR, SECRETARY OF THE INTERIOR/SUPREME COURT
JUSTICE

304. Lamar, L. Q. C.   Papers.   Mississippi Department of
History and Archives, Jackson.   5 vols. and 240 items.

305. Autry, James L.   Papers.   Rice University Library.

306. Bayard, Thomas F.   Papers.   Library of Congress.

307. Bradley, Joseph P.   Papers.   New Jersey Historical
Society.

308. Clay, Clement C.   Papers.   Duke University Library.

309. Cleveland, Grover.   Papers.   Library of Congress.

310. Dawes, Henry L.   Papers.   Library of Congress.

311. Fontaine, Edward.   Papers. Mississippi State University
Library.

312. Jonas, S. A.   Papers.   Mississippi Department of
Archives and History, Jackson.

313. Lee, Stephen D. Papers. Southern Historical Collection, University of North Carolina Library.

314. McCandle, William M. Papers. Mississippi Department of Archives and History, Jackson.

315. Manning, Daniel. Papers. Library of Congress.

316. Mason, James M. Papers. Library of Congress.

317. Phillips Family. Papers. Library of Congress.

318. Read, Keith M. Papers. University of Georgia Library.

319. Reynolds, L. P. Papers. Mississippi Department of Archives and History, Jackson.

320. Saunders, William L. Papers. North Carolina State Department of Archives and History, Raleigh.

321. Stephens, Alexander H. Papers. Library of Congress.

DANIEL S. LAMONT, PRIVATE SECRETARY/SECRETARY OF WAR

322. Lamont, Daniel S. Papers. Cornell University Library. Approximately 1,000 items.

323. ___. Papers. Library of Congress. 17,500 items, many to and from GC during Lamont's long service as GC's private secretary. See: Stewart, Kate MacLean. "The Daniel Scott Lamont Papers." Library of Congress Quarterly Journal 17 (February 1960): 63-83.

324. Bayard, Thomas F.   Papers.   Library of Congress.

325. Cleveland, Grover.   Papers.   Library of Congress.

326. Cooley, Thomas M.   Papers.   University of Michigan Library.

327. Dickinson, Donald M.   Papers.   University of Michigan Library.

328. Frederic, Harold.   Papers.   New York Public Library.

329. Fuller, Melville W.   Papers.   Library of Congress.

330. Hill, David B.   Papers.   Syracuse University Library.

331. Karpinski, Louis C.   Papers.   Bentley Historical Library, University of Michigan.

332. Lamar, L. Q. C.   Papers.   Mississippi Department of Archives and History, Jackson.

333. Lochren, William.   Papers.   Minnesota Historical Society, St. Paul.

334. Manning, Daniel.   Papers.   Library of Congress.

335. Mellen, Charles S.   Papers.   New Hampshire Historical Society, Concord.

336. Olney, Richard.   Papers.   Library of Congress.

337. Sheehan, William F.   Papers.   Syracuse University Library.

338. Wilson, William L.   Papers.   West Virginia University Library.

DANIEL MANNING, SECRETARY OF THE TREASURY

339. Manning, Daniel. Papers. Library of Congress. 900 items.

340. Cleveland, Grover. Papers. Library of Congress.

341. Lamont, Daniel S. Papers. Library of Congress.

J. STERLING MORTON, SECRETARY OF AGRICULTURE

342. Morton, J. Sterling. Papers. Nebraska State Historical Society, Lincoln. 125 feet of material.

343. Abbott, Ned C. Papers. Nebraska State Historical Society, Lincoln.

344. Barus, Carl. Papers. Brown University Library.

345. Blackman, Elmer E. Papers. Nebraska State Historical Society, Lincoln.

346. Evans, Rudolph. Papers. Library of Congress.

347. Kennard, Thomas P. Papers. Nebraska State Historical Society, Lincoln.

348. Lamont, Daniel S. Papers. Library of Congress.

349. Lochren, William. Papers. Minnesota Historical Society, St. Paul.

350. Melville, George W. Papers. Library of Congress.

351. Morton Family. Papers. Chicago Historical Society.

352. Muir, Robert V. Papers. Nebraska State Historical
Society, Lincoln.

353. Olson, James C. Papers. Nebraska State Historical
Society, Lincoln.

354. Pullman, George. Papers. Chicago Historical Society.

355. Show, Arley B. Papers. Nebraska State Historical
Society, Lincoln.

356. Streamer, Francis M. Papers. Washington State
Historical Society Library, Tacoma.

357. Taylor, Frederic W. Papers. Nebraska State Historical
Society, Lincoln.

358. Whitmore, William G. Papers. Nebraska State
Historical Society, Lincoln.

359. Wood, Ben B. Papers. Nebraska State Historical
Society, Lincoln.

RICHARD OLNEY, ATTORNEY GENERAL/SECRETARY OF STATE

360. Olney, Richard. Papers. Library of Congress.
Approximately 28,000 items.

361. ___. Papers. Massachusetts Historical Society,
Boston. 4 vols. and 6 boxes.

362. Bacon, Peter C. Papers. American Antiquarian Society,
Worcester, MA.

363. Bayard, Thomas F. Papers. Library of Congress.

364. Cleveland, Grover. Papers. Library of Congress.

365. Dickinson, Donald M. Papers. Library of Congress.

366. Dickinson, Jacob M. Papers. Tennessee State Archives, Nashville.

367. Ewing, Thomas. Papers. Library of Congress.

368. Foster, John W. Papers. Library of Congress.

369. Fuller, Melville W. Papers. Library of Congress.

370. Hamlin, Charles S. Papers. Library of Congress.

371. Hammond, John Hays. Papers. Yale University Library.

372. Hatch, Albert R. Papers. New Hampshire Historical Society, Concord.

373. Herbert, Hilary A. Papers. Southern Historical Collection, University of North Carolina, Library.

374. Holmes, Conrad. Papers. Virginia Historical Society, Richmond.

375. Lamont, Daniel S. Papers. Library of Congress.

376. Lynch, James D. Papers. Mississippi State University Library.

377. Mellen, Charles S. Papers. New Hampshire Historical Society, Concord.

378. Morton, Levi P. Papers. Syracuse University Library.

379. Phillips Family. Papers. Library of Congress.

380. Rockhill, William W.   Papers.   Houghton Library,
Harvard University.

GEORGE F. PARKER, BIOGRAPHER

381. Parker, George F.   Papers.   Iowa State Department of
History and Archives.   Approximately 1200 items.

WILLIAM E. RUSSELL, FRIEND

382. Russell, William E.   Papers.   Massachusetts Historical
Society.   44 vols. and 20 boxes.

HOKE SMITH, SECRETARY OF THE INTERIOR

383. Smith, Hoke.   Papers.   University of Georgia Library.
Approximately 24,000 items and 30 vols.

384. Brown, Joseph M.   Papers.   University of Georgia
Library.

385. Candler, Warren A.   Papers.   Emory University Library.

386. Cleveland, Grover.   Papers.   Library of Congress.

387. Colquitt, William N.   Papers.   Duke University Library.

388. Lochren, William.   Papers.   Minnesota Historical
Society, St. Paul.

389. Phillips Family. Papers. Library of Congress.

390. Spalding, Mary (Connally). Papers. Atlanta Historical Society.

ADLAI E. STEVENSON, VICE PRESIDENT

391. Alschuler, Samuel. Papers. Illinois State Historical Society, Springfield.

392. Asher, Louis E. Autograph Collection. Library of Congress.

393. Carr, Elias. Papers. East Carolina University Library.

394. Green, Adeline (Burr) Davis. Papers. Duke University Library.

395. Harrison, Carter H. Papers. Newberry Library, Chicago.

396. Lindsay, William. Papers. University of Kentucky Library.

397. Lochren, William. Papers. Minnesota Historical Society, St. Paul.

398. Melville, George W. Papers. Library of Congress.

399. Orme, William W. Papers. University of Illinois Library.

400. Parsons, Lewis B. Papers. Illinois State Historical Society, Springfield.

401. Pierce, Franklin. Papers. New Hampshire Historical
Society, Concord.

402. Sheehan, William F. Papers. Syracuse University
Library.

403. White, Stephen M. Papers. Stanford University
Library.

404. Wolcott, Edward O. Papers. State Historical Society
of Colorado, Denver.

SAMUEL J. TILDEN, DEMOCRATIC PARTY ELDER

405. Tilden, Samuel J. Papers. Columbia University
Libraries. 2 boxes.

406. Bigelow, John. Papers. New York Public Library.

407. Hill, David B. Papers. Syracuse University Library.

408. Marble, Manton. Papers. Library of Congress.

409. Marcy, William L. Papers. Library of Congress.

410. White, Andrew D. Papers. Cornell University Library.

WILLIAM F. VILAS, POSTMASTER GENERAL/SECRETARY OF THE
INTERIOR

411. Vilas, William Freeman. Papers. State Historical
Society of Wisconsin, Madison. 18 vols. and 23 boxes.

412. Anderson, Wendell A. Papers. State Historical Society
of Wisconsin, Madison.

413. Bayard, Thomas F.   Papers.   Library of Congress.

414. Bragg, Edwards S.   Papers.   State Historical Society of Wisconsin, Madison.

415. Hamilton, Alfred K.   Papers.   State Historical Society of Wisconsin, Madison.

416. LaFollette, Robert M.   Papers.   State Historical Society of Wisconsin, Madison.

417. Lamar, L. Q. C.   Papers.   Mississippi Department of Archives and History.

418. Lochren, William.   Papers.   Minnesota Historical Society, St. Paul.

419. Manning, Daniel.   Papers.   Library of Congress.

420. Reinsch, Paul S.   Papers.   State Historical Society of Wisconsin, Madison.

421. Usher, Ellis B.   Papers.   State Historical Society of Wisconsin, Madison.

WILLIAM C. WHITNEY, CAMPAIGN MANAGER/SECRETARY OF THE NAVY

422. Whitney, William C.   Papers.   Library of Congress.   182 vols. and 32 boxes.

423. Bayard, Thomas F.   Papers.   Library of Congress.

424. Camden, Johnson Newlon.   Papers.   West Virginia University Library.

425. Cleveland, Grover. Papers. Library of Congress.

426. Lamont, Daniel S. Papers. Library of Congress.

427. Manning, Daniel. Papers. Library of Congress.

428. Rowan, Stephen C. Papers. Library of Congress.

429. Schoonmaker, Cornelius M. Papers. Library of Congress.

WILLIAM L. WILSON, POSTMASTER GENERAL

430. Wilson, William L. Papers. Washington and Lee University Library, Lexington, Virginia. 550 items.

431. ___. Papers. West Virginia University Library. 3 boxes and 13 microfilm reels.

432. Barbe, Waitman. Papers. West Virginia Library.

433. Camden, Johnson Newlor. Papers. West Virginia University Library.

434. Gibson-Wilson Family. Papers. Bancroft Library, University of California, Berkeley.

435. MacDonald, Marshall. Papers. Duke University Library.

436. McGraw, John T. Papers. West Virginia Library.

CONTEMPORARY U.S. NEWSPAPERS

437. Albany (NY) <u>Argus</u> Daniel Manning's newspaper and therefore pro-GC.

438. Albany (NY) <u>Evening Journal</u> Available on microfilm; anti-GC.

439. Atlanta <u>Constitution</u> Available on microfilm; pro-GC.

440. Baltimore <u>American</u> Began in 1892; available on microfilm; anti-GC.

441. Baltimore <u>Sun</u> Available on microfilm; pro-GC.

442. Boston <u>Daily Globe</u> Available on microfilm; pro-GC.

443. Boston <u>Evening Transcript</u> Available on microfilm; pro-GC.

444. Brooklyn <u>Standard-Union</u> Began in 1887; available on microfilm; anti-GC. (Brooklyn <u>Union</u> 1883-1887).

445. Buffalo <u>Courier</u> Available on microfilm; pro-GC.

446. Buffalo <u>Express</u> Available on microfilm; pro-GC.

447. Buffalo <u>Evening News</u> Available on microfilm; pro-GC.

448. Charleston <u>News and Courier</u> Available on microfilm; pro-GC.

449. Chicago <u>Globe</u> Pro-GC.

450. Chicago <u>Inter-Ocean</u> Anti-GC.

451. Chicago <u>Journal</u> Available on microfilm; anti-GC.

452. Chicago News   Available on microfilm;   pro-GC.

453. Chicago Times later Chicago Times-Herald   Available on microfilm;   pro-GC.

454. Chicago Tribune   Available on microfilm; anti-GC.

455. Cincinnati Commercial-Gazette   1883-1896 on microfilm; anti-GC.

456. Cincinnati Enquirer   Available on microfilm;   pro-GC.

457. Denver News   Anti-GC.

458. Denver Republican   Available on microfilm from 1887 on;   anti-GC.

459. Detroit Free-Press   Available on microfilm;   pro-GC.

460. Detroit Tribune   Available on microfilm; anti-GC.

461. Indianapolis Journal   Available on microfilm; anti-GC.

462. Indianapolis Sentinel   Available on microfilm; pro-GC.

463. Iowa State Register (Des Moines)   Available on microfilm;   anti-GC.

464. Louisville Courier-Journal   Available on microfilm. Henry Watterson's newspaper, it was pro- or anti-GC depending on Watterson's position;   but it was generally anti-GC.

465. Nashville American   Available on microfilm;   pro-GC.

466. New Orleans Picayune Available on microfilm; pro-GC.

467. New York Herald Available on microfilm; pro-GC.

468. New York Sun Available on microfilm; it was at first anti-GC but supported him from 1892 on.

469. New York Times Available on microfilm; pro-GC.

470. New York Tribune Available on microfilm; anti-GC.

471. New York World Available on microfilm; pro-GC.

472. Ohio State Journal (Columbus) Available on microfilm; anti-GC.

473. Philadelphia Inquirer Available on microfilm; anti-GC.

474. Philadelphia Record Available on microfilm; pro-GC.

475. St. Louis Globe-Democrat Available on microfilm; anti-GC.

476. St. Louis Post-Dispatch Available on microfilm; pro-GC.

477. St. Louis Missouri Republican Available on microfilm; pro-GC.

478. San Francisco Chronicle Available on microfilm; anti-GC.

479. San Francisco Examiner Available on microfilm; pro-GC.

480. Springfield (MA) **Republican**   Available on microfilm; generally pro-GC.

481. Toledo **Blade**   Available on microfilm;   anti-GC.

482. Washington **Post**   Available on microfilm;   pro-GC.

CONTEMPORARY FOREIGN NEWSPAPERS

CANADA

483. **British Columbian**   (New Westminster)   Available on microfilm.

484. **Le Courrier du Canada**   (Quebec)   Available on microfilm.

485. **Daily Colonist**   (Victoria, British Columbia) Available on microfilm.

486. Digby **Courier**   (Nova Scotia)   Available on microfilm.

487. Edmonton **Bulletin**   (Alberta)   Available on microfilm.

488. **Le Journal de Quebec**   Available on microfilm.

489. Manitoba **Free Press**   (Winnipeg)   Available on microfilm.

490. **Le Monde**   (Montreal)   Available on microfilm.

491. **Morning Herald**   (Halifax, Nova Scotia)   Available on microfilm.

492. Ottawa **Journal**   Available on microfilm.

493. La Presse (Montreal)   Available on microfilm.

494. Regina Leader (Saskatchewan)   Available on microfilm.

495. St John Daily Sun (New Brunswick)   Available on microfilm.

496. Toronto Daily Mail   Available on microfilm.

497. Toronto Globe   Available on microfilm.

498. Toronto World   Available on microfilm.

ARGENTINA

499. La Nacion (Buenos Aires)   Available on microfilm.

500. La Prensa (Buenos Aires)   Available on microfilm.

BRAZIL

501. O Estado de Sao Paulo   Available on microfilm.

CHILE

502. Mercurio (Valparaiso)   Available on microfilm.

FRANCE

503. La Croix (Paris)   Available on microfilm.

504. L'Echo de Paris   Available on microfilm.

505. Le Figaro   (Paris)   Available on microfilm.

506. Gil Blas   (Paris)   Available on microfilm.

507. L'Intransigeant   (Paris)   Available on microfilm.

508. Journal des Debats   (Paris)   Available on microfilm.

509. La Liberte   (Paris)   Available on microfilm.

510. New York Herald-Tribune   (European edition, Paris)
Available on microfilm.

511. Le Presse   (Paris)   Available on microfilm.

512. Le Temps   (Paris)   Available on microfilm.

GERMANY

513. Der Arbeiterfreund   (Berlin)   Available on microfilm.

514. Frankfurter Zeitung   Available on microfilm.

515. Neue Preussische Zeitung   (Berlin)   Available on
microfilm.

516. Norddeutsche Allgemeine Zeitung   (Berlin)   Available
on microfilm.

517. Vossische Zeitung   (Berlin)   Available on microfilm.

GREAT BRITAIN

518. Daily Telegraph   (London)   Available on microfilm.

519. Economist   (London)   Available on microfilm.

520. Observer   (London)   Available on microfilm.

521. Pall Mall Gazette   (London)   Available on microfilm.

522. Sunday Dispatch   (London)   Available on microfilm.

523. The Times   (London)   Available on microfilm.

ITALY

524. Corriere Della Sera   (Milan)   Available on microfilm.

JAPAN

525. Hochi Shimbun   (Tokyo)   Available on microfilm.

526. Japan Mail   (Tokyo;   published in English)   Available
on microfilm.

MEXICO

527. La Patria   (Mexico City)   Available on microfilm.

RUSSIA

528. St. Petersburger Zeitung   (published in German)
Available on microfilm.

529. Pravitel'stvennyl Vestnik   (St. Petersburg)   Available
on microfilm.

SPAIN

530. Gaceta de Madrid   Available on microfilm.

VENEZUELA

531. Venezuelan Herald   (Caracas, 1896-)   Available on
microfilm.

2
Writings of Grover Cleveland

532. Cleveland, Grover. "Mr. Cleveland's Boston Speech."
Public Opinion 8 (December 21, 1889): 255-8. Excerpt of
December 12, 1889, speech to the Boston Merchant
Association, and the press reaction.

533. ___. "Address at Princeton Celebration." Public
Opinion 21 (October 29, 1896): 550-2. Excerpt of October
22, 1896,speech, and the press reaction.

534. ___. "Education: Ex-President Cleveland's Degree."
Critic 27 (June 1897): 446 and "Ex-President Cleveland's
Degree." Journal of Education 46 (July 22, 1897): 58. Text
of GC's acceptance of a Princeton honorary degree on June
16, 1897.

535. ___. The Self-Made Man in American Life. New York:
Crowell, 1897 and Reed, Thomas B. (ed.) Modern Eloquence. 9
vols. Philadelphia: John D. Morris, 1900, I, 249-54 and
Gilder Joseph B. (ed.) The American Idea As Expounded by
American Statesmen. New York: Dodd, Mead, 1902, 238-61.
Text of October 1897 speech at Princeton's 150th anniversary
celebration.

536. ___. American Citizenship . . . . Laurenceville, NJ:
The Trustees of the Laurenceville School, 1898. The June
21, 1898, Founders' Day address calling on the students to
cultivate "assertive and constant moral courage" (p. 18)
which is not seduced by "thoughtless popular sentiment." (p.
19)

537. ___. "Ex-President Cleveland on the Questions of the
Day." Public Opinion 24 (June 30, 1898): 805-6. Text of
Laurenceville School speech, and press reaction.

45

538. ___. "Does a College Education Pay?" Saturday Evening
Post 172 (May 26, 1900): 1089-90. Yes, as long as the
nation needs "intelligence" and "pure patriotism, obedience
to quickened conscience and disinterested discharge of
duty."

539. ___. "Independence of the Executive." Atlantic Monthly
85 (June 1900): 721-32;   86 (July 1900): 1-14 and The
Independence of the Executive. Princeton: Princeton
University Press, 1913. GC's defense of his stance in the
Tenure of Office Act controversy of his first term.

540. ___. "The Plight of the Democracy." Saturday Evening
Post 173 (December 22, 1900): 1-2 and Pacific Monthly 5
(January 1901): 151-4. Democratic party leaders need to
follow the rank and file and return to the party's true
principles.

541. ___. "The Young Man in Politics." Saturday Evening
Post 173 (January 26, 1901): 1-2. "Every young man should
regard political conviction and activity as a prime factor
of his citizenship" but should insist that his party be true
to its principles.

542. ___. "The Uses of Adversity, Taking the Living the
World Owes You." Saturday Evening Post 173 (March 9, 1901):
1-2. A young man should battle adversity not for success or
money but to serve others.

543. ___. "Venezuelan Boundary Controversy." Century 62
(June-July 1901): 283-97, 405-19 and The Venezuelan Boundary
Controversy Princeton: Princeton University Press, 1913.
Text of March 27, 1901, Princeton University lecture.

544. ___. "The Strength and Needs of Civil Service Reform."
Saturday Evening Post 173 (March 30, 1901): 1-2. Praises
previous civil service reformers and calls for continued
progress.

545. ___. "The Waste of Public Money." Saturday Evening
Post 173 (June 1, 1901): 1-2. Extravagant expenditures and
paternalism are not natural to government.

546. Bryan, William Jennings (ed.) The World's Famous
Orations. 10 vols. New York: Funk and Wagnalls, 1906. GC's
September 19, 1901, Princeton eulogy of William McKinley and
GC's First Inaugural Address (vol. 10, pp. 130-40).

547. Cleveland, Grover. "The Safety of the President."
Saturday Evening Post 174 (October 5, 1901): 1-2; reprint
in 248 (May/June 1976): 42-3, 105. Blames anarchists and
abusive press and politicians for the growing threat to the
president's life.

548. ___. "Duty of the Citizen to Public Charities."
Charities 7 (September 7, 1901): 201-3. Patriotism
includes supporting those in need.

549. ___. "A Defense of Fishermen." Saturday Evening Post
174 (October 19, 1901): 3-4. Defends fishermen's
brotherhood against accusations of laziness and
untruthfulness.

550. ___. "The Serene Duck Hunter." Saturday Evening Post
174 (April 26, 1902): 1-2. Criticizes people who shoot
ducks indiscriminately for market and praises "serene duck
hunters."

551. ___. "The President and His Patronage." Saturday
Evening Post 174 (May 24, 1902): 1-2. Office seekers cause
presidents to support civil service.

552. ___. "The Address for the Board of Trustees [at
Inauguration of Woodrow Wilson]." Princeton Alumni Weekly 3
(November 1, 1902): 98-102. "Princeton's conservatism is
one of her chief virtues." (p. 100) Promises the new
president the Board's support in maintaining the school's
greatness.

553. ___. "Adversity as an Aid to Success." New York
World, March 15, 1903, editorial section. Hard times are
not necessarily bad.

554. ___. "Word to Fisherman." Independent 55 (June 4,
1903): 1297-8. The benefits and joys of recreational
fishing.

555. ___. "The Civic Responsibility of Youth." Youth's
Companion 77 (July 2, 1903): 318. The nation's children
should be taught good citizenship.

556. ___. "The Mission of Fishing and Fishermen." Saturday
Evening Post 176 (December 5, 1903): 1-2. Fishing betters
man's nature.

557. ___. "The Shadow of the City, The Decadence of Rural
Political Independence." Saturday Evening Post 176
(September 19, 1903): 1-2. Defends small town values
against bad aspects of urban culture.

558. ___. "The Democracy's Opportunity." Saturday Evening
Post 176 (February 20, 1904): 1-2. Democratic party will do
well in 1904 elections because it has returned to its roots.

559. ___. "Ex-President Cleveland's Platform." Outlook 76
(February 27, 1904): 484-5. Synopsis of February 20, 1904,
article.

560. ___. "The Cleveland Bond Issues." Saturday Evening
Post 176 (May 7, 1904): 1-4, 17-20. Long, detailed defense
of his negotiations with bankers during the Panic of 1893.

561. ___. "Word for Forestry." Century 68 (June 1904): 308.
Expresses support for forest preservation on the occasion of
the centennial celebration of the Louisiana Purchase.

562. ___. "Summer Shooting." Independent 56 (June 2, 1904):
1228-31. The pleasure of shore bird shooting at Cape Cod.

563. ___. "Government in the Chicago Strike of 1894."
McClure's 23 (July 1904): 226-1904 and Fortnightly Review
82 (July 1904): 1-19 and The Government In the Chicago
Strike. Princeton: Princeton University Press, 1913.   GC's
version of the Pullman Strike.

564. ___. "Steady, Democrats, Steady." Collier's 33 (July
23, 1904): 6. Is pleased with 1904 Democratic convention,
especially nominee A. B. Parker's support of the gold
standard.

565. ___. "Some Fishing Pretenses and Affectations."
Saturday Evening Post 177 (September 24, 1904): 1-2. The
overemphasis on fly fishing should not overshadow
place-fishing for black bass.

566. ___. "Why a Young Man Should Vote the Democratic
Ticket." Saturday Evening Post 177 (October 8, 1904): 1-2.
The Democratic party has returned to its traditional
philosophy and is a sound vehicle for the protection of
American life.

567. ___. Presidential Problems. New York: Century, 1904.
Four essays: on Tenure of Office Act controversy, Pullman
Strike, Panic of 1893 bond sales, and Venezuelan Boundary
dispute.

568. ___. "Mission of Sport and Outdoor Life." Country
Calendar 1 (May 1905): 17-18. The social value of hunting
and fishing as good recreation in the open air.

569. ___. "Woman's Mission and Woman's Clubs." Ladies Home
Journal 22 (May 1905): 304-5. Woman should not punish
husband's neglect by "their own home-neglecting resort to
club pursuits or diversions."

570. ___. "Word Concerning Rabbit Hunting." Independent 58
(June 1, 1905): 1216-8. Rabbit hunting is a worthwhile
hunting pursuit.

571. ___. "Old-Fashioned Honesty and the Coming Man."
Saturday Evening Post 178 (August 5, 1905): 1-2. "Firm
conservatism, forbearance and appeal to sober thoughtfulness
are the needs of the hour," particuarly for college men.

572. ___. "Would Woman Suffrage Be Unwise?" Ladies Home
Journal 22 (October 1905): 7-8. The vote for women would
deal a blow to true womanhood.

573. ___. "The Integrity of American Character." Harpers
Magazine 112 (December 1905): 67-70. Americans will
preserve their nation and institutions because of their
strong inner fiber and patriotism.

574. ___. "The Country Lawyer in National Affairs." Youth's
Companion 80 (February 8, 1906): 63-4. The superiority of
country lawyers to city lawyers. Cites the 18
lawyer-presidents.

575. ___. "Quail Shooting." Independent 60 (June 7, 1906):
1317-23. Health and food value.

576. ___. "Honest American Marriage, A Plea for Honest
Building." Ladies Home Journal 23 (October 1906): 7. Calls
for "greater simplicity in living, and for more
home-building throughout our land."

577. ___. Fishing and Shooting Sketches. New York: Outing,
1906. GC's obvious love for the outdoors is clear in his
discussion of fishing and duck, rabbit, and quail hunting.

578. Collins, Varnum Lansing. Princeton. American College
University Series. New York: Oxford University Press,
1914. Excerpt of GC's November 1906 speech in opening
University Faculty Council Chambers (p. 278).

579. Cleveland, Grover. "Directors That Do Not Direct."
Saturday Evening Post 179 (December 1, 1906): 3-4. Bank and
business directors must be more willing to meet their
obligations to safeguard the stockholders' investments.

580. ___. Compulsory Investment Legislation. New York:
The Association of Life Insurance Presidents, 1907. An 8
page argument against any legislation to force insurance
companies to invest where they do business. This is bad
business and an affront to state sovereignty.

581. ___. "Patriotism and Holiday Observance," North
American Review 184 (April 1907): 683-93. Text of
Washington's Birthday Union League Club of Chicago speech
urging all Americans to express patriotism.

582. ___. "Shooting in Season." Independent 62 (June 6,
1907): 1310-4. Hunters must obey all written and unwritten
rules.

583. ___. Good Citizenship. Philadelphia: H. Alternus,
1908. Address on good citizenship delivered to Chicago
Commercial Club, October 1903, and the one on patriotism and
holiday observance before Chicago Union League Club,
February 22, 1907.

584. ___. "Our People and Their Ex-Presidents." Youth's
Companion 82 (January 2, 1908): 3-4. The nation should
offer financial support to former presidents in need. GC
says he is not.

585. ___. "Does the World Owe You a Living?" Great Orations
Delivered at Peirce Commencements . . . . Philadelphia:
Peirce School, 1910. It does not. Educated men should
serve society.

586. ___. Cleveland's Last Message: Life Insurance and Its
Relationship to Our People. New York: Spectator, 1908.
People need its protection.

3
Biographical Publications

587. Nevins, Allan. Grover Cleveland, A Study in Courage .
New York: Dodd, Mead, 1932. This is the standard GC
biography. It established the view of GC as the only
stand-out president of the Gilded Age.

588. Merrill, Horace Samuel. Bourbon Leader: Grover
Cleveland and the Democratic Party. Boston: Little, Brown,
1957. A critical biography which characterizes GC as a
"Bourbon Leader," "Reluctant Reformer," "Cautious
Politician," and "Defender of the Status Quo. "

589. Lynch, Denis T. Grover Cleveland: A Man Four-Square.
New York: H. Liveright, 1932. A detailed favorable
biography of GC, superceded by Nevins' book.

590. McElroy, Robert. Grover Cleveland, The Man and the
Statesman. An Authorized Biography. 2 vols. Introduction
by Elihu Root. New York: Harper and Brothers, 1923. A
favorable biography of GC, superceded by Nevins' book.

591. Tugwell, Rexford G. Grover Cleveland. New York:
Macmillan, 1968. The former New Dealer argues that GC was a
failure as a president because he lacked personal and
political experience.

592. Parker, George F. Recollections of Grover Cleveland.
New York: Century, 1909. A favorable biography by a friend
who also wrote numerous articles on various aspects of GC's
personal and political life. Includes letters by and about
GC.

51

593. Whittle, James L. Grover Cleveland. Public Men of
Today. London: Bliss, Sands, 1896. Strong British point
of view in this popular and very dated GC biography.

594. Smyth, Clifford. Grover Cleveland, Who Put Independent
Thinking into Party Politics. Builders of America, vol. 22.
New York: Funk and Wagnalls, 1931. A brief, dated, popular
biography.

595. Wilson, James Grant. (ed.) The Presidents of the
United States 1789-1914. 4 vols. New York: Scribners,
1914. A sketch of GC and his presidency appears in vol. 3.

596. Hugins, Roland. Grover Cleveland: A Study in Political
Courage. Admirable Americans. Washington: Anchor-Lee,
1922. A very brief biography, but also includes GC speeches
and letters, including some unavailable elsewhere.

597. McGuire, James K. The Democratic Party of the State of
New York. 3 vols. New York: U.S. History Co., 1905. A
brief sketch of GC and his political career with no emphasis
on his New York career. (vol. II, chap. 2)

598. The Presidents: Their Lives, Families and Great
Decisions As Told by the Saturday Evening Post.
Indianapolis: Curtis, 1980. Excerpts from articles by and
about GC. (pp. 76-81)

599. Roberts, Randy. "Grover Cleveland." The American
Presidents: The Office and the Men. 2 vols. Edited by
Frank N. Magill. Pasadena, California: Salem Press, 1986.
A modern biographical sketch. (vol. II, pp. 411-25).

600. Garraty, John A. "Grover Cleveland." in The
Presidents: A Reference History. Edited by Henry F. Graff.
New York: Scribner's, 1984, 337-49. A good short account of
GC's political career which concludes that he was "rather
limited" but had few equals among American presidents "in
industriousness and in devotion to principle and to the
public good as he saw it." (p. 348)

601. DeGregorio, William A. The Complete Book of U.S.
Presidents. New York: Dembner Books, 1984. Synopsis of
GC's life, election campaigns, cabinets, and presidential
terms. (pp. 319-29, 345-52)

602. Paxson, Frederic L. "Cleveland, Stephen Grover."
Dictionary of American Biography. Edited by Allen Johnson
and Dumas Malone. New York: Charles Scribner's Sons, 1930.
Sketch and dated bibliography. (vol. IV, pp. 205-12.)

603. Kane, Joseph N. Facts about the Presidents: A
Compilation of Biographical and Historical Information. 4th
ed. New York: H. W. Wilson, 1981. Basic information on GC
and his two terms.

604. Taylor, Tim. The Book of Presidents. New York: Arno
Press, 1972. Basic facts on GC, his parents, and his wife.
Also a detailed chronology of his administrations and his
post-presidential life.

605. Sobel, Robert, and Raimo, John (eds.) Biographical
Directory of the Governors of the United States 1789-1978.
Westport, CT: Meckler, 1978. Sketch of GC's life and
political career. (vol. III, pp. 1089-90)

606. Bullard, Thomas R. "Grover Cleveland." Biographical
Directory of American Mayors. Edited by Melvin G. Holli and
Peter d'A Jones. Westport, CT: Greenwood, 1981. A brief
biographical sketch.

607. Archer, Robert L. "President Who Came Back." National
Republic 23 (January, February 1936): 3-4, 20-1. A sketch
of GC's life praising his courage and sound judgment.

608. Mott, Frank H. "Grover Cleveland: An Appreciation."
American Bar Association Journal 13 (October 1927): 587-90.
A speech at the national ABA meeting in Buffalo extolling
GC's life and virtues.

609. Rice, William G. "Grover Cleveland; Intimate
Unpublished Recollections." Century 116 (October 1928):
740-50. Stories about GC from his early Buffalo days to his
post-presidential Princeton period, discovered and passed on
by his former U.S. Civil Service commissioner and assistant
private secretary.

610. Russell, William E. "Grover Cleveland." in The
Presidents of the United States 1789-1894. New York: D.
Appleton, 1894. A sketch of GC's life to his 1892 election
written by a leading Democratic politician and friend.
Includes many excerpts from his speeches.

4
Childhood and Early Development

BIRTHPLACE

611. "Cleveland's Birthplace. " Americana 7 (February
1912): 150-3. A brief account of GC's Caldwell, NJ
birthplace including a photograph of the house.

612. Hampton, William Judson. Presidential Shrines from
Washington to Coolidge. Boston: Christopher, 1928. Photo
and description of GC's birthplace. (pp. 191-7)

613. Grover Cleveland's Birthplace. Proceedings at the
Passing of Title to the 'Old Manse' Caldwell, New Jersey,
March 18, 1913. Caldwell: Grover Cleveland Birthplace
Memorial Association, 1913. Photos and speeches.

GENEALOGY

614. Cleveland, Edmund Janes, and Cleveland, Horace Gilette.
The Genealogy of the Cleveland and Cleaveland Families. 3
vols. Hartford: Case Lockwood and Brainard, 1899.

615. Cleveland, H. G. Excerpts from Genealogical Records
Showing Lineage of Hon. Grover Cleveland. n.p.: n.p.,
1887. A four page listing going back to the early 15th
century.

616. Watkins, Walter K. New England Ancestry of Grover Cleveland.... Salem: Salem Press, 1892.

617. Falley, Margaret D. "Richard Falle-Falley and Some of His Descendants including Grover Cleveland." New England Historical and Genealogical Register 108 (January-June 1954): 39-46, 96-105, 193-202.

618. Burke's Presidential Families of the United States of America. London: Burke's Peerage, 1975. Detailed chapter on GC's family background.

619. Faber, Doris. The Presidents' Mothers. New York: St. Martin's Press, 1978. A short sketch of GC's mother, Ann Neal Cleveland. (pp. 224-6)

620. Metcalf, Henry H. "Grover Cleveland." Bay State Monthly 2 (November 1884): 61-9. GC's genealogy and life to his first election.

621. Pessen, Edward. The Log Cabin Myth. The Social Backgrounds of the Presidents. New Haven: Yale University Press, 1984. GC's family background, his early life, and work.

BOYHOOD

622. "The Boyhood of President Cleveland." Review of Reviews 7 (April 1893): 299-302. Based on interviews with a former school teacher and classmates.

623. Allen, W. C. "Personal Reminiscences of the Boyhood and Early Manhood of Grover Cleveland." National Monthly 4 (January-March 1913): 196-7, 216-7, 256-7. A cousin of the same age details GC's early life, including many personal anecdotes.

624. Chamberlain, Eugene T. Early and Public Services of Grover Cleveland . . . . Chicago: Caxton, 1884. A campaign biography revised by GC himself and especially valuable on his early years.

5
Early Career

625. Crosby, Fanny J. "Cleveland as a Teacher in the
Institution for the Blind." McClure's 32 (April 1909):
581-3. A fellow teacher discusses GC's year (1853-4).

626. Weyand, Paul. "Beecher and Cleveland: A Sermon That
Made a President." Methodist Review 95 (September 1913):
764-8. Influence of an 1854 sermon by Henry Ward Beecher on
17 year old GC.

627. "A Famous Old Law Office." Buffalo Historical Society
Publications 24 (1920): 388-9. A brief discussion of the
first law firm GC worked for in Buffalo beginning in 1855.

628. The Savings Accounts of Successful Buffalonians.
Buffalo: Erie County Savings Bank, 1937. GC's 1868 bank
deposit signature. (p. 5)

6
Mature Years

629. Armitage, Charles H. Grover Cleveland as Buffalo Knew Him. Buffalo: Buffalo Evening News, 1926. GC's early Buffalo days and his later relationship to Buffalo people, based on contemporary reminiscences, letters, and newspaper files.

630. Parker, George F. "Grover Cleveland's Career in Buffalo, 1855-1882." Saturday Evening Post 193 (August 28, 1920): 6-7, 76-90. GC's early years in Buffalo and their influence on his later political career.

631. Walter, Francis J. Grover Cleveland and Buffalo. Adventures in Western New York History, Vol. 11. Buffalo: Buffalo and Erie County Historical Society, 1963. A 20 page account of GC's relationship to Buffalo.

632. Dunn, Walter S., Jr. (ed.) History of Erie County, 1870-1970. Buffalo: Buffalo and Erie County Historical Society, 1972. GC as mayor of Buffalo. (chap. 4)

633. Milburn, John G. "Cleveland's View of Public Life." Scribner's 81 (April 1927): 344-8. A Buffalo lawyer-friend reminisces particularly about GC's Buffalo years and his New York governorship.

634. ___. "Grover Cleveland: Address Delivered at the
Unveiling of the Memorial Tablet at the Buffalo Historical
Society, May 20, 1912." Buffalo Historical Society
Publications 17 (1913): 121-6. A eulogy by an old Buffalo
friend.

635. Bissell, Wilson S. "Cleveland as a Lawyer; By His Law
Partner." McClure's 32 (April 1909): 583-5. An August 1,
1892 letter from GC's Buffalo law partner describing GC
during these early Buffalo years.

636. Goodyear, Anson C. Family History By A Descendant.
Parts I, II, and III. Buffalo: privately printed, Parts I
and II, n.d. Part III, 1976. In this history of an
important Buffalo family, Parts I and II include Appendix I,
"Correspondence with Grover Cleveland [1880s to 1906]."
Part III includes references to GC and his wife.

637. Wickser, Philip J. "Grover Cleveland: His Character,
Background and Legal Career." American Bar Association
Journal 33 (April 1947): 327-30, 408-9. A Buffalo lawyer's
account of GC's pre-presidential life --- based primarily on
the Nevins biography and Armitage book.

638. Scott, Henry W. Distinguished American Lawyers.
Webster, New York: Charles L. Webster, 1891. A sketch of
GC's life with emphasis on his Buffalo years. (pp. 161-72)

639. Abbott, John S. C., and Conwell, Russell H. Lives of
the Presidents . . . . Rev. ed. Portland, Maine: H.
Hallett, 1885. Chapter 22 of this subscription book is a
sketch of GC, emphasizing his Buffalo years.

640. "Historic Relic." Time 28 (November 30, 1936): 14.
An account of GC's hanging of two men in Buffalo when he was
sheriff in the 1870s and the gallows recently discovered in
1936.

641. Larned, Josephus N. History of Buffalo 2
vols. New York: Progress of the Empire State, 1911. GC is
mentioned only in passing, but these volumes contain
valuable information on Buffalo during his years.

642. Walter, Francis J. "A Social and Cultural History of Buffalo, New York, 1865-1901." Ph.D. diss., Western Reserve University, 1958. Buffalo during GC's era.

643. Glazier, Willard. Peculiarities of American Cities. Philadelphia: Hubbard Brothers, 1884. Buffalo during GC's time as mayor. (chap. 3)

GOVERNOR OF NEW YORK

644. Parker, George F. "Grover Cleveland as Governor of New York." Saturday Evening Post 194 (June 24, 1922): 30-40. A detailed account of his two year term.

645. Lincoln, Charles Z. (ed.) Messages From the Governors. Albany: J. B. Lyon, 1909, VII, 815-1126. Contains all GC's messages while governor.

646. Alexander, DeAlva. A Political History of the State of New York. 4 vols. New York: Henry Holt, 1923. GC's meteoric rise in New York State politics in the early 1880s (vol. I) and his governorship and political battles with David B. Hill and other New Yorkers during his presidential campaigns (vol. IV).

647. Flick, Alexander C. Samuel Jones Tilden: A Study in Political Sagacity. New York: Dodd, Mead, 1939. GC's early New York State political career and his 1884 presidential nomination.

648. Fitch, James Monroe. The Ring Buster, A Story of the Erie Canal. New York: Fleming H. Revell, 1940. A fictional account of GC's mayoral and gubernatorial battles against corruption and the impact on the 1884 presidential campaign.

649. Tyler, Moses Coit. In Memoriam E. K. Apgar. Ithaca, New York: privately printed, 1886. This important New York Democrat played an important role in GC's 1882 gubernatorial and 1884 presidential nominations.

650. Downey, Matthew T. "Grover Cleveland and Abram S. Hewitt: The Limits of Factional Consensus." New York Historical Society Quarterly 54 (July 1970): 222-40. "The Hewitt-Cleveland relationship [1880s] suggests that consensus within party factions did not extend much beyond general agreement on public issues." (p. 240)

651. Putnam, Carleton. Theodore Roosevelt, The Formative Years, 1858-1886. New York: Charles Scribner's Sons, 1958. GC's governorship and 1884 presidential election from Roosevelt's perspective.

652. Hurwitz, Howard L. Theodore Roosevelt and Labor in New York State, 1880-1900. Studies in History, Economics, and Public Law, Columbia University, No. 500, 1943. GC as governor and his on and off relationship with Assemblyman Roosevelt.

653. Bishop, Joseph B. Theodore Roosevelt and His Times Shown in His Own Letters. 2 vols. New York: Charles Scribner's Sons, 1920. Numerous references and a few letters to GC.

654. Roosevelt, Theodore. The Letters of Theodore Roosevelt. Edited by Elting E. Morrison. 8 vols. Cambridge: Harvard University Press, 1951-1954. GC from the days of his governorship to the Roosevelt presidency. Includes several TR letters to GC.

655. ___. Theodore Roosevelt. Introduction by Elting E. Morrison. 1913. Reprint. New York: Da Capo, 1985. Brief mentions of GC as governor (pp. 75, 82) and during the 1902 coal strike. (pp. 482, 488)

656. Pringle, Henry F. Theodore Roosevelt, A Biography. New York: Harcourt, Brace, 1931. Roosevelt's perspective on GC from the time of GC's governorship through a labor dispute in Roosevelt's presidency.

657. Norcross, Grenville H. (ed.) "Letters." Massachusetts Historical Society Proceedings 63 (1931): 230. An October 22, 1884,GC to Herman W. Chaplin letter, inviting him to dinner at the New York governor's residence.

658. Mitchell, Edward P. Memoirs of an Editor, Fifty Years of American Journalism. New York: Charles Scribner's Sons, 1924. New York Sun's on and off relationship with GC, beginning with his governor days.

659. Benson, Lee. Merchants, Farmers, and Railroads: Railroad Regulation and New York Politics 1850-1887. Cambridge: Harvard University Press, 1955. GC as New York governor and his role in the elevated railroad fare issue.

660. Congressional Quarterly. Guide to U.S. Elections. Washington: Congressional Quarterly, 1975. Includes information on GC's gubernatorial and presidential races.

7
The Presidential Elections
of 1884, 1888, and 1892

661. Schlesinger, Arthur M., Jr.; Israel, Fred L.; Hansen, William P. (eds.) History of American Presidential Elections, Vol. II: 1848-1896. New York: Chelsea House, 1971. Extended sketch and documents about the 1884 election by Mark D. Hirsch; 1888 election by Robert F. Wesser; and the 1892 election by H. Wayne Morgan.

662. Roseboom, Eugene H., and Eckles, Alfred E., Jr. A History of Presidential Elections From George Washington to Jimmy Carter. 4th ed. New York: Macmillan, 1979. Election statistics.

663. Presidential Elections Since 1789. 2nd. ed. Washington: Congressional Quarterly, 1979. Election statistics.

664. Burnham, Walter Dean. Presidential Ballots, 1836-1892. Baltimore: Johns Hopkins, 1955. Election statistics.

665. Petersen, Svend. A Statistical History of the American Presidential Elections. New York: Unger, 1963.

Grover Cleveland ran for the presidency three times. General material on these campaigns is located here; specific material on the individual campaigns of 1884, 1888, and 1892 is located in Sections 9, 11, and 12 respectively.

666. Congressional Quarterly. Presidential Candidates from
1788 to 1964, Including Third Parties, 1832-1964, and
Popular Electoral Vote: Historical Review. Rev. ed.
Washington: Congressional Quarterly, 1964. Election
statistics.

667. David, Paul T. Party Strength in the United States,
1872-1970. Charlottesville: University Press of Virginia,
1972.

668. Congressional Quarterly. National Party Conventions,
1831-1980. Washington: Congressional Quarterly, 1982.
Convention statistics.

669. McKee, Thomas Hudson. The National Conventions and
Platforms of All Political Parties, 1789 to 1905:
Convention, Popular, and Electoral Vote. Also the Political
Complexion of Both Houses of Congress at Each Biennial
Period. 6th ed. Baltimore: Friedenwald, 1906.

670. Porter, Kirk H., and Johnson, Donald Bruce. (comp.)
National Party Platforms, 1840-1964. Urbana: University of
Illinois Press, 1972.

671. Chester, Edward W. A Guide to Political Platforms.
Hamden, CT: Archon, 1977.

672. Eaton, Herbert. Presidential Timber: A History of
Nominating Conventions, 1868-1960. New York: Free Press of
Glencoe, 1964.

673. McClure, Alexander K. Our Presidents and How We Make
Them. New York: Harper and Brothers, 1900. Election
campaigns according to this famous magazine publisher.

674. Byrne, Gary C., and Marx, Paul. The Great American
Convention: A Political History of Presidential Elections.
Palo Alto, California: Pacific Books, 1976. The 1884 and
1892 conventions according to the authors' "choice model" of
election prediction.

675. Zorilla, Luis G. Historia De Las Relaciones Entre
Mexico y Los Estados Unidos De America 1800-1958. 2 vols.
Mexico City: Editorial Porrua, S.A., 1966. Brief
references to GC's three presidential elections. (vol. 2)

676. Reuter, William C. "Anglophobia in American Politics,
1865-1900." Ph.D. diss., University of California-Berkeley,
1966. In the 1884 and 1888 campaigns, Republicans used
Anglophobia to argue for a high tariff and to gain Irish
votes. In the 1890s, free silverites used Anglophobia
against GC's hard money "British" policy.

677. Cordell, Christobel M. (comp.) Presidential Elections.
Portland, ME: J. Weston Walch, 1965. Eighteen posters from
the Bettman Archive including ones from the 1884, 1888, and
1892 election campaigns.

678. Reynolds, John F. and McCormick, Richard L. "Outlawing
'Treachery': Split Tickets and Ballot Laws in New York and
New Jersey, 1880-1910." Journal of American History 72
(March 1986): 835-58. Electoral statistical information on
two key states (GC's places of birth, career, and
retirement) including the 1882 NY governor's race and the
1884, 1888, and 1892 presidential elections.

679. Parker, Albert C. E. "Beating the Spread: Analyzing
American Election Outcomes." Journal of American History 67
(June 1980): 61-87. The GC election campaigns within the
context of the author's mobilization ratio model. (pp.
75-8, 82-4)

680. Lichtman, Allan J. "Political Realignment and
Ethnocultural Voting in the Late Nineteenth Century
America." Journal of Social History 16 (Spring 1983):
55-82. Statistical information and analysis on the 1888,
1892, and 1896 elections which concludes that the latter did
not realign politics as sometimes argued.

681. DeSantis, Vincent P. "Catholicism and Presidential
Elections, 1865-1900." Mid-America 42 (April 1960): 67-79.
"Rum, Romanism, and Rebellion" and anti-Catholic accusations
against GC in 1884 and pro-Catholic charges in 1892. (pp.
73-5, 78)

682. O'Connor, Joseph. The Case of Cleveland, Considered in Two Letters, Bearing Date May 26, 1888 and May 26, 1892 . . . . . Rochester: Post-Express, 1892. Opposition to GC's nominations both years.

683. Sievers, Harry. Benjamin Harrison: Hoosier Statesman; Hoosier President. 3 vols. New York: University Publishers, 1959 and Indianapolis: Bobbs-Merrill, 1968. GC's election campaigns and administrations from the perspective of his chief Republican presidential opponent. (vols. 2, 3)

684. Socolofsky, Homer E., and Spetter, Alan B. The Presidency of Benjamin Harrison. Lawrence: University of Kansas Press, 1987. Harrison's two election campaigns against GC and his perspective on the issues of both terms.

685. Fischer, Roger A. Tippecanoe and Trinkets Too. The Material Culture of American Presidential Campaigns, 1828-1984. Champaign: University of Illinois Press, 1988. Modern analysis of the memorabilia of presidential campaigns, including GC's.

686. Papale, Henry. (comp.) Banners, Buttons, and Songs: A Pictorial Review and Capsule Almanac of America's Presidential Campaigns. Cincinnati: World Library Publications, 1968. Photos and material from GC's three presidential campaigns.

8
The Presidency: 1885-1889, 1893-1897

ILLUSTRATED OVERVIEWS

687. Lorant, Stefan. The Glorious Burden: The History of the Presidency and Presidential Elections from George Washington to James Earl Carter, Jr. Lenox, MA: Authors Edition, 1976. Excellent contemporary cartoons and several photographs with a good sketch of events. (pp. 366-91, 411-28)

688. Durant, John, and Durant, Alice. Pictorial History of American Presidents. New York: Castle Books, 1975. Photographs and sketches of major events from the GC years. (pp. 182-7, 194-7)

689. ___ . The Presidents of the United States: A History . . . With an Encyclopedic Supplement on the Office and Powers of the Presidency: Chronologies, and Records of Presidential Elections. 2 vols. Miami: A. A. Gache, 1976. Photographs and cartoons on GC's presidency. (Vol. I)

Material pertinent to both presidential terms is located here; material on the individual terms is located in Sections 10 and 13 respectively.

INAUGURATIONS

690. Durbin, Louise. Inaugural Cavalcade. New York: Dodd,
Mead, 1971. GC's two inaugurations. (pp. 114-16, 120-2)

691. Kittler, Glenn D. Hail to the Chief! The Inauguration
Days of Our Presidents. Philadelphia: Chilton Books, 1965.
GC's two inaugurations including photos of each. (pp.
118-23, 129-33)

692. Chase, Edward W. "Beyond the Rhetoric: A New Look at
Presidential Inaugural Addresses." Presidential Studies
Quarterly 10 (Fall 1980): 571-82. A brief comparision of
GC's two inaugural addresses with those of other presidents
of the age. (p. 575)

693. MacNeil, Neil. The President's Medal, 1789-1977. New
York: C. N. Potter, 1977. GC's inauguration medals and
badges. (pp. 36-9, 46-9)

REMINISCENCES

694. Barry, David S. Forty Years in Washington. Boston:
Little, Brown, 1924. GC and his presidency, particularly
contemporary anecdotes about the cabinet and other political
personalities.

695. Cortissoz, Royal. The Life of Whitelaw Reid. 2 vols.
London: Thornton, Butterworth, 1921. This New York Tribune
reporter and politician discusses GC's two terms negatively.

696. Cox, James M. Journey Through My Years. New York:
Simon and Schuster, 1946. This memoir of the 1920
Democratic party presidential candidate includes a favorable
evaluation of GC and discussions of his second term cabinet
and other leading politicians of that day.

697. Harrison, Benjamin. This Country of Ours. New York:
Charles Scribner's Sons, 1897. Mentions GC only in regard

to Tenure of Office Act controversy (pp. 101-3) and the
Wilson-Gorman Tariff. (p. 129)

698. Hudson, William C. Random Recollections of an Old
Political Reporter . . . . Introduction by St. Clair
McKelway. New York: Cupples and Leon, 1910. Much material
on GC, his presidential campaigns, and his political
attitudes.

699. Peck, Harry Thurston. Twenty Years of the Republic,
1885-1905. New York: Dodd, Mead, 1932. A detailed
favorable discussion of GC's first term, the 1892 election,
and GC's second term.

700. ___ . "Twenty Years of the Republic (1885-1905) Parts I
- XII." Bookman 20 (January-February 1905): 422-46,
519-40; 21 (March-August 1905): 31-58, 142-59, 293-304,
368-79, 472-95, 616-34; 22 (September-December 1905):
39-56, 111-30, 242-55, 334-58. These segments from Peck's
book discuss GC's two presidential terms in a favorable
light.

701. Sherman, John. Recollections of Forty Years in the
House, Senate, and Cabinet. 2 vols. Chicago: Werner,
1895. Vol. 2 includes this Ohio Republican Senator/Cabinet
member's view of GC and his presidential policies.

702. Stealey, Orlando Oscar. Twenty Years in the Press
Gallery. New York: By author, 1906. Generally favorable
evaluation of GC as president. (pp. 28-30)

703. Stoddard, Henry L. As I Knew Them: Presidents and
Politics from Grant to Coolidge. New York: Harper, 1927.
A newspaper reporter's memoirs discuss both of GC's terms.

GENERAL HISTORIES

704. Welch, Richard E., Jr., The Presidencies of Grover
Cleveland. American Presidency Series. Lawrence:
University Press of Kansas, 1988. Modern in-depth study of
GC's two terms.

705. Agar, Herbert. The People's Choice, From Washington to Harding: A Study in Democracy. New York: Houghton Mifflin, 1933. A brief survey of GC's two terms praising his honesty but criticizing his stubbornness.

706. Andrews, Elisha B. History of the Last Quarter of a Century in the United States. 2 vols. New York: Charles Scribner's, 1896. Vol. 2, Chap. 3-6 and 10-11 of this social history discuss GC's elections and two terms.

707. Boller, Paul F., Jr. Presidential Anecdotes. New York: Oxford University Press, 1981. Mostly humorous stories about GC and his presidency. (pp. 177-82)

708. Dewey, Davis Rich National Problems, 1885-97. American Nation Series. New York: Harper Brothers, 1907. A dated, detailed favorable account of the two GC presidential terms.

709. Dictionary of American History. 7 vols. Rev. ed. New York: Scribners, 1976. Provides information on "Cleveland Democrats," the "Campaign of 1892," "Pullman Strike," and other events and terminology of the GC presidency.

710. Ford, Henry Jones. The Cleveland Era, A Chronicle of the New Order in Politics. The Chronicles of America Series, vol. 44. New Haven: Yale University Press, 1919. Detailed, dated account of GC's presidency.

711. Ginger, Ray. Age of Excess: The United States from 1877 to 1914. New York: Macmillan, 1965. Basic information on major issues of GC's two terms.

712. Josephson, Matthew C. The Politicos, 1865-1896. New York: Harcourt Brace, 1938. This opinionated study of Gilded Age politicians discusses GC's role as opposition leader to the dominant Republicans and to the Silver Democrats.

713. Keller, Morton. Affairs of State: Public Life in Late Nineteenth Century America. Cambridge: Harvard University Press, 1977. Chaps. 14 and 15 contain information about GC's presidency.

714. Kleppner, Paul. The Cross of Culture: A Social
Analysis of Midwestern Politics, 1850-1900. New York: Free
Press, 1970. GC is only mentioned once, but this is an
important book for understanding the politics of his era.

715. ___. The Third Electoral System, 1853-1892: Parties,
Voters, and Political Cultures. Chapel Hill: University of
North Carolina Press, 1979. Like the author's earlier book,
this is an important study of Gilded Age politics.

716. Marcus, Robert D. Grand Old Party, Political Structure
in the Gilded Age, 1880-1896. New York: Oxford University
Press, 1971. GC is mentioned frequently but in passing in
this study of the Republican party's lack of organization in
the Gilded Age.

717. McClure, Alexander K. Col. Alexander K. McClure's
Recollections of Half a Century. Salem, MA: Salem Press,
1902. "Cleveland's Three Contests and Two Administrations."
(pp. 124-33)

718. Merrill, Horace Samuel. Bourbon Democracy of the
Middle West 1865-1896. Baton Rouge: Louisiana State
University Press, 1953. GC, his two terms, and Midwest
Democratic party leaders.

719. Morgan, H. Wayne. From Hayes to McKinley, National
Party Politics, 1877-1896. Syracuse: Syracuse University
Press, 1969. Several detailed chapters on the politics of
GC's election campaigns and two terms.

720. Morison, Samuel Eliot. The Oxford History of the
American People. New York: Oxford University Press, 1965.
Includes a delightfully written analysis of the GC
presidency.

721. Nevins, Allan. The Evening Post: A Century of
Journalism. New York: Boni and Liveright, 1924. The
mugwump New York Evening Post's support during the 1884
election and GC's two terms in office.

722. Oberholtzer, Ellis Paxson. History of the United
States Since the Civil War. 5 vols. New York: Macmillan,
1917-1937. Detailed coverage of GC's election campaigns and
presidency. (vols. 4, 5)

723. Painter, Nell Irwin. Standing at Armageddon, The
United States 1877-1919. New York: Norton, 1987. This
interpretive history of the United States discusses GC's
role in the nation's struggle to deal with the anxieties of
a society changing from rural to industrial.

724. Rhodes, James Ford. History of the United States from
Hayes to McKinley. new ed. New York: Macmillan, 1919.
Much detail on the GC presidency.

725. Stanwood, Edward. A History of the Presidency. Rev.
ed. 2 vols. Boston: Houghton Mifflin, 1928. GC's
election campaigns and two terms. (vol. 1, chaps. 27-8, 30)

726. White, Leonard D. The Republican Era, 1869-1901: A
Study in Administrative History. New York: Macmillan,
1958. GC is mentioned briefly concerning laissez faire,
pensions, Tenure of Office Act, office seekers, civil
service, and cabinet procedure.

727. Williams, R. Hal. The Democratic Party and California
Politics, 1880-1896. Stanford: Stanford University Press,
1973. California's dissatisfaction with GC's two terms.

OFFICIAL PUBLICATIONS

728. U.S. Attorney General. Digest of Official Opinions.
Washington: Government Printing Office, 1789-1921.

729. U.S. Congress. Congressional Record. Washington:
Government Printing Office, 1874 to present. Transcript of
congressional debate, often edited by the speakers before
publication.

730. ___. House Journal. Washington: Government Printing
Office, 1789 to present. Outline of daily business.

731. ___. Journal of the Executive Proceedings of the
Senate of the United States of America. Washington:
Government Printing Office, 1828 to present. Outline of
closed sessions.

732. ___. List of Treaties Submitted to the Senate,
1789-1934. Washington: Government Printing Office, 1935.
Those accepted and rejected.

733. ___. Senate Journal. Washington: Government Printing
Office, 1789 to present. Outline of daily business.

734. U.S. National Archives. Papers of the United States
Senate Relating to Presidential Nominations, 1789-1901.
Record Group 46. Washington: Government Printing Office,
1964. Includes GC's nominations in both terms. See,
especially, in regards to Tenure of Office Act controversy.

735. U.S. State Department. Treaties, Conventions,
International Acts, Protocols, and Agreements Between the
U. S. A. and Other Powers, 1776-1937. Washington: Government
Printing Office, 1910-1938.

736. United States Statutes-at-Large. Washington:
Government Printing Office, 1789 to present. Laws.

737. U. S. Supreme Court. Supreme Court Reporter. St.
Paul, MN: West, 1883 to present. Opinions and decisions.

738. U. S. Supreme Court. United States Reports.
Washington: Government Printing Office, 1790 to present.
Opinions and decisions.

739. U. S. Treasury Department. Digest of Decisions of the
Second Comptroller. Washington: Government Printing
Office, 1817-1894. Includes only half of GC's second term.

740. ___. Synopsis of Decisions. Washington: Government
Printing Office, 1868-1898.

SERIAL SET

The House and the Senate Documents and the House and the
Senate Reports, organized into volumes and numbered
consecutively, are called the serial set. They are indexed
and are also available on microform. The following entries
are selected examples of the kind of material available on
the GC presidency in this valuable source.

741. CIS U.S. Serial Set Index. 36 vols. Washington:
Congressional Information Service, 1976.

742. U.S. Congress. House of Representatives. Foreign
Relations of the United States. 49th Cong., 1st Sess. to
50th Cong., 2nd Sess., 53rd Cong., 1st Sess. to 54th Cong.,
2nd Sess., 1886-1888, 1894-1898. H. Exec. Docs. Serials
2368, 2430, 2432, 2626-27, 3197, 3292, 3369, 3477. Primary
sources on the diplomatic issues of GC's two terms.

743. ___. Reform in Civil Service. Report to accompany
H.R. 2248. 48th Cong., 1st Sess., 1888. H. Rept. 1955.
Serial 2259. Tenure of Office Act controversy.

744. ___. To Repeal the Tenure of Office Act. Report to
accompany S. 512. 49th Cong., 2nd Sess., 1887. H. Rept.
3539. Serial 2500.

745. ___. Report of the Interstate Commerce Commission.
50th Cong., 1st Sess., 1888. H. Exec. Doc. 1. Serial 2541.

746. ___. Letter from Secretary of the Treasury, January
12, 1888. 50th Cong., 1st Sess., 1888. H. Exec. Doc. 71.
Serial 2557. Correspondence regarding tariff revision.

747. ___. Reciprocity with Canada. Resolution to Committee
on Ways and Means. 50th Cong., 1st Sess., 1889. H. Misc.
Doc. 397. Serial 2570.

748. ___. Intervention by United States Government . . . in
the Affairs of the Hawaiian Government. Resolution referred
to the House calendar. 53rd Cong., 2nd Sess., 1893. H.
Misc. Doc. 44. Serial 3229.

749. U.S. Congress. Senate. Report of the Chicago Strike
of June-July 1894, By Strike Commission. 53rd Cong., 3rd
Sess., 1895. S. Exec. Doc. 7. Serial 3276.

TARIFF

750. Terrill, Tom E. The Tariff, Politics, and American
Foreign Policy, 1874-1901. Westport, CT: Greenwood, 1973.
Thorough study of tariff issues in both terms. (chap. 6, 8)

751. Taussig, Frank W. The Tariff History of the United
States. 8th ed. New York: G. P. Putnam's 1931. Chapters
5 and 6 in this standard work discuss tariff measures
associated with GC.

752. Stanwood, Edward. American Tariff Controversies in the
Nineteenth Century. 2 vols. Boston: Houghton, Mifflin,
1903. The tariff issues of GC's two terms. (vol. II,
chaps. 15, 16)

753. Tarbell, Ida M. The Tariff in Our Times. New York:
Macmillan, 1911. The tariff issues of GC's two terms.
(chap. 6, 9)

FOREIGN AFFAIRS

754. Young, George B. "The Influence of Politics on
American Diplomacy during Cleveland's Administrations
1885-1889, 1893-1897." Ph.D. diss., Yale University, 1939.
"Cleveland's diplomacy was permeated with the pernicious
influence of party politics" (p. 287), but more in the first
than in the second term.

755. Iriye, Akira. From Nationalist to Internationalism, U.S. Foreign Policy to 1914. London: Routledge and Kegan Paul, 1977. Foreign affairs during GC's two terms. (chap. 3)

756. LaFeber, Walter. The New Empire: An Interpretation of American Expansion, 1860-1898. Ithaca: Cornell University Press, for the American Historical Association, 1963. GC was an economic expansionist in both his presidential terms. The second term is emphasized.

757. Zevin, Robert. "An Interpretation of American Imperialism." Journal of Economic History 32 (March 1972): 316-60. GC's first term "heralds an escalation of imperialist activity on all fronts." (p. 327) The Venezuelan Boundary dispute of the second term is also discussed. (pp. 328-29)

758. Crapol, Edward P., and Schonberger, Howard. "The Shift to Global Expansion, 1865-1900." In From Colony to Empire, Essays in the History of American Foreign Relations. Edited by William Appleman Williams. New York: John Wiley, 1972. How GC and other administrations of these years used domestic issues like the tariff, silver, merchant marine, railroads, and agricultural protest in foreign policy terms.

759. Holt, W. Stull. Treaties Defeated by the Senate. Baltimore: Johns Hopkins Press, 1933. The various treaties of GC's two terms. (chap. 7)

760. Williams, William Appleman. (ed.) The Shaping of American Diplomacy. Chicago: Rand McNally, 1956. Documents on Korea (1885), Samoa (1886), Latin America (1886), and Hawaii (1893). (chap. 7)

761. Johnson, Willis Fletcher. America's Foreign Relations. 2 vols. New York: Century, 1916. GC's diplomacy and a list of nineteenth century U.S. overseas representatives, (vol. II, chaps. 27-31, 34 and Appendix I)

762. Wreston, Henry Merritt. Executive Agents in American Foreign Relations. Baltimore: The Johns Hopkins Press, 1929. GC's use of executive agents (plenipotentiaries) in his foreign policy.

763. Willson, Beckles. America's Ambassadors to England
(1785-1928), A Narrative of Anglo-American Diplomatic
Relations. London: John Murray, 1928. U.S. ambassadors to
Great Britain during GC's two terms (chap. 19, 20);
Venezuelan Boundary dispute. (pp. 405-11)

764. White, Elizabeth Brett. American Opinion of France.
From Lafayette to Poincare. New York: Alfred A. Knopf,
1927. "The Third Republic" (chap. 7) includes the French
view of the GC years including the Liberian and African
issues and the Statue of Liberty.

765. Willson, Beckles. America's Ambassadors to France
(1777-1927), A Narrative of Franco-American Diplomatic
Relations. London: John Murray, 1928. French ambassadors
to U.S. during GC's two terms (chaps. 19. 20) and the 1895
French ban on imported cattle. (pp. 362-63)

766. ___. Friendly Relations. A Narrative of Britain's
Ministers and Ambassadors to America (1791-1930). Boston:
Little, Brown, 1934. GC, the Irish vote, and
Sackville-West. (chap. 16) Venezuelan Boundary dispute.
(pp. 267-72)

767. Stolberg-Wernigerode, Otto. Germany and the United
States During the Era of Bismarck. Translated from the
German by Otto E. Lessing. Reading, PA: Henry Janssen
Foundation, 1937. German perspective on GC's foreign policy
including Samoa, Hawaii, and Venezuelan Boundary dispute.

768. Callcott, Wilfrid Hardy. The Caribbean Policy of the
United States 1890-1920. Baltimore: Johns Hopkins Press,
1942. GC's role in various Latin American foreign policy
issues of his two terms, including Cuba but especially the
Venezuelan Boundary dispute.

769. Tate, Merze. Hawaii: Reciprocity or Annexation. East
Lansing: Michigan State University Press, 1968. GC and
Hawaii during both terms: reciprocity during the first and
refusal to annex during the second.

770. Kuykendall, Ralph S. The Hawaiian Kingdom, 1874-1893:
The Kalakaua Dynasty. Honolulu: University of Hawaii
Press, 1967. A few references to GC's policy toward Hawaii

during his first term and a brief overview of his second term opposition to annexation.

771. McWilliams, Tennant S. "The Lure of Empire: Southern Interest in the Caribbean, 1877-1900." Mississippi Quarterly 29 (Winter 1975-76): 43-63. Southern reaction to GC's tariff policy, his navy construction program, and the Venezuelan Boundary dispute.

772. Young, Marilyn B. "American Expansion, 1870-1900: The Far East." In Towards A New Past: Dissenting Essays in American History. Edited by Barton J. Bernstein. New York: Pantheon, 1968. GC's cautious attitude toward a U.S. governmental role in China. Richard Olney, at least, allowed U.S. ministers to aid American companies trying to establish themselves there. (pp. 186-88)

773. Battistini, Lawrence H. Japan and America, From Earliest Times to the Present. New York: John Day, 1954. The 1886 extradition convention (pp. 40-41) and Japanese pleasure at U.S. neutrality in the Sino-Japanese War. (pp. 46-47)

774. Grayson, Benson Lee. (ed.) The American Image of China. New York: Frederick Ungar, 1979. GC's condemnation of 1886 anti-Chinese violence (pp. 12, 127-29); Sino-Japanese War. (p. 13)

775. Campbell, Charles S., Jr. Anglo-American Understanding 1898-1903. Baltimore: Johns Hopkins Press, 1957. Brief references to Sackville-West problems (p. 126) and the Venezuelan Boundary dispute. (pp. 5, 7, 270)

776. Brebner, John Bartlett. North Atlantic Triangle, The Interplay of Canada, the United States, and Great Britain. New Haven: Yale University Press, 1945. The failed 1888 Bayard-Chamberlain fisheries treaty, Sackville-West, and the Venezuelan Boundary dispute. (pp. 247, 249-51)

777. Dunning, William A. The British Empire and the United States. A Review of Their Relations During the Century of Peace Following the Treaty of Ghent. New York: Charles Scribner's Sons, 1914. The fisheries question, Sackville-West, and the Venezuelan Boundary dispute from the British perspective. (chap. 7)

778. Godshall, Wilson Leon. American Foreign Policy,
Formulation and Practice. Ann Arbor MI: Edwards Brothers,
1937. Selected documents on the Venezuelan Boundary dispute
(pp. 161-75); GC's statement on the isthmian canal (p.
190); the 1888 Pan-American Act (p. 275); Hawaii (pp.
364-69).

779. Graber, Doris A. Crisis Diplomacy. A History of U.S.
Intervention Policies and Practices. Washington: Public
Affairs Press, 1959. GC and Cuba, Hawaii, Samoa, Berlin
Conference, Turkey, and the Venezuelan Boundary dispute.

780. Peterson, Harold F. Argentina and the United States,
1810-1960. New York: State University of New York, 1964.
GC and the Falkland Islands, Argentine wool tariff relief,
South American trade, Argentine boundary dispute with
Brazil, and the Olney Corollary.

781. Stuart, Graham H. Latin America and the United States.
2nd ed. New York: D. Appleton Century, 1928. Brief
discussion of GC and Monroe Doctrine, isthmian canal,
Argentina, Brazil, and Cuba.

MISCELLANEOUS ISSUES

782. Altschuler, Glenn C. Andrew D. White: Historian,
Diplomat. Ithaca: Cornell University Press, 1979.
Mugwumps and GC's 1884 election. (chap. 9) Venezuelan
Boundary commission. (chap. 13)

783. Bensel, Richard Franklin. Sectionalism and American
Political Development, 1880-1980. Madison: University of
Wisconsin Press, 1984. GC and the tariff, pensions, and
blacks. (pp. 63-69)

784. Burch, Philip H., Jr. Elites in American History.
Vol. II: The Civil War to the New Deal. New York: Holmes
and Meier, 1981. GC's appointment policy during his two
terms was pro-business, particularly pro-railroad. (pp.
86-91, 96-103)

785. Corwin, Edward S. The President: Office and Powers
1787-1984. 5th ed. New York: New York University Press,
1984. In this important work on the presidency, the author
mentions GC in reference to the Pullman Strike,
Spanish-American War, and the Tenure of Office Act
controversy.

786. Gillett, Frederick H. George Frisbie Hoar. Boston:
Houghton Mifflin, 1934. A leading Republican's view of GC's
role in Chinese immigration, Tenure of Office Act,
fisheries, tariff, Cuba, Hawaii, and 1888 election.

787. "Great Example." Nation 55 (November 10, 1892): 346.
GC's 1887 tariff message and his 1891 silver letter were
both bold and courageous statements.

788. Haynes, George Henry. The Senate of the United States:
Its History and Practice. New York: Russell and Russell,
1960. GC and the Tenure of Office Act, Venezuelan Boundary
dispute, Hawaii, and rejected Supreme Court Nominations.

789. Myers, Margaret G. A Financial History of the United
States. New York: Columbia University Press, 1970.
Financial issues of GC's two terms. (chaps. 9, 10)

790. Ridge, Martin. Ignatius Donnelly. Chicago:
University of Chicago Press, 1962. First term patronage
squabbles and second term silver issue.

791. Sageser, A. Bower. The First Two Decades of the
Pendleton Act. Lincoln: University of Nebraska Press,
1935. The civil service record of the two GC presidential
terms. (chaps 3, 5)

792. Skowronek, Stephen. Building a New American State:
The Expansion of National Administrative Capacities,
1877-1920. Cambridge: Cambridge University Press, 1982.
GC, civil service reform, and the 1894 Pullman Strike.

793. Tebbel, John, and Watts, Sarah Miles. The Press and
the Presidency: From George Washington to Ronald Reagan.
New York: Oxford University Press, 1985. GC's stormy
relationship with the press. (pp. 256-78, 287-95)

9
The Election of 1884

794. Chamberlain, Eugene T. Early Life and Public Services of Grover Cleveland. Chicago: Claxton, 1884. Revised by GC himself.

795. Babcock, Benjamin F. The Presidential Favorites 1888 . . . . Chicago: Babcock, Fort, 1884. Biographical sketches of all possible candidates.

796. Barnum, Augustine. The Lives of Grover Cleveland and Thomas A. Hendricks, Democratic Presidential Candidates of 1884 . . . . . Hartford: Hartford, 1884.

797. Black, Chauncey F. (ed.) Two Great Careers, The Lives of Grover Cleveland and Thomas A. Hendricks . . . . Philadelphia: H. L. Warren, 1884. Written by Pennsylvania's lieutenant governor.

798. Boyd, James P. Building and Ruling the Republic. Philadelphia: Garretson, 1884. GC's characteristics, personality, and work habits. (Part 4)

Consult Section 7 for additional material on this campaign.

799. Dorsheimer, William, and Hensel, W. U. Life and Public
Services of Hon. Grover Cleveland. Also, A Biographical
Sketch of Hon. Thomas A. Hendricks. New York: Hubbard,
1884.

800. Goodrich, Frederick E. The Life and Public Services of
Grover Cleveland. Boston: B. B. Russell, 1884.

801. Grover Cleveland. The Open Record of an Honest Man.
New York: Clarke, 1884. Newspaper clippings on GC's
political positions.

802. Handford, Thomas W. Early Life and Public Services of
Hon. Grover Cleveland. Also, The Life of Hon. Thomas A.
Hendricks . . . . Chicago: Belford, Clarke, 1884.

803. King, Pendleton. Life and Public Services of Grover
Cleveland. New York: G. P. Putnam's, 1884.

804. LeFevre, Benjamin. Biographies of S. Grover Cleveland,
the Democratic Candidate for President, and Thomas A.
Hendricks, the Democratic Candidate for Vice-President . . .
. Philadelphia: Fireside, 1884. Written by an Ohio
Democratic congressman.

805. Life of Grover Cleveland. A Record of Incompetency,
Demagoguery and Mediocrity . . . . Philadelphia: John D.
Avil, 1884. A campaign attack.

806. The Lives of the Four Candidates . . . . Chicago:
Elder, 1884. Democratic and Republican slates.

807. McClure, James B. (ed.) The Life of Honorable Grover
Cleveland . . . . Chicago: Rhodes and McClure, 1884.

808. Our Next President: Sketches and Portraits of the
Prospective Candidates for President . . . . Providence:
J. A. and R. A. Reid, 1884.

809. Portraits of Republican and Democratic Candidates With
the Nominating Speeches, and Sketches of the Lives of the
Candidates . . . . Chicago: Vandercook, 1884.

810. The Political Reformation of 1884. A Democratic
Campaign Book. New York: National Democratic Committee,
1884.

811. Triplett, Frank. The Authorized Pictorial Lives of
Stephen Grover Cleveland and Thomas Andrews Hendricks.
Philadelphia: A. Groton, 1884.

812. Welch, Deshler. Life of Grover Cleveland With Sketch
of Life of Thomas Andrews Hendricks. New York: John W.
Lovell, 1884.

813. "Grover Cleveland." Nation 39 (September 4, 1884):
205-6. A review of four campaign biographies.

THE CAMPAIGN

814. Official Proceedings of the National Democratic
Convention . . . 1884. New York: Taylor's Democratic
Printing House, 1884. Factual information on GC's
nomination.

815. Gronowicz, Anthony B. "Revising the Concept of
Jacksonian Democracy: A Comparison of New York Democrats in
1844 and 1884." Ph.D. diss., University of Pennsylvania,
1981. By 1884, skilled workmen were no longer well
represented in party circles.

816. Parker, George F. "Cleveland Nomination and Election
Campaign of 1884." Saturday Evening Post 195 (August 19,
1922): 28-38. A detailed account of GC's first run for the
presidency.

817. Rice, William G. "Cleveland's First Election."
Century 84 (June 1912): 299-310. GC's assistant private
secretary discusses GC's first presidential run. Also
mentions 1888 and 1892 elections.

818. Rosenberg, Marvin, and Rosenberg, Dorothy. "The Dirtiest Election." American Heritage 13 (August 1962): 4-9, 97-100. Concludes that GC carried "the wounds of this campaign for the rest of his life." (p. 100)

819. Ambrose, Stephen E. "The Blaine-Cleveland Election." American History Illustrated 1 (October 1966): 32-40. "Perhaps the dirtiest in American history." (pp. 32-3)

820. Tugwell, Rexford G. How They Became President: Thirty-Five Ways to the White House. New York: Simon and Schuster, 1965. GC became president due to "sheer character." (pp. 270-84)

821. Osborne, Thomas J. "What Was the Main Reason for Cleveland's Election Victory in 1884?" Northwest Ohio Quarterly 45 (Spring 1973): 67-71. Blaine might have captured Oneida County and won New York in the 1884 election except for Roscoe Conkling.

822. Jordon, David M. Roscoe Conkling of New York: Voice in the Senate. Ithaca: Cornell University Press, 1971. This New York Republican's 1884 support for GC. (pp. 420-1)

823. Thomas, Harrison C. The Return of the Democratic Party to Power in 1884. New York: Columbia University Press, 1919. A dated study of GC's first election in 1884 and his first term.

824. Pletcher, David M. The Awkward Years: American Foreign Relations Under Garfield and Arthur. Columbia: University of Missouri Press, 1962. 1884 election and foreign policy. (chap. 14)

825. Pocock, Emil. "Wet or Dry? The Presidential Election of 1884 in Upstate New York." New York History 54 (April 1973): 174-90. GC carried New York and thus won election because Prohibition Party candidate took votes from Blaine. Downplays mugwump bolt, rains that held down turn-out, and "Rum, Romanism and Rebellion" remark.

826. Rice, William Gorham, and Stetson, Francis L. "Was New York's Vote Stolen?" North American Review 199 (January 1914): 79-92. No, it was not. No evidence.

827. "Personal and Pertinent." Harper's Weekly 51 (April 20, 1907): 564. Some anecdotes about GC and a reporter in 1884.

OPPONENTS

828. Ford, Throwbridge H. "The Political Crusade Against Blaine in 1884." Mid-America 57 (January 1975): 38-55. The English-Irish issue helped GC and hurt Blaine.

829. Muzzey, David S. James G. Blaine: A Political Idol of Other Days. New York: Dodd, Mead, 1934. GC's 1884 campaign from Blaine's perspective.

830. Russell, Charles E. Blaine of Maine. New York: Cosmopolitan, 1931. GC's 1884 campaign from Blaine's perspective.

831. Taylor, John M. "Everyone Wanted Blaine from Maine." Yankee 48 (November 1984): 126-33. A popular account of the 1884 election, mainly from Blaine's perspective.

832. James, Edward T. "Ben Butler Runs for President: Labor, Greenbackers, and Anti-Monopolists in the Election of 1884." Essex Institute Historical Collections 113 (April 1977): 65-88. Butler failed to stop GC's nomination and election despite support from the three groups cited in the title.

833. Raymond, Harold B. "Ben Butler's Last Hurrah: The Presidential Campaign of 1884." Colby Library Quarterly 10 (March 1973): 26-38. Butler was not a mere stalking horse for Blaine.

834. Trefousse, Hans L. "Ben Butler and the New York
Election of 1884." New York History 37 (April 1956):
185-96. New York Republicans and dissident Tammany Hall
Democrats supported Butler against GC.

835. Malcolm, James. "Lively Political Campaign of 1884;
When Grover Cleveland Was Denounced on the Stump by Senator
Grady . . . ." State Service 8 (December 1924): 116-9. A
New York senator's vociferous anti-GC support for Butler.

ISSUES

836. Jeansonne, Glen. "Caricature and Satire in the
Presidential Campaign of 1884." Journal of American
Culture. 3 (Summer 1980): 238-47. The cartoons and
ridicule used against Blaine and GC represented a new
plateau for political satire.

837. Hunt, Irma. Dearest Madame, The President's
Mistresses. New York: McGraw Hill, 1978. Maria Halpin,
the mother of GC's illegitimate child, and the impact of the
issue on GC. (pp. 75-109)

838. Miller, Hope Ridings. Scandals in the Highest Office:
Facts and Fictions in the Private Lives of Our Presidents.
New York: Random House, 1973. A popular account of the
illegitimate child matter. (pp. 153-64)

839. Olssen, Erik. "Sex, Scandal, and Suffrage in the
Gilded Age." Historian 42 (February 1980): 225-43. GC's
illegitimate child problem. (pp. 228-9)

840. Chase, Philip P. "The Attitude of the Protestant
Clergy in Massachusetts during the Election of 1884."
Massachusetts Historical Society Proceedings 64 (1932):
467-98. Comments and stand on the GC illegitimate child
issue.

841. Clarke, Clifford E., Jr. Henry Ward Beecher: Spokesman
for a Middle-Class America. Urbana: University of Illinois
Press, 1978. This famous minister's support for GC on the
illegitimate child issue. (pp. 251-4)

842. Farrelly, David. "Rum, Romanism, and Rebellion
Resurrected." Western Political Quarterly 8 (June 1955):
262-70. A discussion of Supreme Court Justice John Marshall
Harlan's sympathetic memorandum concerning James G. Blaine's
inadequate reaction to this political issue.

843. Harlan, Richard D. "The Phrase That Beat Blaine."
Outlook 126 (December 8, 1920): 649-51. The "Rum,
Romanism, and Rebellion" remark and GC's later friendly
meeting with its author.

844. Boller, Paul F. Jr. "Religion and the U.S.
Presidency." Journal of Church and State 21 (Winter 1979):
5-21. GC's non-church going Presbyterianism and the "Rum,
Romanism, and Rebellion" controversy. (pp. 16-17)

845. Bishop, Joseph B. Presidential Nominations and
Elections. New York: Charles Scribner's Sons, 1916.   The
1884 campaign and the patronage issue. (chap. 9)

MUGWUMPS

846. Dobson, John M. "The Mugwump Protest in the Election
of 1884." Ph.D. diss., University of Wisconsin, Madison,
1966, The causes for and the significant pro-GC activities.

847. McFarland, Gerald W. Mugwumps, Morals, and Politics,
1884-1920. Amherst: University of Massachusetts Press,
1975. GC, the election of 1884, and his presidency from the
perspective of these reformers. (chaps. 3, 4)

848. Dobson, John M. "George William Curtis and the
Election of 1884: The Dilemma of the New York Mugwumps."
New York Historical Society Quarterly 52 (July 1968):
215-34. The New York Mugwumps supported GC primarily
because of their opposition to Blaine.

849. McFarland, Gerald W. "The New York Mugwumps of 1884:
A Profile." Political Science Quarterly 78 (March 1963):
40-58. GC's home state reform supporters.

850. ___. "Gilded Age Connecticut: Blaine Men, Butlerites,
and Mugwumps in 1884." Connecticut Historical Society
Bulletin 49 (Spring 1984): 61-74. GC's illegitimate child
problem kept Connecticut Mugwumps from supporting him.

RESULTS

851. Hurlburt, William Henry. "The Democratic Victory in
America." Eclectic Magazine 104 (February 1885): 183-202.
The meaning of GC's 1884 victory from the perspective of
other 19th century presidents.

852. Belmont, August. Letters, Speeches, and Addresses of
August Belmont. n.p.: n.p., 1890. A speech by this
leading New York Democrat on GC's election. (pp. 230-1)

853. Bradley, Arthur G. "Southern View of the Election of
Cleveland." Macmillan 51 (March 1885): 372-4. There was
great happiness in the white South over GC's victory and the
defeat of the alleged Negrophile Republicans.

854. Avary, Myrta L. Dixie After the War. Boston:
Houghton Mifflin, 1906. Southern black fright at GC's
election.

855. Leach, Duane M. "The Tariff and the Western Farmer,
1860-1890." Ph.D. diss., University of Oklahoma, 1965. Not
until GC's 1884 election did the farm and tariff issue
become a national concern and a focus of farmer criticism.

856. Klein, Maury. The Life and Legend of Jay Gould.
Baltimore: Johns Hopkins University Press, 1986. A Blaine
supporter, Gould had a cheery public and a concerned private
reaction to GC's election (pp. 335-37), but by 1887 he had
come to admire him. (p. 392)

857. Perkins, Norman C. A Man of Destiny . . . . Chicago:
Clarke, 1885. December 1884 to March 1885 letters addressed
to GC, printed in the Chicago Inter-Ocean.

858. Yearley, Clifton K. The Money Machines: The Breakdown
and Reform of Governmental and Party Finance in the North,
1860-1920. Albany: State University of New York Press,
1970. The cost of the 1884 GC election to the New York
Democratic party. (p. 105)

10
The First Term, 1885-1889

859. "The President's Installation." Saturday Review 59 (March 7, 1885): 298-9. GC's inauguration was an "imposing spectacle," but there are problems for him ahead.

860. U.S. Congress, Senate. Committee on Arrangements for the Inauguration, 1885. Arrangements for the Inauguration of the President of the United States, on the Fourth of March, 1885. Washington: Government Publication Office, 1885. Eight pages of official arrangements.

861. Washington, D. C. Inauguration Committee, 1885. Cleveland and Hendricks Inauguration, March 4, 1885 . . . . Washington: R. O. Polkinhorn, 1885. A twenty four page set of rules by the city Committee of 50.

862. ___ . Final Report of the Executive Committee of the Inauguration Ceremonies of March 4, 1885 and Resolutions of the General Committee. Washington: C. W. Brown, 1885. Nineteen page final report.

Consult Sections 8 and 13 for additional material on GC's presidency.

863. Kintz, Henry J. The Inauguration of Grover Cleveland,
the President-Elect, March 4, 1885. Philadelphia: W. F.
Fell, 1885. Souvenir book.

864. Papers Read Before The Cleveland Democracy of Buffalo,
1884-5 Including An Account of the Club's Celebration of the
Inauguration of President Cleveland. Buffalo: privately
printed, n.d. Papers on various topics.

865. Durbin, Louise. "Inauguration Was No Big Deal At
First." Smithsonian 7 (January 1977): 101-11. Photograph
of an Inauguration Democratic rooster souvenir with GC's
head on it and the words "Our Bird." (p. 109)

866. Cable, Mary. The Avenue of the Presidents. Boston:
Houghton Mifflin, 1969. Grandstands for watching the
inauguration parade were first set up for GC's inauguration.

POLITICS: AN OVERVIEW

867. Shannon, Fred A. The Centennial Years: A Political
and Economic History of America from the Late 1870s to the
Early 1890s. Edited by Robert H. Jones. Garden City:
Doubleday, 1967. Election of 1884 and GC's first term.
(chaps. 8, 9)

868. Poore, Ben Perley. Perley's Reminiscences of Sixty
Years in the National Metropolis. Philadelphia: Hubbard
Brothers, 1886. GC and how he conducted the day to day
business of his first term. (chaps. 43, 44). GC's wedding.
(chap. 46)

869. Powderly, Terrence V. The Path I Trod. The
Autobiography of Terrence V. Powderly. Edited by Harry J.
Carman, Henry David, and Paul N. Guthrie. New York:
Columbia University Press, 1940. This labor leader's
memoirs discuss in Chap. 21 "A Day With Grover Cleveland"
and GC's offer of the post of Commissioner of Labor.

870. Damon, Allan L. "Presidential Accessibility."
American Heritage 25 (April 1974): 60-3, 97. Policemen
first guarded the White House gates during GC's first term,
and GC personally answered the telephone.

871. LaFollette, Robert M. Robert LaFollette's
Autobiography: A Personal Narrative of Political
Experience. Madison: Robert M. LaFollette Co., 1911.
Brief description and evaluation of GC during the early days
of his first term. (pp. 52-3, 55)

872. Adams, Henry. Letters of Henry Adams, 1858-1891. 2
vols. Edited by W. C. Ford. Boston: Houghton Mifflin,
1930. Scattered political references to GC's first term
especially in vol. 2.

873. Bryce, Lord James. American Commonwealth. 2 vols.
New York: Macmillan, 1893. Scattered references to GC and
his first term.

874. Belmont, Perry. An American Democrat. The
Recollections of Perry Belmont. New York: Columbia
University Press, 1940. GC is mentioned throughout this
leading Democrat's book.

875. Lindsey, David. "Sunset" Cox: Irrepressible Democrat.
Detroit: Wayne State University Press, 1959. The first
term relationship of GC and this longtime Democratic
congressman.

876. Cullom, Shelby M. Fifty Years of Public Service.
Chicago: A. C. McClurg, 1911. GC's first term and this
Republican senator's role in it. (chaps. 16, 18)

877. Pepper, Charles M. The Life and Times of Henry
Gassaway Davis, 1823-1916. New York: Century, 1920. GC
and this leading businessman/Democratic politician. (chaps.
9, 10)

878. Lambert, John R. Arthur P. Gorman. Baton Rouge:
Louisiana State University Press, 1953. GC's relationship
with this important Maryland Democratic Senator.

879. Horton, Louise. Samuel Bell Maxey: A Biography.
Austin: University of Texas, 1974. Chapter 9, "Under
President Cleveland," discusses this Texas Democratic
politician's role in GC's first term.

880. Lee, R. Alton. A History of Regulatory Taxation.
Lexington: University Press of Kentucky, 1973. GC is
mentioned several times in regard to the oleomargarine and
opium laws passed in his first term.

881. Halsell, Willie D. "Appointment of L. Q. C. Lamar to
the Supreme Court; A Political Battle of Cleveland's
Administration." Mississippi Valley Historical Review 28
(December 1941): 399-412. The political battle over GC's
1887 appointment of this Southern Secretary of the Interior
to the Supreme Court.

882. "The President's Visit to Richmond." Public Opinion 2
(October 30, 1886): 43-5. Newspaper reactions to GC's
visit, particularly his decision not to bring Mrs. GC.

883. "The President's Message." Public Opinion 2 (December
11, 1886): 161-4. Newspaper reaction to GC's 1886 annual
message.

884. Jones, Howard Mumford. The Age of Energy: Varieties
of American Experience. New York: Viking, 1970. Quote
from GC's 1887 Constitution Centennial speech in
Philadelphia. (pp. 37-8)

885. Rossiter, Clinton. Conservatism in America: The
Thankless Persuasion. New York: Knopf, 1962. GC's speech
at the 1887 Philadelphia Constitution Centennial is an
example of his and other conservatives' deification of
laissez-faire. (p. 146)

886. McCullogh, David G. "Hail Liberty!" American Heritage
17 (February 1966): 22-3, 96-9. GC's participation in the
October 28, 1886, unveiling of the Statue of Liberty.

TENURE OF OFFICE ACT

887. Fisher, Louis. "Grover Cleveland Against the Senate."
Congressional Studies 7 (Spring 1979): 11-25. GC's battle
with the Senate over his right of appointment and rejection
centered on differing interpretations of his act.

888. Marszalek, John F. "Grover Cleveland and the Tenure of
Office Act." Duquesne Review 15 (Spring 1970): 206-19. GC
saw this contest with the Senate as a matter of executive
freedom. The Senate saw it as partisan politics.

889. Hoar, George F. Autobiography of Seventy Years. 2
vols. New York: Charles Scribner's Sons, 1903. This
memoir of a leading Republican includes discussion of the
Tenure of Office Act controversy and GC's judicial
nominations.

890. Breckinridge, Adam C. The Executive Privilege:
Presidential Control Over Information. Lincoln: University
of Nebraska Press, 1974. The Tenure of Office Act
controversy and its meaning. (pp. 46-8, 101-2)

891. Ford, Henry Jones. The Rise and Growth of American
Politics: A Sketch of Constitutional Development. New
York: Macmillan, 1900. Tenure of Office Act controversy
and its effect. (p. 268)

892. Adler, Selig. "The Senatorial Career of George
Franklin Edmunds, 1866-1891." Ph.D. diss., University of
Illinois, 1934. Includes information on the Tenure of
Office Act controversy.

893. Shepherd, Edward M. Defense of Grover Cleveland in
Regard to His Treatment of the United States Attorneys in
Pennsylvania and Missouri. New York: privately printed,
1887.

PENSION VETOES AND VETERANS

894. Copeland, Gary W. "When Congress and the President
Collide: Why Presidents Veto Legislation." Journal of
Politics 45 (August 1983): 696-710. GC was "one of the
all-time veto champions." (p. 698)

895. Lee, Jong R. "Presidential Vetoes from Washington to
Nixon." Journal of Politics 37 (May 1975): 522-46. Of all
presidential vetoes, more than one half were GC's and FDR's.

896. Damon, Allan L. "Veto." American Heritage 25
(February 1974): 12-15, 81. As of 1974, GC (along with
FDR, Truman, and Eisenhower) accounted for 72% of all
presidential vetoes, and GC was second only to FDR.

897. Robertson, P. L. "Cleveland's Constructive Use of the
Pension Vetoes." Mid-America 44 (January 1962): 33-45.
GC's pension vetoes had a positive impact including a growth
in presidential power.

898. Jackson, Carlton. Presidential Vetoes, 1792-1945.
Athens: University of Georgia Press, 1967. GC's pension
and other vetoes. (Chap. 11)

899. Tobin, Richard L. Decisions of Destiny. Cleveland:
World, 1961. "Grover Cleveland Dignifies the Presidential
Veto." (chap. 6)

900. Fisher, Louis. President and Congress: Power and
Policy. New York: Free Press, 1973. The pension vetoes
controversy. (pp. 96-7)

901. ___ . Presidential Spending Power. Princeton
University Press, 1975. The pension vetoes controversy and
GC's other attempts to cut spending. (pp. 25-7, 165, 174)

902. "The Pension Vetoes." Nation 43 (July 15, 1886): 48.
Supports GC's pension vetoes.

903. "President Cleveland and the Soldiers." Nation 45
(July 14, 1887): 26-7. Defends GC's pension vetoes.

904. Dearing, Mary R. Veterans in Politics, The Story of
the G.A.R. Baton Rouge: Louisiana State University Press,
1952. The Civil War pension vetoes issue, the Confederate
battle flag controversy, and the veterans' views of GC.

905. Lankevich, George J. "The Grand Army of the Republic
in New York State, 1865-1898." Ph.D. diss., Columbia
University, 1967. GC had good relations with the New York
G.A.R. until the Confederate battle flag issue angered the
veterans. Their animosity contributed to GC's 1888 defeat.

906. Ross, Sam. "A Biography of Lucius Fairchild of
Wisconsin (1831-1893)." Ph.D. diss., University of
Wisconsin, Madison, 1955. The most in-depth account of the
G.A.R. commander who attacked GC for ordering return of
Confederate battle flags to southern states.

907. Davies, William E. "Was Lucius Fairchild a Demagogue?"
Wisconsin Magazine of History 31 (June 1948): 418-28. A
brief account of the battle flags dispute.

908. "The President's Journey." Nation 45 (October 27,
1887): 326. A favorable overview of GC's three week
national tour stimulated by his visit to the St. Louis
G.A.R. encampment.

909. Pusateri, C. Joseph. "Public Quarrels and Private
Plans: The President, The Veterans, and the Mayor of St.
Louis." Missouri Historical Review 62 (October 1967):
1-13. The GC-G.A.R conflict which delayed GC's visit to St.
Louis hurt GC politically but helped David R. Francis become
Missouri governor.

910. Stevens, Walter B. "When Cleveland Came to St. Louis."
Missouri Historical Review 21 (January 1927): 145-55. GC's
October 1887 visit to St. Louis after the G.A.R.controversy
had prevented an earlier trip.

CIVIL SERVICE AND REFORMERS

911. Doenecke, Justus. "Grover Cleveland and the
Enforcement of the Civil Service Act." Hayes Historical
Journal 4 (Spring 1984): 45-58. No lasting effect to GC's
generally pro-civil service actions.

912. Fowler, Dorothy G. "Precursors of the Hatch Act."
Mississippi Valley Historical Review 47 (September 1960):
147-62. GC's important 1886 circular on the Pendleton Civil
Service Act's meaning in regard to office holder
participation in politics. (pp. 256-58)

913. Blodgett, Geoffrey. "The Mupwump Reputation, 1870 to
the Present." Journal of American History 66 (March 1980):
867-87. Includes information on their relationship with GC.

914. ___. The Gentle Reformers: Massachusetts Democrats in
the Cleveland Era. Cambridge: Harvard University Press,
1966. A case study of the attitudes, successes, and
ultimate failure of the reformers who formed the core of the
Cleveland supporters.

915. Baum, Dale. "'Noisy But Not Numerous': The Revolt of
the Massachusetts Mugwumps." Historian 41 (February 1979):
241-56. The Mugwumps were not nearly as important in the
1880s as many historians have believed.

916. Sproat, John G. "The Best Men": Liberal Reformers in
the Gilded Age. New York: Oxford University Press, 1968.
GC receives extensive mention.

917. Hoogenboom, Ari. Outlawing the Spoils, A History of
the Civil Service Reform Movement, 1865-1883. Urbana:
University of Illinois Press, 1961. Includes information on
GC's civil service activities as governor and president.

918. Van Riper, P. P. History of the United States Civil
Service. Evanston: Row, Peterson, 1958. Chapter 6,
"Morality in Office: 1883-1897," includes full and
favorable discussion of GC.

919. Foulke, William D. Fighting the Spoilsmen: Reminiscences of the Civil Service Reform Movement. New York: G. P. Putnam, 1919. This book by a contemporary reformer includes information on GC's civil service reform attitudes and actions.

920. Fish, Carl Russell. Civil Service and the Patronage. Cambridge: Harvard University Press, 1904. GC's civil service attitude and behavior and the Tenure of Office Act controversy.

921. Miller, Larry C. "Dimension of Mugwump Thought, 1880-1920: Sons of Abolitionists as Professional Pioneers." Ph.D. diss., Northwestern University, 1969. The first generation of professional intelligentsia who assumed increased influence in political and economic affairs.

922. Tucker, David M. "The Mugwumps and the Money Question, 1865-1900." Ph.D. diss., University of Iowa, 1965. The reformers acted out of economic self-interest not status anxiety.

923. Persons, Stow. The Decline of American Gentility. New York: Columbia University Press, 1973. An analysis of the kind of "gentlemen" who supported GC.

924. McFarland, Gerald W. Moralists or Pragmatists? The Mugwumps, 1884-1900. New York: Simon and Schuster, 1975. A collection of journal articles.

925. Curtis, George W. Orations and Addresses. 3 vols. Edited by C. E. Norton. New York: Harper and Brothers, 1894. GC is mentioned frequently both favorably and critically. (Vol. 2)

926. "President Cleveland and Civil Service Reform." Public Opinion 3 (August 13, 1887): 369-74. Press reaction to George W. Curtis's August 3, 1887, speech and the National Civil Service Reform League criticism of GC.

927. Godkin, E. L. The Gilded Age Letters of E. L. Godkin. Edited by William M. Armstrong. Albany: State University of New York Press, 1974. These letters of a leading mugwump include letters and numerous references to GC.

928. McFarland, Gerald W.   "Partisan of Nonpartisanship:
Dorman B. Eaton and the Genteel Reform Tradition."   Journal
of American History 54 (March 1968):   806-22. This overview
of the reform career of the long time head of the Civil
Service Commission briefly mentions his problems with other
mugwumps during GC's first term.

929. Ostrogorski, Moisei. Democracy and the Organization of
Political Parties. 2 vols. Translated from the French by
Frederick Clarke. New York: Macmillan, 1902. GC is
mentioned in regard to civil service and tariff. (vol. 2)

930. Hixson, William B., Jr. Moorfield Storey and the
Abolitionist Tradition. New York: Oxford University Press,
1972. Mugwumps early support for GC and their later
disagreement with GC's Venezuelan Boundary dispute position.

931. Howe, M. A. deWolfe. Portrait of an Independent:
Moorfield Storey 1845-1925. Boston: Houghton Mifflin,
1932. The mugwump role in the 1884 election and civil
service issues.

932. Trefousse, Hans L. Carl Schurz: A Biography.
Knoxville: University of Tennessee Press, 1982. GC and
civil service reform.

933. Fuess, Claude M. Carl Schurz, Reformer. New York:
Dodd Mead, 1932. GC and civil service reform.

934. Schurz, Carl. Speeches, Correspondence, and Political
Papers of Carl Schurz. 6 vols. Edited by Frederic
Bancroft. New York: G. P. Putnam, 1913. GC and civil
service reform. (vols. 4-6)

935. ___. Reminscences. 3 vols. New York: McClure, 1907.
GC and civil service reform. (vol. III, 405ff)

936. Wheeler, Everett P. "Grover Cleveland." Independent
65 (July 1902): 11-18. A leading civil service reformer
praises GC's presidential policies.

937. "Democratic Support of Cleveland." Nation 41 (August

13, 1885): 128-9. Southern support of GC's civil service policy as seen in southern newspapers.

938. Eustis, J. B.; Grace, William R.; Roosevelt, Theodore. "The President's Policy." North American Review 141 (October 1885): 374-96. Three contemporary politicians, including a future president, discuss the pros and cons of GC's appointment policy.

939. Cary, Edward. "Would We Do It Again?" Forum 1 (March 1886): 228-34. A mugwump says reformers would support GC again because his first year in office had been so successful.

940. Curtis, William E. "A Day with the President." Lippincott 39 (February 1887): 285-97. A GC day during his first term --- material on office seekers.

941. Abbott, Lawrence F. "Grover Cleveland." Outlook 135 (November 21, 1923): 484-6. A favorable evaluation of GC by an old mugwump on the occasion of the publication of the Robert McElroy biography of GC.

942. Fuller, Wayne E. The American Mail, Enlarger of the Common Life. Chicago History of American Civilization. Chicago: University of Chicago Press, 1972. GC continued post office patronage despite his mugwump support.

943. Merrill, Horace S. "Ignatius Donnelly, James J. Hill, and Cleveland Administration Patronage." Mississippi Valley Historical Review. 39 (June 1952): 505-18. GC's wealthy 1884 supporters like Hill were rewarded with patronage; farmers and labor leaders like Donnelly were not.

944. Kraines, Oscar. "The Cockrell Committee, 1887-1889: First Comprehensive Congressional Investigation into Administration." Western Political Quarterly 4 (December 1951): 583-609. Four years after the creation of the Civil Service Commission, this committee made recommendations for improving administrative reform.

945. Williamson, Hugh P. (ed.) "Correspondence of Senator Francis Marion Cockrell, December 23, 1885 - March 24, 1888." Bulletin of the Missouri Historical Society 25 (1969): 196-305. The ten letters include references to GC.

INDIANS

946. Wise, Jennings C. The Red Man in the New World Drama: A Politico-Legal Study with a Pageantry of American Indian History. Edited by Vine Deloria, Jr. New York: Macmillan, 1971. GC's attitude toward Indians. (pp. 280-5, 295-6)

947. Mardock, Robert Winston. The Reformers and the American Indian. Columbia: University of Missouri Press, 1971. GC's role in the passage of the Dawes Severalty Act (pp. 219-20) and the impact of Helen Hunt Jackson's A Century of Dishonor on GC. (p. 186)

948. Dippie, Brian W. The Vanishing American: White Attitudes and U.S. Indian Policy. Middletown, CT: Wesleyan University Press, 1982. GC's attitude toward Indian reform before and after the Dawes Act. (pp. 141-2, 181)

949. Prucha, Francis. The Great Father, The United States Government and the American Indians. 2 vols. Lincoln: University of Nebraska Press, 1984. The Dawes Act and other Indian aspects of GC's presidency. (vol. II)

950. Washburn, Wilcomb E. (ed.) The American Indian and the United States: A Documentary History. 4 vols. New York: Random House, 1973. Reports of the Commissioners of Indian Affairs during GC's two terms. (vol. 1) First term congressional debate on Indian appropriations and the severalty issue; the texts of two laws passed during GC's first term. (vol. 3) Several court decisions issued during GC's presidency. (vol. 4)

951. ___. The Indian in America. New American Nation Series. New York: Harper and Row, 1975. The Dawes Severalty Act passed during GC's first term. (chap. 11)

952. Otis, Delos Sackett. The Dawes Act and the Allotment of Indian Lands. Edited by Francis Paul Prucha. Norman: University of Oklahoma Press, 1973. Originally published in 1934. An edited reprint of a valuable 1934 report to a House committee.

953. Washburn, Wilcomb E. The Assault on Indian Tribalism: The General Allotment Law (Dawes Act) of 1887. Philadelphia: Lippincott, 1975. An overview of the act's passage and impact, a collection of documents on the law, and a bibliographical essay.

954. Hagan, William T. The Indian Rights Association: The Herbert Welsh Years, 1882-1904. Tucson: University of Arizona Press, 1985. The I.R.A.'s contention that GC was generally unfavorable toward Indians.

FOREIGN AFFAIRS AND THE NAVY

955. Plesur, Milton. American's Outward Thrust: Approaches to Foreign Affairs, 1865-1890. DeKalb: Northern Illinois University Press, 1971. GC and Secretary of State Thomas F. Bayard "were expansionists in their own way." (p. 235)

956. Parker, George F. "How Cleveland and Whitney Made the New Navy." Saturday Evening Post 195 (May 19, 1923): 42-54. A biographical sketch of William C. Whitney and how he, with GC's support, helped create the modern U.S. fleet.

957. Herrick, Walter R., Jr. The American Naval Revolution. Baton Rouge: Louisiana State University Press, 1966. GC's role in the development of the new navy and his anti-expansionist views.

958. Spring-Rice, Sir Cecil Arthur. Letters and Friendships of Sir Cecil Spring-Rice. London: Constable, 1929. Vol. 1 of these letters of Great Britain's minister to the U.S. contains many references to GC.

959. Hagan, Kenneth J. American Gunboat Diplomacy and the Old Navy, 1877-1889. Westport, CT: Greenwood, 1973. Although GC is only mentioned in passing, this book

discusses his first administration's role in naval and
diplomatic affairs.

960. Cooling, Benjamin Franklin. Benjamin Franklin Tracy:
Father of the Modern American Fighting Navy. Hamden, CT:
Archon, 1973. GC's role in the upgrading of the U.S. Navy.

961. ___. Gray Steel and Blue Water Navy: The Formative
Years of America's Military-Industrial Complex, 1881-1917.
Hamden, CT: Archon, 1979. The role of GC's Secretaries of
the Navy, William Whitney and Hilary Herbert, in building up
the American steel fleet.

962. Sprout, Harold, and Sprout, Margaret. The Rise of
American Naval Power, 1776-1918. Annapolis: Naval
Institute, 1966. GC's presidency in the creation of the new
navy and the expansionism that developed with it. (chaps.
12, 13)

963. Burnette, Allen L., Jr. "The Senate Foreign Relations
Committee and the Diplomacy of Garfield, Arthur, and
Cleveland." Ph.D. diss., University of Virginia, 1952.
Diplomacy of GC's first term.

964. Campbell, Charles S. "Edward J. Phelps and
Anglo-American Relations." In Contract and Connection,
Bicentennial Essays in Anglo-American History. Edited by
Henry C. Allen and Roger Thompson. Athens: Ohio University
Press, 1976. GC's first term minister to Great Britain, he
handled the diplomatic problems of the first term poorly.
(pp. 210-24)

965. Dozer, Donald M. "The Opposition to Hawaiian
Reciprocity, 1876-1888." Pacific Historical Review 14 (June
1945): 157-83. GC's administration successfully pressed
for continuation of Chester A. Arthur's policy to extend the
reciprocity agreement. (pp. 177-81)

966. Tate, Merze. "British Opposition to the Cession of
Pearl Harbor." Pacific Historical Review 29 (November
1960): 381-94. British acquiescence to GC's acquisition of
naval rights to Pearl Harbor.

967. Tansill, Charles C. Diplomatic Relations Between the United States and Hawaii, 1885-1889. New York: Fordham University Press, 1940. U.S. policy toward Hawaii during GC's first term was expressed by Secretary of State Bayard as "simply a matter of waiting until the apple should ripen and fall." (p. 44)

968. Marti Y Perez, Jose Julian. Hombres de Norteamerica. Havana: Patronato del Libro Popular, 1961. Mostly newspaper articles (1881-1888) by the NY correspondent of La Nacion (Buenos Aires) on contemporary Americans including GC.

969. Ealy, Lawrence O. Yanqui Politics and the Isthmian Canal. University Park: Pennsylvania State University Press, 1971. GC, an isthmian canal, and rejection of the Frelinghuysen-Zavala Treaty. (pp. 38-43)

970. Parks, E. Taylor. Colombia and the United States, 1765-1934. Durham, NC: Duke University Press, 1935. Numerous references to GC's attitude toward intervention and a possible canal.

971. Bermann, Karl. Under the Big Stick, Nicaragua and the United States Since 1848. Boston: South End Press, 1986. GC's rejection of the Frelinghuysen-Zavala Treaty and his refusal to consider canal possibilities. (pp. 117-118)

972. Wicks, Daniel H. "Dress Rehearsal: United States Intervention on the Isthmus of Panama, 1885." Pacific Historical Review 49 (November 1980): 581-605. GC's sending of troops to Panama during the early days of his first term set a precedent for Theodore Roosevelt's 1903 intervention.

973. LaFeber, Walter. The Panama Canal, The Crisis in Historical Perspective. New York: Oxford University Press, 1978. Despite his anti-imperialist reputation, GC conducted the nation's largest military landing operation between the Mexican War and the Spanish-American War. (pp. 26-27)

974. Vivian, James F. "The Pan American Conference Act of
May 10, 1888: President Cleveland and the Historians."
Americas 27 (October 1970): 185-92. Despite the
discrepancy between the Congressional Record and
Statutes-at-Large over whether GC signed this bill, he did.

975. Kennedy, Paul. The Samoan Tangle: A Study in
Anglo-German-American Relations, 1878-1900. New York:
Barnes and Noble, 1974. GC's role in this long debate.
(chaps.2, 3)

976. Ryden, George Herbert. The Foreign Policy of the
United States in Relation to Samoa. New Haven: Yale
University Press, 1933. GC's attitude and actions toward
Samoa. (chaps. 9-14)

977. Vagts, Alfred. Deutschland und die Vereinigten Staaten
in der Weltpolitik. 2 vols. New York: Macmillan, 1935.
German perspective on imperialism, for example, Samoa.
(vol. I, chap. 10)

978. Jonas, Manfred. The United States and Germany, A
Diplomatic History. Ithaca, NY: Cornell University Press,
1984. The negative impact on German-American relations of
the GC administration's role in Samoa. (pp. 44-49)

979. Schwelien, Joachim H. Encounter and Encouragement, A
Bicentennial Review of German-American Relations. Bonn:
Bonner Universitats-Bruchdruckerei, 1976. Samoa did not
spoil good German-American relations. (p. 76)

980. Levi, Werner. American-Australian Relations.
Minneapolis: University of Minnesota Press, 1947. GC saw
the Samoan problem as punishment for U.S. overseas activity.
(p. 79)

981. Logan, Rayford W. The Diplomatic Relations of the
United States with Haiti, 1776-1891. Chapel Hill:
University of North Carolina Press, 1941. The GC
administration took a hands off attitude toward Haiti for
policy, not racial prejudice, reasons. (chap. 13, 14)

982. Hall, Luella J. The United States and Morocco,
1776-1956. Metuchen, NJ: Scarecrow Press, 1971. GC
mentioned Liberia in his first annual message, but he had no
African policy. He did not, for example, follow through on
the earlier Berlin Conference. (pp. 232-33)

983. Cooper, Allan D. U.S. Economic Power and Political
Influence in Namibia, 1700-1982. Boulder, CO: Westview
Press, 1982. Berlin Conference and Namibia. (pp. 12-13)

984. Yeselson, Abraham. United States-Persian Diplomatic
Relations, 1883-1921. New Brunswick, NJ: Rutgers
University Press, 1956. Persia mentioned in GC's second and
final annual messages, and a legation was established there.
(pp. 33, 39)

985. Sherwood, Morgan B. Exploration of Alaska, 1865-1900.
New Haven: Yale University Press, 1965. GC's 1885
initiation of an Alaskan boundary survey. (pp. 136-7)

986. Lee, Yur-Bok. Diplomatic Relations Between the United
States and Korea, 1866-1887. New York: Humanities Press,
1970. GC's first term Far East diplomacy. (chaps, 4, 5)

987. Dulles, Foster Rhea. China and America, The Story of
Their Relations Since 1784. Port Washington, NY: Kennikat
Press, 1946. Brief comment on GC and 1888 Chinese Exclusion
Bill. (p. 91)

988. McKee, Delber. Chinese Exclusion Versus the Open Door
Policy, 1900-1906. Clashes Over China Policy in the
Roosevelt Era. Detroit: Wayne State University Press,
1977. GC and the 1888 Chinese Exclusion Bill. (p. 24)

989. Karlin, Julius A. "Anti-Chinese Outbreaks in Seattle,
1885-1886." Pacific Northwest Quarterly 39 (April 1948):
103-30. The GC administration had to send troops to quell
the disturbance.

990. O'Grady, Joseph P. "The Roman Question in American
Politics: 1885." Journal of Church and State 10 (No. 3,
1968): 365-77. The controversy surrounding GC's minister
to Italy, Anthony M. Keily, and its impact on GC's Catholic
and southern support.

CANADIAN FISHERIES AND RECIPROCITY

991. Tansill, Charles C. Canadian-American Relations, 1875-1911. New Haven: Yale University Press, 1943. Detailed study which has much material on all aspects of GC's presidency and its diplomatic relations with Canada.

992. Callahan, James Morton. American Foreign Policy in Canadian Relations. New York: Macmillan, 1937. GC and the fisheries and reciprocity issues of first term; pelagic sealing, Alaskan Boundary dispute, and other issues of both terms. (chaps 15, 18)

993. Brown, Robert Craig. Canada's National Policy, 1883-1900. A Study in Canadian-American Relations. Princeton, NJ: Princeton University Press, 1964. Alaskan Boundary dispute, pelagic sealing and reciprocity.

994. Campbell, Charles S., Jr. "American Tariff Interests and the Northeastern Fisheries, 1883-1888." Canadian Historical Review 45 (September 1964): 212-18. Despite his inability to obtain a fisheries treaty, GC's actions helped keep the peace until the 1912 agreement.

995. Craig, Gerald M. The United States and Canada. Cambridge: Harvard University Press, 1968. Brief references to GC's 1888 fisheries treaty which the Senate rejected. (p. 158)

996. Creighton, Donald. John A. MacDonald, The Old Chieftain. Toronto: Macmillan of Canada, 1955. Fisheries, reciprocity, Sackville-West, and Bering Sea controversies from this Canadian statesman's perspective.

997. Falconer, Sir Robert. The United States As a Neighbour from a Canadian Point of View. Cambridge, England: At the University Press, 1925. Fisheries and Venezuelan Boundary disputes from the Canadian perspective. (pp. 92-95, 127-29)

998. Hutchinson, Bruce. The Struggle for the Border.
Toronto: Longmans, Green, 1955. Brief discussion of GC,
reciprocity, and fisheries from the Canadian perspective.
(p. 424)

999. Keenleyside, Hugh L., and Brown, Gerald S. Canada and
the United States. Some Aspects of Their Historical
Relations. Rev. ed. New York: Alfred A. Knopf, 1952.
Fisheries controversy. (chap. 7)

1000. Martin, Lawrence. The Presidents and the Prime
Ministers. Washington and Ottawa Face to Face: The Myth of
Bilateral Bliss, 1867-1982. Toronto: Doubleday Canada
Limited, 1982. Fisheries and reciprocity controversies.
(pp. 39-46)

1001. McInnis, Edgar W. Canada, A Political and Social
History. New York: Holt Rinehart and Winston, 1963.
Fisheries and reciprocity controversies. (pp. 356, 358-59)

1002. ___. The Unguarded Frontier, A History of
American-Canadian Relations. Garden City, NY: Doubleday,
Doran, 1942. Fisheries and reciprocity controversies, and
Canada's desire and the U.S. refusal to arbitrate the
Alaskan Boundary in 1898 based on the Venezuelan Boundary
precedent. (pp. 289-91, 313)

1003. Saunders, Edward M. (ed.) The Life and Letters of the
Rt. Hon. Sir Charles Tupper Bart, K.C. M.G. 2 vols.
London: Cassell, 1916. "The Fishery Commission (1886-88)"
and this Canadian statesman's participation on it. (vol.
II, chap. 7)

1004. Garvin, James L. The Life of Joseph Chamberlain. 3
vols. London: Macmillan, 1933. His 1887-1888 visit to the
U.S. concerning the fisheries question and his eventual
marriage to Mary, the daughter of GC's Secretary of War,
William C. Endicott. (vol. II)

1005. Short, Adam, and Doughty, Arthur G. (eds.) Canada and
Its Provinces. 23 vols. Toronto: Edinburgh University
Press for the Publishers Associates of Canada Limited, 1914.
Fisheries and reciprocity controversies. (vol. 9, pp. 158,
163-64)

1006. Tupper, Sir Charles. Recollections of Sixty Years in
Canada. London: Cassell, 1914. The fisheries controversy
from the perspective of this major Canadian statesman.
(chap. 9)

1007. Warner, Donald F. The Idea of Continental Union:
Agitation for the Annexation of Canada to the United States,
1849-1893. Lexington: University of Kentucky Press for the
Mississippi Valley Historical Association, 1960. Canadian
perspective on fisheries, reciprocity, Venezuelan Boundary
dispute, and the talk of U.S. annexation of Canada. (pp.
180, 186, 238)

1008. Wittke, Carl. A History of Canada. Rev. ed. New
York: F.S. Crofts, 1941. Fisheries and reciprocity
controversies. (pp. 282-83)

TARIFF

1009. McCormick, Richard L. The Party Period and Public
Policy. American Politics from the Age of Jackson to the
Progressive Era. New York: Oxford University Press, 1986.
GC's 1887 tariff message "stands as the Gilded Age's
equivalent to Jackson's Bank veto." (p. 323)

1010. "The Effect of the Message." Nation 46 (January 19,
1888): 44. GC's tariff message, the first real state paper
since Abraham Lincoln's time.

1011. "President Cleveland's Message." Saturday Review 64
(December 10, 1887): 785-6. Importance of the 1887 tariff
message.

1012."A Republican. "Two Messages." North American Review
146 (January 1888): 1-13. Criticizes GC's 1887 tariff
message.

1013. Blaisdell, Thomas C., Jr., et. al. The American
Presidency in Political Cartoons, 1776-1976. Salt Lake
City: Peregrine Smith, 1976. An 1894 Judge cartoon
lampooning GC's tariff position. (p. 139)

1014. Smith, Ballard. "The Political Effect of the
Message." North American Review 146 (February 1888): 211-18.
Praises GC's tariff message.

1015. Stephenson, Nathaniel W. Nelson W. Aldrich, A Leader
in American Politics. New York: Charles Scribner's Sons,
1930. The tariff controversy of GC's first term from the
perspective of this leading Republican senator.

INTERSTATE COMMERCE COMMISSION

1016. Kolko, Gabriel. Railroad and Regulation: 1877-1916.
Princeton: Princeton University Press, 1965. GC's
pro-railroad appointments to the newly formed commission.
(pp. 46-8)

1017. "The President and the Republicans." Nation 44 (March
31, 1887): 264. GC's appointments to the new commission
provoked this pro-GC, anti-opponent statement.

1018. Neilson, James W. Shelby M. Cullom: Prairie State
Republican. Urbana: University of Illinois Press, 1962.
GC and the Interstate Commerce Act, and Cullom's defense of
GC's anti-silver stand.

BLACKS

1019. Grossman, Lawrence. The Democratic Party and the
Negro: Northern and National Politics, 1868-92. Urbana:
University of Illinois Press, 1976. GC's attitude and
policy toward blacks resembled that of Southern Redeemers,
though, in practice, he acted better.

1020. Sinkler, George. The Racial Attitudes of American
Presidents, From Abraham Lincoln to Theodore Roosevelt.
Garden City: Doubleday, 1971. GC showed some concern for
non-whites, but shared the racial prejudice of his age.
(chap. 6)

1021. Logan, Rayford W. The Negro in American Life and Thought: The Nadir, 1877-1901. New York: Macmillan, 1954. Chapter 3, "Dead Center Under Cleveland."

1022. Steinfield, Melvin. Our Racist Presidents: From Washington to Nixon. San Ramon, California: Consensus Publishers, 1972. Document 25 is an excerpt from the Rayford Logan book cited above.

EVALUATIONS

1023. Parker, George F. "Grover Cleveland's First Administration as President." Saturday Evening Post 195 (April 7, 1922): 46-56. Detailed favorable overview of GC's first term.

1024. Garraty, John A. The New Commonwealth 1877-1890. New American Nation Series. New York: Harper and Row, 1968. Good short synopsis and analysis of the 1884 election and GC's first term.

1025. Ketchersid, William L. "The Maturing of the Presidency, 1877-1889." Ph.D. diss., University of Georgia, 1977. GC played the major role in these years in expanding presidential power.

1026. Buck, Paul H. The Road to Reunion: 1865-1900. Boston: Little, Brown, 1937. A brief overview of GC's first term and its calming effect on northern apprehensions over a Democratic presidency.

1027. House, Albert V. "Republicans and Democrats Search for New Identities, 1870-1890." Review of Politics 31 (October 1969): 466-76. GC's term was crucial in turning the Democratic party from Civil War questions to issues that would carry it into the twentieth century.

1028. DiBacco, Thomas V. "A Heavy-Laden President of 100 Years Ago." Wall Street Journal, April 7, 1987, p. 34. GC's problems at the end of his first term.

1029. Eaton, Donald B. "Possible Presidents: President Cleveland." North American Review 145 (December 1887): 629-44. GC's successful first term accomplished more than anyone ever had "for reform in administration and manhood in politics." (p. 644)

1030. Ralphdon, Harold Fulton. Age of Cleveland. New York: F. A. Stokes, 1888. A very critical review of GC and his first term.

1031. Nixon, William P. (ed.) A Man of Destiny. Chicago: Belford, Clarke, 1885. A series of fictitious letters attacking GC and the Democratic party.

1032. "The President's Message." Nation 43 (December 7, 1886): 468. Praises GC's annual message.

1033. Richmond, Arthur. "Letters to Prominent Persons. No. 5 - To the President." North American Review 143 (December 1886): 616-27. A very critical evaluation of the first two years of the GC presidency.

1034. Piatt, Don. "Arthur Richmond and the President." North American Review 144 (January 1887): 111-2. Attacks Arthur Richmond's anti-GC article cited above.

1035. "What Mr. Cleveland Has Done." Nation 44 (March 10, 1887): 202. A favorable evaluation of the first two years of the GC presidency emphasizing his courage and honesty.

1036. "Two Years of Democratic Administration." Public Opinion 2 (March 19, 1887): 487-90. Newspaper reaction to GC's first two years in office.

1037. Larremore, Wilbur. "Popular Leaders - Grover Cleveland." Arena 3 (January 1891): 147-56. Favorable analysis of GC's first term, particularly praising his principle and courage.

1038. Fairman, Charles. Mr. Justice Miller and the Supreme
Court. New York: Russell and Russell, 1939. Justice
Miller's late 1880s negative opinion of GC. (pp. 429-30)

11
The Election of 1888

CAMPAIGN BIOGRAPHIES AND FACT BOOKS

1039. Stoddard, William O. Grover Cleveland. The Lives of the Presidents Series. New York: Frederick A. Stokes and Brothers, 1888. The best of the campaign biographies.

1040. Boyd, James P. Biographies of Pres. Grover Cleveland and Hon. Allen G. Thurman . . . . Philadelphia: Franklin News Co., 1888.

1041. Dieck, Herman. Life and Public Services of Our Great Reform President, Grover Cleveland and ... Allen G. Thurman . . . . New York: Hill and Harvey, 1888.

1042. Goodrich, Frederick E. The Life and Public Services of Grover Cleveland . . . . Boston: Lindsay, 1888.

1043. Graphic Life and History of Grover Cleveland. New York: Daily Graphic, July 1888. Newspaper sketch.

1044. Hensel, William U. Life and Public Services of Grover Cleveland . . . . Philadelphia: Edgewood, 1888.

Consult Section 7 for additional material on this campaign.

1045. Norton, Charles B. The President and His Cabinet . .
. Grover Cleveland. Boston: Cupples and Hurd, 1888.

1046. The Presidential Candidates. Sketches and Portraits of
the Nominees of All Parties. Providence: J. A. and R. A.
Reid, 1888.

1047. The Campaign Text Book of the Democratic Party of the
United States for the Presidential Election of 1888 . . . .
Prepared by Direction of the National Democratic Committee.
New York: Brentanos, 1888.

1048. Contest of 1888. Lives of the Candidates, Election
Statistics and Party Platforms . . . . Detroit: F. B.
Dickerson, 1888.

1049. "Democracy Photographed. The Record of a Bogus
Reformer. President Cleveland, A Wanton Pledge-breaker."
New York Tribune Extra, No. 100, 1888.

1050. Mistakes of Grover and Allan. Showing the Follies and
Weaknesses of the Past Administration. A Great Political
Satire . . . . Detroit: Darling, 1888. Ridicule of GC's
first term activities.

1051. Facts and Figures Relating to the Presidential
Campaign of 1888. Chicago: Lane Bridge and Iron Works,
1888.

1052. Herringshaw, Thomas W. The Biographical Review . . .
All the Presidential Candidates for 1888 . . . . Chicago:
Lewis, 1888.

1053. Our Presidents From Washington to Cleveland . . . and
Portraits and Sketches of the Lives of the Present
Candidates. Chicago: E. J. Lehmann, 1888.

1054. National Contest, Containing Portraits and Biographies
of Our National Favorites . . . . Detroit: Darling
Brothers, 1888.

THE CAMPAIGN

1055. Official Proceedings of the National Democratic
Convention . . . 1888. St. Louis: Woodward and Treanan,
1888. Factual information on GC's nomination.

1056. "Democratic Candidates and Platform." Public Opinion
5 (June 16, 1888): 214-9. Press reaction to GC's
nomination and the party platform.

1057. "Supporting Cleveland." Nation 46 (June 14, 1888):
482-3. Supports GC not because of tariff but because he
will bring civil service reform.

1058. "The Presidential Campaign." Public Opinion 5
(September 15, 1888): 485-90. Further press reaction to
GC's nomination acceptance.

1059. Reed, Thomas B. "The President's Letter." North
American Review 147 (October 1888): 385-93. The Republican
Speaker of the House uses the occasion of GC's nomination
acceptance to attack his and Democratic party positions on
the major issues of the day.

1060. McDaniel, John Edgar, Jr. "The Presidential Election
of 1888." Ph.D. diss., University of Texas, 1970. GC was
not cheated; he lost the election because of his tariff
stand.

1061. Bernardo, Carmelo J. "The Presidential Election of
1888." Ph.D. diss., Georgetown University, 1950. A
detailed, dated, but still useful, account.

1062. Baumgardner, James L. "The 1888 Presidential
Election: How Corrupt?" Presidential Studies Quarterly 14
(Summer 1984): 416-27. This election was not one of the
most corrupt in U.S. history.

1063. Campbell, Charles S., Jr. "The Dismissal of Lord
Sackville." Mississippi Valley Historical Review 44 (March
1958): 635-48. The British recalled Sackville-West too
precipitously because of the GC administration's

pressure which was based on political considerations and an incorrect knowledge of the British position.

1064. Sackville-West, Vita. Pepita. London: Virago Press, 1986. Sackville-West's granddaughter discusses the 1888 election and the Murchison letter, concluding that her grandfather was tricked and it "cost him his career." (pp. 167-73)

1065. Hinckley, Ted C. "George Osgoodby and the Murchison Letter." Pacific Historical Review 27 (No. 4, 1958): 359-70. This obscure California fruit grower was the author of the Murchison letter to which Lord Lionel Sackville-West penned his controversial reply.

1066. Adams, Charles Kendall. "Defeat of President Cleveland." Contemporary Review 55 (February 1889): 283-300. Why GC lost the election.

1067. Brooks, Frank H. "A Story of Cleveland's First Defeat." Harper's Weekly 48 (October 1, 1904): 1518. A newsman says he predicted GC's defeat after visiting influential NY Democrats during the campaign.

1068. Fredman, Lionel E. The Australian Ballot: The Story of an American Reform. East Lansing: Michigan State University Press, 1968. David B. Hill-GC election conflict and GC's tariff speech. (pp. 28-9, 56-7)

1069. Thieme, Otto Charles. "'Wave High the Red Bandanna': Some Handkerchiefs of the 1888 Presidential Campaign." Journal of American Culture 3 (Winter 1980): 686-705. Descriptions and photos of GC and Harrison campaign handkerchiefs.

1070. Pickens, Donald K. "The Historical Images in Republican Campaign Songs, 1860-1900." Journal of Popular Culture 15 (Winter 1981): 165-74. The text of a campaign song castigating GC for sending a substitute to fight for him in the Civil War. (p. 169)

1071. Cleveland and Thurman 1888 Campaign Songster; The Best and Most Popular Songs. n.p.: W. F. Shaw, 1888. "Tariff Reform" is printed at the head of the title page.

12
The Election of 1892

CAMPAIGN BIOGRAPHIES AND FACT BOOKS

1072. Parker, George F. A Life of Grover Cleveland with a
Sketch of Adlai E. Stevenson. New York: Cassell, 1892. A
campaign biography by a later prolific GC historian. Also
includes a pro-GC letter by Richard Gilder.

1073. Boyd, James P. Men and Issues of 1892 . . . . n.p.:
Publishers Union, 1892.

1074. Campbell-Copeland, Thomas. Cleveland and Stevenson.
Their Lives and Record . . . . New York: Charles L.
Webster, 1892.

1075. Fulton, Chandos. The History of the Democratic Party .
. . . Lives of Cleveland and Stevenson. New York: P. F.
Collier, 1892.

1076. Grady, John R. The Life and Public Services of the
Great Reform President, Grover Cleveland . . . . To Which
is Added the Life and Public Services of Adlai E. Stevenson
. . . . Philadelphia: National Publishing Company, 1892.

Consult Section 7 for additional material on this campaign.

121

1077. Hensel, William U. Life and Public Services of Grover
Cleveland . . . . Also, A Sketch of the Life and Services
of Hon. Adlai E. Stevenson . . . . By Professor Charles
Morris. n.p.: Edgewood, 1892.

1078. Life of Hon. Grover Cleveland, Ex-President, U.S.A . .
. With A Sketch of the Life and Public Services of Hon.
Adlai E. Stevenson . . . . n.p.: Political Publishing Co.,
1892.

THE CAMPAIGN

1079. Parker, George F. "How Grover Cleveland Was Nominated
and Elected President." Saturday Evening Post 192 (April
24, 1920): 22-3, 168-82. GC's activities during the four
years he was out of office (1889-1893).

1080. Official Proceedings of the National Democratic
Convention . . . 1892. Chicago: Cameron, Amberg, 1892.
Factual information on GC's nomination.

1081. Halstead, Murat. "The Chicago Convention of 1892."
Cosmopolitan 13 (September 1892): 585-91. A famous
reporter's description of the Democratic convention.

1082. Johnson, Tom L. My Story. Edited by Elizabeth J.
Hauser. New York: B. W. Huebsch, 1913. GC and William C.
Whitney's reaction to the free trade plank in the 1892
platform, and Johnson's insistence that Whitney had little
to do with GC's nomination. (pp. 72-3)

1083. "The Presidential Campaign." Public Opinion 13 (July
2, 1892): 295-9. Press reaction to Democratic and
Republican nominees and platform.

1084. "Mr. Cleveland's Candidacy." Nation 54 (June 30,
1892): 480. Praises the nomination of GC.

1085. "The Presidential Campaign." Public Opinion 13
(October 1, 1892): 613-7. Synopsis of GC's nomination
acceptance letter and press reaction.

1086. The Cleveland Democracy of Erie County. Constitution and By-Laws, Officers and By-Laws. Buffalo: Hutchinson, 1890. List of all members.

1087. Knoles, George H. The Presidential Campaign and Election of 1892. Stanford: Standford University Press, 1942. The most thorough analysis of GC's second victorious campaign.

1088. Russell, Charles E. These Shifting Scenes. New York: Hodder and Stoughton, George H. Doran, 1914. How GC won the 1892 Democratic nomination. (pp. 227-44)

1089. Parker, George F. "Grover Cleveland, A Character Sketch." Review of Reviews 6 (August 1892): 28-42. GC, the man and the politician, on the eve of the 1892 election.

1090. "Grover Cleveland." Introduction by Albert Shaw. Review of Reviews 6 (August 1892): 541-8. GC, the man and the politician, on the eve of the 1892 election. Includes photos, sketches, and cartoons.

1091. Schlup, Leonard. "Grover Cleveland and His 1892 Running Mate." Studies in History and Society 2 (1977): 60-74. Adlai Stevenson's political activity from 1888 to his crucial rule in the 1892 campaign.

1092. ___. "Adlai Stevenson and the Southern Campaign of 1892." Quarterly Review of Historical Studies [India] 17 (1977/1978): 7-14. Stevenson's successful attempts to keep the South in the Democratic camp.

1093. ___. "Adlai E. Stevenson and the 1892 Campaign in Alabama." Alabama Review 29 (January 1976): 3-15. Stevenson's efforts helped blunt the Populists and carry the state for the GC ticket.

1094. ___. "Adlai E. Stevenson's Campaign Visits to Kentucky in 1892." Register of the Kentucky Historical Society 75 (April 1977): 112-20. Stevenson was born in Kentucky, campaigned there twice, and GC carried the state.

1095. ___. "Adlai E. Stevenson and the 1892 Campaign in Virginia." Virginia Magazine of History and Biography 86 (July 1978): 345-54. Stevenson's energetic campaign helped carry the state for the GC ticket.

1096. ___. "Adlai E. Stevenson's Campaign Visits to West Virginia." West Virginia History 38 (January 1977): 126-35. Stevenson's 1892 and 1900 visits and how he became "the Democratic Talleyrand of his age." (p. 135)

1097. Miller, Carl. (comp.) Marches of the Presidents, 1789-1909: Authentic Marches and Campaign Songs, Arranged for Piano. New York: Chappell, 1968. "Up With the Red Bandanna," a Democratic campaign march in 1892. (pp. 52-3)

1098. Gibson, Florence E. Attitudes of the New York Irish Toward State and National Affairs, 1848-1892. Studies in History, Economics, and Public Law, No. 563. New York: Columbia University Press, 1951. GC's turbulent relationship with Tammany Hall and Irish voters throughout his political career from Buffalo to the election of 1892.

1099. "Mr. Cleveland and Tammany." Nation 55 (November 24, 1892): 384. GC did not promise favors in return for support.

1100. "How Richard Croker Helped William C. Whitney Elect Grover Cleveland." American Magazine 66 (August 1908): 412-6. Boss Croker supported GC in 1892 in repayment for Whitney's earlier support against an unfair murder charge.

1101. Dillon, Charles. "Grover Cleveland --- As Seen by a Telegraph Operator Who Handled His Political Secrets." American Magazine 66 (October 1908): 618-9. Boss Croker's support in 1892 was expected, not a surprise, as the previous article argues.

1102. Adams, Charles Francis. "What Mr. Cleveland Stands For." Forum 13 (July 1892): 662-70. Though a Republican, Adams supported GC because he felt he was a courageous statesman, while Harrison was a failure as president.

1103. Harrison, Carter H. Growing Up with Chicago. Chicago: Ralph Fletcher Seymour, 1944. GC asked for Harrison's and Chicago Times support in the 1892 election campaign. Includes GC letters. (pp. 263-5)

1104. McJimsey, George T. Genteel Partisan: Manton Marble, 1834-1917. Ames: Iowa State University Press, 1971. GC and this N.Y. World editor, international bimetalist, and 1892 David B. Hill supporter.

1105. Parker, George F. "Some Decisive Quarrels and Jealousies in American Politics." Saturday Evening Post 193 (September 4, 1920): 6-7, 160-9. Includes GC's political battles with David B. Hill.

1106. Ellis, David M.; Frost, James A.; Syrett, Harold C.; and Carman, Harry J. A History of New York State. Ithaca: Cornell University Press, 1957. Political battles between N.Y. Democratic politicians GC and David B. Hill. (pp. 367-73)

1107. Buss, Dietrich G. Henry Villard: A Study of Transatlantic Investments and Interests, 1870-1895. New York: Arno, 1978. Villard gathered the important German vote in GC's 1892 election and later supported GC on the silver issue. (pp. 240-5)

1108. Luebke, Frederick C. Immigrants and Politics: The Germans of Nebraska, 1880-1900. Lincoln: University of Nebraska Press, 1969. GC was considered in 1892 "a great friend of Germans and an opponent of prohibition and of all forms of nativism." (p. 153)

1109. Harvey, George B. Henry Clay Frick, The Man. New York: privately printed, 1928. Andrew Carnegie believed that GC's election was good for manufacturers. (p. 157)

1110. "Useful Reminder." Nation 55 (December 15, 1892): 444. GC is another Lincoln who understands the American people because he represents their basic virtues.

13
The Second Term, 1893-1897

DOMESTIC MATTERS

INAUGURATION

1111. "Grover Cleveland President-Elect." Harper's Weekly 36 (November 19, 26, 1892): 1105, 1130. GC's election and the major issues he will have to face during his second term.

1112. Washington, D.C. Inauguration Committee, 1893. Cleveland and Stevenson Inauguration Ceremonies, March 4, 1893 . . . . Washington: n.p., 1893. Sixty page listing of inauguration officials and rules for the ceremony and celebration.

1113. Nelson, Henry L. "Inauguration of President Cleveland." Harper's Weekly 37 (March 18, 1893): 245, 251-3. Description of the inauguration including photos of the swearing-in and the parade.

1114. "Mr. Cleveland as Prophet." Spectator 70 (March 11, 1893): 313-5. GC's inaugural address was "one of the most noteworthy speeches ever spoken to the American people." (p. 312)

Consult Sections 8 and 10 for additional material on GC's presidency.

1115. "President Cleveland's Inaugural Address." Harper's
Weekly 37 (March 11, 1893): 222. Favorable evaluation.

1116. "Comment on the Inaugural Address." Public Opinion 14
(March 11, 1893): 536. Press reaction.

1117. Dustenberg, Richard B. The Official Inaugural Medals
of the Presidents of the United States. 2nd ed.
Cincinnati: Medallion Press, 1976. Picture and description
of GC's 1893 inauguration badge, the forerunner of later
inauguration medals. (pp. 14-16)

1118. Washington, D.C. Inauguration Committee, 1893.
Inauguration Ceremonies of Grover Cleveland . . . and Adlai
E. Stevenson . . . March 4, 1893. Final Report . . . .
Washington: J. F. Sheiry, 1893. Forty eight pages.

1119. Erickson, Julius. "Astrological Forecast of the
Administration of President Cleveland." With comment by B.
O. Flower. Arena 10 (September 1894): 536-41. A prediction
three weeks after GC's inauguration that he, his party, and
their policies would all fail.

1120. Smith, Godwin. "Situation at Washington." Nineteenth
Century 34 (July 1893): 131-44. This British journal
presents its view of GC and the U.S.A. at the beginning of
GC's second term.

1121. "The Cleveland Cabinet." Public Opinion 14 (February
25, March 4, 1893): 491-4, 511-3. Press reaction to GC's
choice of cabinet members.

1122. "Meaning of Mr. Cleveland's Cabinet." Nation 56
(February 23, 1893): 137-8. Defends GC's choice of cabinet
members as bipartisan.

1123. Wilson, Woodrow. "Mr. Cleveland's Cabinet." Review
of Reviews 7 (April 1893): 286-97. A future president
evaluates GC's cabinet and its forthcoming role in GC's
second term. Includes photographs and signatures of all
cabinet members.

1124. Hoxie, R. Gordon. "The Cabinet in the American Presidency, 1789-1984." Presidential Studies Quarterly 14 (Spring 1984): 209-30. GC believed that a cabinet should be subordinate to the president. (p. 220)

1125. Parker, George F. "Return to the White House and the Second Cabinet." McClure's 32 (March 1909): 457-72. The 1892 campaign and GC's relationship with his cabinet.

PANIC OF 1893

1126. Sullivan, Mark. Our Times. The United States 1900-1925. New York: Charles Scribner's Sons, 1926. Some material on GC and the Panic of 1893, but it is most valuable for its social history of the 1890s. (Vol. I)

1127. Nugent, Walter T. K. From Centennial to World War: American Society, 1876-1917. The History of American Society. Indianapolis: Bobbs-Merrill, 1976. GC and the Panic of 1893. (pp. 103-8)

1128. Wiebe, Robert. The Search for Order: 1877-1920. The Making of America Series. New York: Hill and Wang, 1967. GC's failure to deal with the Panic of 1893 and the political repercussions. (pp. 93-5)

1129. Hoffman, Charles. The Depression of the Nineties, An Economic History. Westport, CT: Greenwood, 1970. An in depth economic account of the Panic of 1893.

1130. ___. "Depression of the Nineties." Journal of Economic History 16 (June 1956): 137-64. A detailed short account of the economics of the Panic of 1893.

1131. Steeples, Douglas W. "Five Troubled Years: A History of the Depression, 1893-1897." Ph.D. diss., University of North Carolina, 1961. The Panic affected wide areas of American life but caused no real rejection of the nation's traditional values.

1132.___. "The Panic of 1893: Contemporary Reflections and Reactions." Mid-America 47 (July 1965): 155-75. The Panic's impact on public opinion and attitudes.

1133. Bard, Mitchell. "Ideology and Depression Politics I: Grover Cleveland (1893-1897)." Presidential Studies Quarterly 15 (No. 1, 1985): 77-88. GC's conservatism's influence on his anti-panic policies.

1134. Fels, Rendigs. American Business Cycles, 1865-1897. Chapel Hill: University of North Carolina Press, 1959. "The Cycle of 1894-97" (chap. 11) and "The Depression of the Nineties" (chap. 12).

1135. Reszneck, Samuel. "Unemployment, Unrest, and Relief in the United States during the Depression of 1893-1897." Journal of Political Economy 41 (August 1953): 324-45. The effect of the Panic on American society.

1136. Darling, Arthur B. "Grover Cleveland and National Finances." American Scholar 3 (1934): 144-54. GC's inflexible monetary policy in the context of the economic crisis of the Panic.

1137. Grant, H. Roger. Self-Help in the 1890s Depression. Ames: Iowa State University Press, 1983. A brief overview of GC's financial policy (pp. 11-12) in this book about how people tried to cope with the crisis.

1138. Schwantes, Carlos A. Coxey's Army, An American Odyssey. Lincoln: University of Nebraska Press, 1985. Attorney General Richard Olney played the major role in the GC administration's negative view of this movement. (pp. 161ff)

1139. Woodward, C. Vann. Origins of the New South, 1877-1913. A History of the South. Baton Rouge: Louisiana State University Press, 1951. Southern perspective on the GC presidency, especially the Panic.

1140. Kinley, David. The Independent Treasury of the United States and Its Relations to the Banks of the Country. Washington: Government Printing Office, 1910. Its role in the Panic of 1893. (chaps. 8, 9)

1141. Hovey, Carl. The Life Story of J. Pierpont Morgan. New York: Sturgis and Walton, 1911. This banker's role in the financial crisis of the 1890s. (chaps. 8, 9)

1142. Allen, Frederick L. The Great Pierpont Morgan. New York: Harper and Brothers, 1949. GC, Morgan, and the gold reserve crisis of the Panic.

1143. Corey, Lewis. The House of Morgan. New York: G. Howard Watt, 1930. Morgan's role in the Panic's financial crisis. (chap. 18)

1144. Noyes, Alexander Dana. Forty Years of American Finance . . . 1865-1907. New York: G. P. Putnam, 1907. GC and financial issues like silver and the Panic bond issue. (chaps. 4, 6-10)

1145. White Gerald T. The United States and the Problem of Recovery after 1893. University of Alabama Press, 1982. GC believed the maintenance of the gold standard would restore good times.

1146. McSeveney, Samuel T. The Politics of Depression: Political Behavior in the Northeast, 1893-1896. New York: Oxford University Press, 1972. GC and the Cleveland Democrats, the Panic, and GC's home region's reaction.

1147. Nye, Russel B. Midwestern Progressive Politics: A Historical Study of its Origins and Development 1870-1950. East Lansing: Michigan State College, 1951. GC's handling of the Panic and its impact on the rise of Populists. (pp. 78ff)

1148. Salisbury, Robert S. "The Republican Party and Positive Government: 1860-1890." Mid-America 68 (January 1986): 15-34. GC's and Democrats' "negative government laissez faire precepts" (p. 28) were in contrast to the GOP's more positive approach.

1149. Degler, Carl N. Out of Our Past: The Forces that Shaped Modern America. Rev. ed. New York: Harper and Row, 1970. GC's continuance of traditional Democratic limited

government attitude helped create party sympathy for the
Populists. (pp. 335-6)

1150. Palmer, Bruce. "Man Over Money": The Southern
Populist Critique of American Capitalism. Chapel Hill:
University of North Carolina Press, 1980. GC is often
mentioned in this book from a critical Southern Populist
perspective.

SPECIAL SESSION AND SILVER

1151. Villard, Henry. Memoirs of Henry Villard: Journalist
and Financier, 1835-1900. 2 vols. New York: Da Capo
Press, 1969. Reprint. Villard's role in GC's 1892 campaign
and his pressure on GC to call a special session of
Congress. (pp. 362ff)

1152. "The President's Message." Social Economist 5
(September 1893): 129-34. GC's message to the Special
Session of Congress was a "signal failure" (p. 129) and
forewarned disaster for the nation.

1153. Dewey, Davis Rich. Financial History of the United
States. New York: Longmans, Green, 1909. GC's financial
policies.

1154. Nichols, Jeannette P. "The Politics and Personalities
of Silver Repeal in the United States Senate." American
Historical Review 41 (October 1935): 26-53. The battle in
the Senate over the repeal of the Sherman Silver Purchase
Act.

1155. Burlin, Paul T. "American Monetary Reform and
Expansion, 1893-1905." Ph.D. diss., Rutgers University,
1984. In the monetary debate of the 1890s, both sides
claimed their metal represented the nation's salvation.

1156. Hepburn, A. Barton. History of Currency in the United
States. Rev. ed. New York: Macmillan, 1924. The silver
issue and the impact of the Panic of 1893 on the American
currency system. (chap. 20)

1157. Devine, Jerry W. "Free Silver and Alabama Politics, 1890-1896." Ph.D. diss., Auburn University, 1980. The Alabama state Democratic leadership's battle over GC's anti-silver stand.

1158. Byars, William V. An American Commoner: The Life and Times of Richard Parks Bland. Columbia: University of Missouri Press, 1900. A critical evaluation of GC by a leading silver Republican.

1159. Glass, Mary Ellen. Silver and Politics in Nevada: 1892-1902. Reno: University of Nevada Press, 1969. Nevada opposition to GC because of his anti-silver stand.

1160. Pyle, Joseph G. The Life of James J. Hill. Garden City: Doubleday, Doran, 1917. This railroad magnate's letters to GC in opposition to Coxey's Army and free silver.

1161. Robinson, William A. Thomas B. Reed, Parliamentarian. New York: Dodd, Mead, 1930. Republican House Speaker "Czar" Reed's views of GC on the tariff and silver.

1162. Stewart, William M. Reminiscences of Senator William M. Stewart of Nevada. Edited by George Rothwell Brown. New York: Neale, 1908. A critical evaluation of GC, especially his anti-silver stance. (chaps. 34-6)

1163. Wooldridge, William C. "The Sound and Fury of 1896: Virginia Democrats Face Free Silver." Virginia Magazine of History and Biography 75 (January 1967): 97-108. The split in the Virginia Democratic party over silver which saw one state Democratic convention delegate call GC "a party wrecker." (p. 99)

1164. Werner, Morris R. Bryan. New York: Harcourt Brace, 1929. GC-Bryan differences over silver. (pp. 43ff)

1165. Malone, Preston S. "The Political Career of Charles Frederick Crisp." Ph.D. diss., University of Georgia, 1962. This Democratic member of Congress from Georgia (1883-1896) and Speaker during 52nd and 53rd Congresses broke with GC over the silver issue.

1166. Archer, Robert L. "Cleveland and Gold Standard."
National Republic 21 (February 1934): 5, 31. GC fought to
maintain the gold standard without Congress's help.

1167. Rothman, David. Politics and Power: The United
States Senate, 1869-1901. Cambridge: Harvard University
Press, 1966. GC and the Sherman Silver Purchase Act and
Wilson-Gorman Tariff. (pp. 93, 102-5)

1168. Barnes, James A. "The Gold Standard, Democrats, and
the Party Conflict." Mississippi Valley Historical Review
17 (December 1930): 422-50. The Democratic party's
monetary debate leading to the 1896 split into GC Gold
Democrats and Bryan Silver Democrats.

1169. Faulkner, Ronnie W. "North Carolina Democrats and
Silver Fusion Politics, 1892-1896." North Carolina
Historical Review 59 (July 1982): 230-51. The North
Carolina Democratic party-Populist fusion over silver.

1170. "Our National Object Lesson." Social Economist 5
(July 1893): 1-10. GC's retrogressive policies will teach
the nation a lesson it will not soon have to be re-taught.

1171. Edwards, Elisha J. "The Personal Force of Cleveland."
McClure's 1 (November 1893): 493-500 and Review of Reviews
8 (December 1893): 691-2. GC's strength and personal
integrity make him a great president.

1172. "Taft and Cleveland, 1893 and 1911." Nation 93
(August 24, 1911): 158. Compares GC's and Taft's calling
of special sessions of Congress to GC's benefit.

PULLMAN STRIKE

1173. United States Strike Commission, Report of the Chicago
Strike of June-July, 1894. Washington: Government Printing
Office, 1895. Reprinted by Augustus M. Kelley, 1972.
Verbatim testimony.

1174. "How Cleveland Dealt With the Chicago Strike."
Harper's Weekly 48 (July 16, 1904): 1083-4. Favorable
commentary on GC's 1904 McClure's article about his
handling of the strike.

1175. Lindsey, Almont. The Pullman Strike. Chicago:
University of Chicago Press, 1942. The most detailed
account available of this event and GC's role in it.

1176. Eggert, Gerald G. "The Great Pullman Strike."
American History Illustrated 6 (April 1971): 32-47. An
accurate popular account.

1177. Taft, Philip. Organized Labor in American History.
New York: Harper and Row, 1964. A good extended account of
the strike. (chap. 11)

1178. Rayback, Joseph G. A History of American Labor. New
York: Macmillan, 1959. A good extended account of the
strike. (chap. 14)

1179. Dulles, Foster Rhea. Labor in America, A History.
New York: Thomas Y. Crowell, 1949. A good extended
account.

1180. Taft, Philip. The A. F. of L. in the Time of Gompers.
New York: Harper and Brothers, 1957. Several page account
of the strike. (pp. 75ff)

1181. Hillquit, Morris. History of Socialism in the United
States. 5th ed. New York: Funk and Wagnalls, 1910. Brief
account. (pp. 284-6)

1182. Newborn, Newton N. "Restrictions on the Right to
Strike on the Railroads: A History and Analysis (I), (II)."
Labor Law Journal 24 (March, April, 1973): 142-63, 234-50.
A brief account of the strike and the Supreme Court case In
Re Debs. (pp. 144-6)

1183. Raphalides, Samuel J. "The Presidents' Use of Troops
in Civil Disorders." Presidential Studies Quarterly 8
(Spring 1978): 80-7. Includes GC and the strike.

1184. Blackman, John L., Jr.   Presidential Seizure in Labor Disputes. Cambridge, MA: Harvard University Press, 1967. Includes GC and strike.

1185. Berman, Edward. Labor Disputes and the Presidents of the United States. Studies in History, Economics and Public Law, No. 111. Columbia University, 1924. A detailed and critical account of GC and the strike. (Chap. 1)

1186. Altgeld, John Peter. The Mind and Spirit of John Peter Altgeld, Selected Writings and Addresses. Edited by Henry M. Christman. Urbana: University of Illinois Press, 1960. Altgeld's 1896 New York speech defending his position in the strike; some correspondence between him and GC. (pp. 124-74)

1187. Browne, Waldo R.   Altgeld of Illinois. New York: B. W. Huebsch, 1924. Chapter 15, "The Altgeld-Cleveland Controversy," includes the correspondence between the two men.

1188. Barnard, Harry. "Eagle Forgotten," The Life of John Peter Altgeld. New York: Dodd, Mead, 1938. Includes controversy with GC.

1189. Wish, Harvey. "The Administration of Governor John Peter Altgeld of Illinois, 1893-1897." Ph.D. diss., Northwestern University, 1936. Includes strike information.

1190. Ginger, Ray. Altgeld's America: The Lincoln Ideal Versus Changing Realities. Chicago: Quadrangle Books, 1965. A critical evaluation of GC's role in the strike. (pp. 158ff)

1191. Salvatore, Nick. Eugene V. Debs: Citizen and Socialist. Urbana: University of Illinois Press, 1982. The strike from the perspective of the most influential labor leader involved.

1192. Ginger, Ray.   The Bending Cross, A Biography of Eugene Victor Debs. New Brunswick: Rutgers University Press, 1949. The strike from the perspective of the most influential labor leader involved.

1193. Brommel, Bernard J. "Eugene V. Debs: Blue-Denim Spokesman." North Dakota Quarterly 41 (Spring 1973): 12-28. Debs' speeches and the newspaper coverage during the strike. (pp. 15-20)

1194. Coleman, McAlister. Eugene V. Debs, A Man Unafraid. New York: Greenberg, 1930. An oversimplified version of GC and the strike. (pp. 132-41)

1195. Darrow, Clarence. The Story of My Life. New York: Charles Scribner's Sons, 1932. Calls GC one of his idols but mentions him only in passing, even in his discussion of the strike.

1196. Jernigan, E. Jay. Henry Demarest Lloyd. Boston: Twayne, 1976. Lloyd's reaction to the Pullman Strike. (pp. 96-102)

1197. Martin, Albro. James J. Hill and the Opening of the Northwest. New York: Oxford University Press, 1976. This railroad man's relationship with GC was never as politically productive as he would have wished. (pp. 305-9, 425-7)

1198. Miles, Nelson A. Serving the Republic. New York: Harper and Brothers, 1911. GC, the Army, and the strike. (pp. 254, 257)

1199. Cooper, Jerry M. "The Army as Strikebreaker --- The Railroad Strikes of 1877 and 1894." Labor History 18 (Spring 1977): 179-96. The Army's role in these two labor disputes reflected middle class American desires for social order and the sanctity of property.

1200. ___. The Army and Civil Disorder: Federal Military Intervention in Labor Disputes, 1877-1900. Westport, CT: Greenwood, 1980. The Pullman Strike (chaps 5, 6) and GC's use of troops in the West, 1885 and 1886. (pp. 87-90)

1201. Hacker, Barton. "The U.S. Army as a National Police Force: The Federal Policing of Labor Disputes 1877-1898." Military Affairs 33 (April 1969): 255-64. Sixteen thousand troops out of a twenty five thousand man army were made

available to protect the railroads during the strike.   (p.
261)

1202. Fabiano, Gerald J.   "The Analysis and Interpretation
of the Use of Presidential Authority to Order United States
Armed Forces into Military Action to Quell Domestic
Disturbances."   Ph.D. diss., New York University, 1962.
Includes GC's use of federal troops in the strike.

1203. Thorelli, Hans B.   The Federal Antitrust Policy,
Origination of an American Tradition.   Baltimore: Johns
Hopkins Press, 1955.   The influence of Attorneys General
Olney and Harmon and the Pullman Strike on GC's attitude
toward large corporations.

1204. Kleiler, Frank M.   "White House Intervention in Labor
Disputes."   Political Science Quarterly 68 (June 1953):
227-40.   GC's intervention in the strike is an example of
the complexity of executive action.

1205. Eggert, Gerald G.   Railroad Labor Disputes: The
Beginnings of Federal Strike Policy.   Ann Arbor: University
of Michigan Press, 1967.   GC's labor attitude and actions
with special attention to the strike.

1206. ___.   "A Missed Alternative: Federal Court Arbitration
of Railway Labor Disputes, 1877-1895."   Labor History 7
(Fall 1966):   287-306.   "The climax of the development of
the labor injunction came with the Pullman Boycott Strike"
(p. 302), while arbitration was a missed alternative during
these same years.

1207. Leiby, James.   Carroll Wright and Labor Reform.
Cambridge: Harvard University Press, 1960.   The foremost
labor commissioner of the era, 1890 census taker, and head
of the Pullman Strike Investigating Committee.

1208. Foner, Philip S.   American Labor Songs of the
Nineteenth Century.   Urbana: University of Illinois Press,
1975.   Includes the lyrics to several anti-GC songs.

WILSON-GORMAN TARIFF ACT

1209. Wilson, Warren H.   "Grover Cleveland and the
Wilson-Gorman Tariff." Masters thesis, University of Texas,
1977. An excellent analysis.

1210. Ratner, Sidney. American Taxation. New York: W. W.
Norton, 1942. The economic issues of GC's two terms from
the perspective of the income tax issue which culminated in
the income tax provision of this tariff.

1211. Waltman, Jerold. "Origins of the Federal Income Tax."
Mid-America 62 (October 1980): 147-60. Conditions leading
to the tariff act. (pp. 151-54)

1212. Seligman, Edwin Robert Anderson. The Income Tax. New
York: Macmillan, 1914. Passage of the income tax provision
of this tariff act. (chap. 4)

1213. Mills, Roger Q. "The Wilson Bill." North American
Review 158 (February 1894): 235-44. This Texas senator
urges the amendment and passage of this bill.

1214. Palmer, John M. Personal Recollections of John M.
Palmer, The Story of an Earnest Life. Cincinnati: Robert
Clarke, 1901. An 1894 letter to GC urging him to sign the
tariff bill. (p. 558)

PATRONAGE

1215. "Anxiety of the Tammany Machine." Harper's Weekly 37
(March 18, 1893): 246-7. Suppports GC in his steadfastness
against Tammany Hall.

1216. "Emancipation Proclamation Against Office Seekers."
Nation 56 (May 11, 1893): 340. Praise for GC's May 8,
1893, statement limiting the access of office seekers.

1217. "Mr. Cleveland and the New York Democracy." Harper's
Weekly 37 (December 2, 1893): 1142. GC should use his

appointments not to battle Tammany Hall but to get good
appointments and thus thwart boss rule.

1218. McGurren, James E. Bourke Cockran, A Free Lance in
American Politics. New York: Charles Scribner, 1948.
Chapter 6, "Cleveland and Tammany," and later pages of this
book discuss GC's on and off relationship with this New York
machine politician.

1219. Bloom, Florence T. "The Political Career of William
Bourke Cockran." Ph.D. diss., City University of New York,
1970. He regularly battled GC but agreed with him on the
tariff issue.

1220. Simkins, Francis B. Pitchfork Ben Tillman. Baton
Rouge: Louisiana State University Press, 1944. This South
Carolina demagogue's inability to receive patronage and his
resulting opposition and "pitchfork" comment against GC.
(p. 315)

1221. Morgan, James F. "William Cary Renfrow: Governor of
Oklahoma Territory." Chronicle of Oklahoma 53 (No. 1,
1975): 46-65. GC made Renfrow the first Democrat and the
first former Confederate to be territorial governor of
Oklahoma.

1222. Werking, Richard Hume. The Master Architects:
Building the United States Foreign Service, 1890-1913.
Lexington: University Press of Kentucky, 1977. GC's 1895
executive order attempting to establish civil service for
consulate appointments. (pp. 38-40)

1223. Paterson, Thomas G. "American Businessmen and
Consular Service Reform, 1890's to 1906." Business History
Review 40 (Spring 1966): 77-97. Business reaction to GC's
1895 consular reform executive order. (pp. 87-9)

1224. Blodgett, Geoffrey. "A New Look at the American
Gilded Age." Historical Reflections 1 (Winter 1974):
231-44. GC, the Mugwumps, and the 1890s collapse of the
Cleveland coalition.

1225. McFarland, Gerald W. "The Breakdown of Deadlock: The
Cleveland Democracy in Connecticut, 1884-1894." Historian
31 (May 1969): 381-97. In 1884, the Democratic party had
gained new converts. The Panic of 1893 drove them away.

CONSERVATION

1226. McCarthy, G. Michael. "The Forest Reserve
Controversy: Colorado under Cleveland and McKinley."
Journal of Forest History 20 (April 1976): 80-90. GC's
prominent role in the first major conservation battle
between the Federal government and the West.

1227. Robbins, Roy M. Our Landed Heritage: The Public
Domain, 1776-1936. Princeton: Princeton University Press,
1942. GC's conservation activities and the creation of
federal forest preserves. (chaps. 17, 18, 19)

1228. Stevens, Walter B. "When A Missourian Forced a
Special Session of Congress." Missouri Historical Review 23
(October 1928): 44-8. GC's February 22, 1897 proclamation
taking 21 million acres of public domain for forest
reserves.

1229. Pinchot, Gifford. Breaking New Ground. New York:
Harcourt Brace, 1947. Theodore Roosevelt's leading
conservationist praises GC and his Secretary of the Interior
Hoke Smith for establishing forest reserves.

BLACKS

1230. Washington, Booker T. Up From Slavery, An
Autobiography. Garden City: Doubleday, 1900. A GC letter
and Washington's favorable evaluation of GC based on his
experience with him at the 1895 Atlanta Exposition. (pp.
227-8)

1231. Harlan, Louis R. Booker T. Washington. 2 vols. New
York: Oxford University Press, 1972, 1983. GC and Atlanta
Exposition speech (vol. I, p. 224) and GC's racist comment

at 1903 Tuskegee fund raising rally in New York. (vol.II,
p. 134)

1232. Washington, Booker T. The Booker T. Washington
Papers. 12 vols. Edited by Louis R. Harlan et. al.
Urbana: University of Illinois Press, 1972-1982. Numerous
references to GC and several GC letters from 1895 to the
fund raising years of GC's post-presidency.

1233. Spencer, Samuel R. J. Booker T. Washington and the
Negro's Place in American Life. The Library of American
Biography. Boston: Little, Brown, 1955. In 1899 GC
offered a $25,000 donation to Tuskegee Institute from an
anonymous donor.

SUPREME COURT

1234. Jager, Ronald E. "The Democracy's Demise: Grover
Cleveland's Rejected Supreme Court Nominations." Ph.D.
diss., University of Texas at Austin, 1972. The rejection
of GC's Supreme Court nominations by a NY Senator David B.
Hill-led Senate faction hurt GC's ability to lead in other
crucial areas and helped kill his influence over party
philosophy.

1235. Godkin, E. L. "Nomination of Mr. Peckham." Nation 58
(January 25, 1894): 61-2. GC's Supreme court nomination
shows he is again fighting for government reform.

1236. Pratt, Walter F. "Rhetorical Styles on the Fuller
Court." American Journal of Legal History 24 (July 1980):
189-220. An in depth study based on 286 Supreme Court cases
from 1895 to 1905.

1237. McCurdy, Charles W. "The Knight Sugar Decision of
1895 and the Modernization of American Corporation Law,
1869-1903." Business History Review 53 (Autumn 1979):
304-42. This Supreme Court decision was not an attempt to
shield a monopoly but the last attempt to retain state
jurisdiction over chartered institutions.

1238. Seager, Henry R., and Gulick, C. A. Trust and
Corporation Problems. New York: Harper Brothers, 1929. GC
said that the E.C. Knight decision made trusts a state
rather than a federal problem. (p. 385)

FOREIGN POLICY MATTERS

OVERVIEWS OF FOREIGN POLICY

1239. Dulebohn, George R. "Principles of Foreign policy
Under the Cleveland Administration." Ph.D. diss.,
University of Pennsylvania, 1940, published by author, 1941.
"The promotion of national security and economic growth
constituted the cardinal principles underlying and governing
his conduct of foreign affairs" (p. v) and "later
developments . . . have vindicated Cleveland's stand." (p.
93)

1240. Grenville, John A. S., and Young, George B. Politics,
Strategy, and American Diplomacy: Studies in Foreign
Policy, 1873-1917. New Haven: Yale University Press, 1966.
Five of the eleven chapters deal with GC and foreign policy,
mostly 2nd term.

1241. Dulles, Foster Rhea. The Imperial Years. New York:
Thomas Y. Crowell, 1956. GC's foreign policy is detailed in
three chapters.

1242. DeConde, Alexander. (ed.) Encyclopedia of American
Foreign Policy: Studies of the Principal Movements and
Ideas. 3 vols. New York: Charles Scribner's Sons, 1978.
Biographical sketches of GC and his Secretaries of State and
references to his Cuban policy, Hawaii, Sackville-West
issue, and Venezuelan Boundary dispute.

1243. Dobson, John M. American Ascent: The United States
Becomes a Great Power, 1880-1914. DeKalb: Northern
Illinois University Press, 1978. GC and anti-imperialism,
Cuba, the Far East, Hawaii, Samoa, and the Venezuelan
Boundary dispute.

1244. Campbell, Charles S. The Transformation of American Foreign Relations, 1865-1900. New York: Harper and Row, 1976. GC's foreign policy attitudes emphasized moralism and anti-expansionism.

1245. Beisner, Robert L. From the Old Diplomacy to the New, 1865-1900. New York: Cromwell, 1975. GC and Cuba, Hawaii, Latin America, and Venezuela.

1246. Callcott, Wilfrid Hardy. The Western Hemisphere, Its Influence on United States Policies to the End of World War II. Austin: University of Texas Press, 1968. GC and Cuba, Venezuelan Boundary dispute, Lord Salisbury, Colombia-Costa Rica Boundary dispute, and isolationism.

1247. Pratt, Julius W. America's Colonial Experiment. How the United States Gained, Governed, and in Part Gave Away a Colonial Empire. New York: Prentice-Hall, 1950. Hawaii, Cuba, Venezuelan Boundary dispute, and anti-imperialism.

1248. Devine, Michael J. John W. Foster: Politics and Diplomacy in the Imperial Era, 1837-1917. Athens: Ohio University Press, 1981. In this biography of a leading American diplomat, GC is mentioned in reference to the major diplomatic issues of his time.

1249. Hofstadter, Richard. The Paranoid Style in American Politics and Other Essays. New York: Random House, 1965. GC and 1890s foreign policy, business, and silver. (Chaps. 5-7)

1250. Dennis, Alfred L. P. Adventures in American Diplomacy, 1896-1906. New York: E.P. Dutton, 1928. Venezuelan Boundary dispute and Hawaii.

1251. Appel, John C. "American Labor and the Annexation of Hawaii: A Study in Logic and Economic Interest." Pacific Historical Review 23 (February 1954): 1-18. Differences in conditions kept labor leaders indifferent to Hawaiian annexation, but the 1895 Cuban revolt caused them to press GC for intervention there.

1252. Dorwart, Jeffrey M. The Pigtail War: American Involvement in the Sino-Japanese War of 1894-1895. Amherst: University of Massachusetts Press, 1975. Secretary of State Walter Gresham set precedents for McKinley, Roosevelt, and Wilson.

1253. ___. "The United States Navy and the Sino-Japanese War of 1894-1895." American Neptune 34 (July 1974): 210-18. The Navy's urging of restraint helped limit the GC administration's military role in this conflict.

1254. ___. "The Independent Minister: John M. B. Sill and the Struggle against Japanese Expansion in Korea, 1894-1897." Pacific Historical Review 44 (November 1975): 485-502. This GC appointee's three year effort to prevent Japanese expansion in Korea and his failure to convince Washington of a Japanese threat.

1255. Koo, Youngnok, and Suh, Dae-Sook. (eds.) Korea and the United States. A Century of Cooperation. Honolulu: University of Hawaii Press, 1984. GC and Korea during the Sino-Japanese War. (pp. 65-66)

1256. Dulles, Foster Rhea. Yankees and Samurai. America's Role in the Emergence of Modern Japan, 1791-1900. New York: Harper and Row, 1965. U.S. friendly neutrality during the Sino-Japanese War made Japan happy. (p. 252)

1257. Young, Marilyn B. The Rhetoric of Empire, American China Policy 1895-1901. Cambridge: Harvard University Press, 1968. The GC administraion tried to be neutral in the Sino-Japanese War, but the American public favored Japan because of her efficiency and China's inefficiency. (p. 15)

1258. Palmer, Spencer J. (ed.) Korean-American Relations. Documents Pertaining to the Far Eastern Diplomacy of the United States. Vol. II The Period of Growing Influence, 1887-1895. Berkeley: University of California Press, 1963. Text of letters to Secretaries of State from U.S. ministers in Korea. Includes GC letters.

1259. Lee, Yur-Bok, and Patterson, Wayne. One Hundred Years of Korean - American Relations, 1882-1982. Tuscaloosa: University of Alabama Press, 1986. During the Sino-Japanese War, the GC administration tried to aid Korea without

intervention. (p. 22)   Also includes brief sketches of U.S.
ministers to Korea. (pp. 63-4)

1260. Cohen, Warren I. America's Response to China: An
Interpretive History of Sino-American Relations. New York:
John Wiley, 1971. GC, Sino-Japanese War, and the China
trade. (pp. 41, 44)

1261. LaFeber, Walter. "United States Depression Diplomacy
and the Brazilian Revolution, 1893-1894." Hispanic American
Historical Review 40 (February 1960): 107-18. The GC
administration's depression-inspired fear that insurgents
would end a favorable commercial treaty caused it to send in
naval forces to crush the uprising.

1262. Burns, E. Bradford. The Unwritten Alliance.
Rio-Branco and Brazilian-American Relations. New York:
Columbia University Press, 1966. GC arbitrates an 1895
Brazil-Argentina boundary dispute which helps US-Brazil
relations and makes GC popular there. (pp. 30-32, 61, 85,
135)

1263. Crane, Daniel M., and Breslin, Thomas A. An Ordinary
Relationship: American Opposition to Republican Revolution
in China. Miami: University Presses of Florida, 1986. GC
made an anti-democracy statement in 1893. (p. 8)

1264. Canby, Henry Seidel. The Age of Confidence: Life in
the Nineties. New York: Farrar and Rinehart, 1934. Some
people in the 1890s considered GC a dangerous free trader.

1265. Lodge, Henry C. Speeches and Addresses, 1884-1909.
Boston: Houghton Mifflin, 1909. Includes speeches on major
issues of GC's second term: free silver, tariff, Hawaii,
Navy, and Venezuela.

1266. Montague, Ludwell Lee. Haiti and the United States,
1714-1938. New York: Russell and Russell, 1966. Haitians
were generally happy with GC. (p. 177) GC and the impact
of the tariff on Haiti. (pp. 167-68)

1267. Sivachev, Nikolai V., and Yakovlev, Nikolai N. Russia and the United States. Chicago: University of Chicago Press, 1979. GC's 1894 annual message called for equality of treatment for insurance companies in Russia. (p. 19)

1268. Churchward, L. G. Australia and America, 1788-1972. An Alternative History. Sydney, Australia: Alternative Publishing Cooperative, 1979. Hoping for a wool tariff concession, Sydney merchants congratulated the U.S. on GC's 1892 election. GC did place wool on the free list in 1894. (p. 75)

1269. Noer, Thomas J. Briton, Boer, and Yankee. The United States and South Africa, 1870-1914. Kent, OH: Kent State University Press, 1978. The arrest of seven U.S. citizens for their role in the 1895 Jameson Raid caught the GC adminstration unprepared. (pp. 48-55)

1270. Reed, James E. "American Foreign Policy, The Politics of Missions and Josiah Strong, 1890-1900." Church History 41 (June 1972): 230-45. The GC administration and the Armenian problem in Turkey.

1271. Evans, Henry Clay, Jr. Chile and Its Relations with the United States. Durham: Duke University Press, 1927. Early in GC's second term, the U.S. embassy in Chile served as a refuge for insurgents. (pp. 152-53)

1272. McCormick, Thomas. "The Wilson-McCook Scheme of 1896-1897." Pacific Historical Review 36 (February 1967): 47-58. The failed attempt by two entrepreneurs to convince the GC and then the McKinley administrations to cooperate with Russia in China.

ANTI-IMPERIALISM, HAWAII, AND CUBA

1273. Tompkins, E. Berkeley. "The Old Guard: A Study of the Anti-Imperialist Leadership." Historian 30 (May 1968): 366-88. The individuals, including GC, who lead the Anti-Imperialist League.

1274. ___. Anti-Imperialism in the United States: The
Great Debate, 1890-1920. Philadelphia: University of
Pennsylvania Press, 1970. GC's anti-imperialist attitude
during and after his presidency.

1275. Welch, Richard E., Jr. "Motives and Policy Objectives
of Anti-Imperialists, 1898." Mid-America 51 (April 1969):
119-29. GC is included in this study of 25 "representative"
anti-imperialists.

1276. Harrington, Fred A. "The Anti-Imperialist Movement in
the United States, 1898-1900." Mississippi Valley
Historical Review 22 (September 1935): 211-30. GC is
mentioned as one of the most prominent members.

1277. Lasch, Christopher. "The Anti-Imperialists, The
Philippines, and the Inequality of Man." Journal of
Southern History 24 (August 1958): 319-31. Many
anti-imperialists were southerners and held racist views
against the annexation of the Philippines.

1278. Calhoun, Charles W. "Rehearsal for Anti-Imperialism:
The Second Cleveland Adminstration's Attempt to Withdraw
from Samoa, 1893-1895." Historian 48 (February 1986):
209-24. Secretary of State Walter Gresham's role in
attempting to disengage the U.S. from Samoa helped initiate
the Anti-Imperialist League.

1279. Schirmer, Daniel B. "Anti-Imperialism and
Neo-Colonialism." Science & Society 35 (Summer 1971):
219-26. GC was a neo-colonialist who "promoted the
expansion of U.S. corporate interests abroad without the
benefit of colonization," as, e.g., in the Venezuelan
Boundary dispute. (pp. 222-3)

1280. ___. "On the Anti-Imperialist Movement: A Rejoinder."
Science & Society 38 (Spring 1974): 85-9.
Anti-imperialist opposition to GC's belligerent Venezuelan
Boundary policy. (p. 86)

1281. Warburg, James P. The United States in a Changing
World. An Historical Analysis of American Foreign Policy.
New York: G. P. Putnam's Sons, 1954. GC's foreign policy
was anti-imperialist, yet it asserted just rights and helped
build up expansionist pressures for later. (pp. 179-88)

1282. McCormick, Thomas J. China Market: America's Quest
for Informal Empire, 1893-1901. Chicago: Quadrangle, 1967.
GC pursued commercial expansionism as a way to deal with
domestic socio-economic problems.

1283. Iriye, Akira. Pacific Estrangement. Japanese and
American Expansion, 1897-1911. Cambridge: Harvard
University Press, 1972. Though an anti-imperialist, GC was
a commercial expansionist. (pp. 33-34)

1284. Schirmer, Daniel B. Republic or Empire: American
Resistance to the Philippine War. Cambridge, MA:
Schenkman, 1972. GC's anti-imperialism in Hawaii and his
Venezuelan Boundary dispute policy, the latter in terms of
Henry Cabot Lodge's imperialism.

1285. Ekrich, Arthur A., Jr. Ideas, Ideals, and American
Diplomacy: A History of Their Growth and Interaction. New
York: Appleton-Century-Crofts, 1966. GC's anti-imperialist
stance and the Olney Corollary.

1286. May, Ernest, R. Imperial Democracy, The Emergence of
America as a Great Power. New York: Harcourt Brace, 1961.
GC's anti-imperialist views and actions.

1287. Beisner, Robert L. Twelve Against Empire: The
Anti-Imperialists, 1898-1900. New York: McGraw-Hill, 1968.
GC's anti-imperialist foreign policy, his early ties to the
Mugwumps, and the split over the Venezuelan Boundary
dispute.

1288. Williams, William Appleman. The Roots of the Modern
American Empire: A Study of the Growth and Shaping of
Social Consciousness in a Marketplace Society. New York:
Random House, 1969. Characterizes GC as a "marketplace
expansionist." (p. 250)

1289. Pratt, Julius W. Expansionists of 1898: The
Acquisition of Hawaii and the Spanish Islands. Baltimore:
Johns Hopkins Press, 1936. GC's anti-imperialism with
special emphasis on Hawaii.

1290. Foner, Philip S. (ed.) The Anti-Imperialist Reader:
A Documentary History of Anti-Imperialism in the United
States. 2 vols. New York: Holmes & Meier, 1984. GC's
"Opposition to Hawaiian Annexation." (vol. I, chap. 2)

1291. Allen, Helena, G. The Betrayal of Liliuokalani: Last
Queen of Hawaii, 1838-1917. Glendale, California: Clark,
1982. GC's withdrawal of the Hawaiian annexation treaty and
his support for the queen.

1292. Osborne, Thomas J. "Empire Can Wait": American
Opposition to Hawaiian Annexation, 1893-1898. Kent, OH:
Kent State University Press, 1981. GC's prominent role.
(chaps. 2, 6)

1293. Tate, Merze. The United States and the Hawaiian
Kingdom: A Political History. New Haven: Yale University
Press, 1965. Chapter 7, "Cleveland's Policy," details his
anti-imperialist actions toward Hawaii.

1294. Stevens, Sylvester K. American Expansion in Hawaii
1842-1898. Harrisburg, PA: Archerse, 1945. GC's role in
stopping Hawaiian annexation.

1295. Alexander, William D. Last Years of the Later Years
of the Hawaiian Monarchy and the Revolution of 1893.
Honolulu: Hawaiian Gazette Company, 1896. Chapter 6,
"President Cleveland's Attempt to Restore the Queen."

1296. Lanier, Osmos J. "'Paramount' Blount: Special
Commissioner to Investigate the Hawaiian Coup, 1893." West
Georgia College Studies in the Social Sciences 11 (1972):
45-55. Congressman James Henderson Blount, GC's "executive
agent" (investigator) of the overthrow of the Hawaiian
monarchy.

1297. Baker, George W., Jr. "Benjamin Harrison and Hawaiian
Annexation: A Reinterpretation." Pacific Historical Review
33 (August 1964) : 295-310. GC's rejection of Hawaiian
annexation. (pp. 308-9)

1298. Devine, Michael J. "John W. Foster and the Struggle
for the Annexation of Hawaii." Pacific Historical Review 46
(February 1977): 29-50. GC's and Secretary of State Walter
Gresham's opposition to Hawaiian annexation. (pp. 46-50)

1299. Kiernan, Victor G. America: The New Imperialism,
From White Settlement to World Hegemony. London: Zed
Press, 1978. GC rejected annexation, but recognized the
republic of Hawaii. (pp. 91, 100)

1300. Bailey, Thomas A. America Faces Russia.
Russian-American Relations from Early Times to Our Day.
Ithaca: Cornell University Press, 1950. Russia favored
U.S. annexation of Hawaii. During the Panic of 1893, she
offered the U.S. a loan of gold and in 1895 asked for a loan
of silver. The U.S. refused both. (p. 160)

1301. Gillis, James A. The Hawaiian Incident; An
Examination of Mr. Cleveland's Attitude Toward the
Revolution of 1893. Boston: Lee and Shepard, 1897. Many
excerpts from official documents to defend GC.

1302. "The Annexation Policy." Harper's Weekly 37 (March
18, 1893): 246. Praises and defends GC for withdrawing the
Hawaiian annexation treaty.

1303. "President's Hawaii Message." Harper's Weekly 37
(December 30, 1893): 1242. Endorses GC's message.

1304. Hammett, Hugh B. "The Cleveland Administration and
Anglo-American Naval Friction in Hawaii, 1893-1894."
Military Affairs 40 (February 1976): 27-32. GC
administration's determination to keep the Navy's Pacific
fleet from dictating foreign policy regarding Hawaiian
annexation.

1305. LaFeber, Walter F. "The Latin American Policy of the
Second Cleveland Administration." Ph.D. diss., University
of Wisconsin-Madison, 1959. GC and his advisers were
anti-colonialists, but the GC administration helped set the
stage for later expansion.

1306. Chadwick, French Ensor. The Relations of the United States and Spain. New York: Charles Scribner's Sons, 1909. A detailed account of GC, his administration, Spain, and Cuba. (chaps. 19-24)

1307. Langley, Lester D. The Cuban Policy of the United States: A Brief History. New York: John Wiley and Sons, 1968. GC tried to keep the U.S. out of the Cuban problems. (pp. 87-95)

1308. Healy, David F. The United States in Cuba, 1898-1902. Generals, Politicians, and the Search for Policy. Madison: University of Wisconsin Press, 1963. GC did not want to intervene in Cuba to help the insurgents; Congress did. (pp. 10-13.

1309. Guggenheim, Harry F. The United States and Cuba, A Study in International Relations. New York: Macmillan, 1934. GC's willingness to help but his refusal to intervene in Cuban problems. (pp. 31-35)

1310. Wisan, Joseph E. The Cuban Crisis as Reflected in the New York Press, 1895-1898. New York: Columbia University Press, 1934. The press's varied response to GC for his anti-intervention stand. (pp. 99-102, 237-42)

1311. Williams, William Appleman. "President and His Critics." Nation 196 (March 16, 1963): 220-8, 236. On the occasion of a 1963 debate over American policy toward Cuba, a historian discusses GC's 1890s actions toward the island.

1312. Cortada, James W. Two Nations Over Time: Spain and the United States, 1776-1977. Westport, CT: Greenwood, 1978. GC's anti-war policy toward Cuba. (p. 113)

1313. Lodge, Henry Cabot. War with Spain. New York: Harper and Brothers, 1899. The Republican expansionist senator's view of GC and Cuba. (chap. 1)

1314. Adams, Henry. Education of Henry Adams. Boston: Houghton Mifflin, 1918. Adams' cynical evaluation of GC in 1892 (pp. 320, 324) and criticism of his Cuba policy. (p. 349)

VENEZUELAN BOUNDARY DISPUTE

1315. Ireland, Gordon. Boundaries, Possessions, and
Conflicts in South America. Cambridge: Harvard Unversity
Press, 1938. Factual and technical information on the
Venezuela-British Guiana boundary. (pp. 230-43)

1316. Venezuelan-British Guiana Boundary Arbitration . . .
1897. 6 vols. New York: Evening Post, 1898. Documents of
the U.S. case, counter-case, and argument.

1317. "Representative Opinions of Cleveland's Message.
Outlook 52 (December 28, 1895): 1134-6. Reactions of
leading Americans to GC's Venezuelan Boundary dispute
message.

1318. "President's Message." Spectator 75 (December 7, 21,
1895): 809-10, 884-5. Favorable review of 1895 annual
message and unfavorable account of Venezuelan boundary
dispute message.

1319. "Homeopathy in Government." Nation 62 (January 30,
1896): 91. Sadly criticizes GC's Venezuelan policy as only
slightly better than Congress's.

1320. Perkins, Bradford. The Great Rapprochement: England
and the United States 1895-1914. New York: Athenaeum,
1968. Excellent analysis of Venezuelan Boundary dispute.
(chap. 2).

1321. Dulles, Foster Rhea. Prelude to World Power:
American Diplomatic History 1860-1900. New York:
Macmillan, 1965. Chapter 8, "Cleveland and Venezuela."

1322. LaFeber, Walter F. "The Background of Cleveland's
Venezuelan Policy: A Reinterpretation." American
Historical Review 66 (July 1961): 947-67. Both
international dangers and the Panic of 1893 played key roles
in GC's Venezuelan Boundary dispute policy.

1323. Holmes, Jack E. The Mood/Interest Theory of American Foreign Policy. Lexington: University Press of Kentucky, 1985. GC was an "introvert" in foreign policy, but he used "extrovert" means in the Venezuelan Boundary dispute. (pp. 42, 132)

1324. Elliot, Arthur D. The Life of George Joachim Goschen, First Viscount of Goschen, 1831-1907. London: Longmans, Green, 1911. GC took his position in the Venezuelan Boundary dispute for political, not diplomatic, reasons. (pp. 203-04)

1325. Schlesinger, Arthur M., Jr. The Cycles of American History. Boston: Houghton Mifflin, 1986. The Venezuelan Boundary dispute was not an economic issue as some historians have argued. (pp. 139-39) GC and laissez faire." (pp. 235, 241)

1326. LaFeber, Walter F. "The American Business Community and Cleveland's Venezuela Message." Business History Review 34 (Winter 1960): 393-402. Contrary to traditional accounts, businessmen approved GC's Venezuelan policy and his expansionist interpretation of the Monroe Doctrine.

1327. Shaw, Albert. International Bearings of American Policy. Baltimore: John Hopkins Press, 1943. An in depth discussion of the Venezuelan Boundary dispute including the British side. (pp. 227-49)

1328. Blake, Nelson M. "Background of Cleveland's Venezuelan Policy." American Historical Review 47 (January 1942): 259-77. GC believed the Monroe Doctrine was at stake but primarily acted because of political and journalistic jingoism.

1329. Hedrick, Edith V. "The Diplomacy of the Venezuelan Boundary Controversy." Ph.D. diss., University of California, 1942. A detailed older study.

1330. Moore, John Bassett. Principles of American Diplomacy. New York: Harper and Brothers, 1918. This leading diplomatic writer's discussion of the Venezuelan Boundary dispute and the Monroe Doctrine.

1331. Bartlett, Ruhl. Policy and Power: Two Centuries of American Foreign Relations. New York: Hill and Wang, 1963. GC's and Richard Olney's corollary to the Monroe Doctrine.

1332. Young, George B. "Intervention Under the Monroe Doctrine: The Olney Corollary." Political Science Quarterly 57 (June 1942): 247-80. Since Richard Olney's statement vindicated the Monroe Doctrine, it deserves to be called a corollary.

1333. Smith, Theodore C. "Secretary Olney's Real Credit in the Venezuelan Affair." Massachusetts Historical Society Proceedings 65 (1933): 112-47. An indepth discussion of Olney's major role.

1334. Crabb, Cecil V., Jr. The Documents of American Foreign Policy. Their Meaning, Role, and Future. Baton Rouge: Louisiana State University Press, 1982. Olney Corollary. (pp. 33, 37-38)

1335. Bemis, Samuel Flagg. The Latin American Policy of the United States. An Historical Interpretation. New York: Harcourt, Brace, and World, 1943. The Olney Corollary to the Monroe Doctrine and the Venezuelan Boundary dispute. (chap. 7) GC's anti-imperialist policies. (chap. 8)

1336. Barclay, Thomas. Thirty Years of Anglo-French Reminiscences (1876-1906). Boston: Houghton, Mifflin, 1914. In 1903 Richard Olney told the author that the U.S. had had to speak out during the Venezuelan Boundary dispute because Great Britain and others were not taking the Monroe Doctrine seriously enough. (p. 128)

1337. Seitz, Don C. Joseph Pulitzer, His Life and Letters. New York: Simon and Schuster, 1924. GC's letter praising the New York World's role in his elections (p. 149); also, an in depth discussion of Venezuelan Boundary controversy.

1338. Rojas, Armando. Historia De Las Relaciones Diplomaticas Entre Venezuela y Los Estados Unidos -I- 1810-1899. Caracas: Ediciones De La Presidencia De La Republica, 1979. The Venezuelan Boundary dispute from the Venezuelan perspective. (chap. 11)

1339. Allen, Harry C. Great Britain and the United States. A History of Anglo-American Relations (1783-1952). New York: St. Martin's Press, 1955. Anglo-American diplomacy, particularly the Venezuelan Boundary dispute, from the British perspective. (chap. 14)

1340. Ions, Edmund. James Bryce and American Democracy, 1870-1922. London: Macmillan, 1968. GC's three election campaigns and the Venezuelan Boundary dispute from the perspective of this famed British interpreter of American society. (pp. 153-61)

1341. Bourne, Kenneth. Britain and the Balance of Power in North America, 1815-1908. Berkeley: University of California Press, 1967. The Venezuelan Boundary dispute from the British side, including a long quote from Lord Dufferin, British ambassador to France. (pp. 319, 339-40)

1342. Anderson, Stuart. Race and Rapprochement. Anglo-Saxonism and Anglo-American Relations, 1895-1904. Rutherford, NJ: Fairleigh Dickinson University Press, 1981. "The Venezuelan Boundary Dispute and the Olney-Pauncefote Treaty: Anglo-Saxonism Emerges as an Influence on Anglo-American Relations." (chap 5)

1343. Nicholas, Herbert G. The United States and Britain. Chicago: University of Chicago Press, 1975. A brief analysis of the Venezuelan Boundary dispute emphasizing British-American national similarities. (pp.52-4)

1344. Campbell, Alexander E. Great Britain and the United States, 1895-1903. London: Macmillan, 1960. Venezuelan Boundary dispute from the British perspective; argues that the British made most of the concessions. (chap. 2)

1345. Ward, Adolphus W, and Gooch, George Peabody. (eds.) The Cambridge History of British Foreign Policy, 1783-1919. 3 vols. New York: Macmillan, 1923. Lord Salisbury's wise willingness to compromise solved the Venezuelan Boundary dispute. (vol. 3, pp. 225-26)

1346. Whitridge, Arnold. "The Monroe Doctrine." History Today 6 (June 1956): 376-86. The Venezuelan Boundary dispute from the British perspective.

1347. Wheelwright, John T. "President Cleveland's
Foresight; The Venezuelan Message." University
Magazine(Montreal) 17 (December 1918): 506-12. GC's
Venezuelan Boundary policy helped later British-U.S.
relations, especially the U.S. entering World War I on the
British side.

1348. Grenville, John A. S. Lord Salisbury and Foreign
Policy. The Close of the Nineteenth Century. London: The
Athlone Press, 1964. The British perspective on the
Venezuelan Boundary dispute which concludes that it all
worked out for the best despite early hard feelings. (chap
3)

1349. Sloan, Jennie A. "Anglo-American Relations and the
Venezuelan Boundary Dispute." Hispanic American Historical
Review 18 (November 1938): 486-506. Because of a complex
of problems between Great Britain and the United States, war
seemed imminent, but the Venezuelan Boundary dispute
settlement caused a significant rapprochement.

1350. Mathews, Joseph J. "Informal Diplomacy in the
Venezuelan Crisis of 1896." Journal of American History 50
(September 1963): 195-212. Unofficial channels of
communication kept the GC administration and Great Britain
from moving toward war.

1351. Slosson, Preston W. "The Venezuela Dispute."
Independent 81 (March 15, 1915): 387-8. A quick overview
of this issue as part of an eight part series "On the
Hundred Years of Peace Among English-Speaking Peoples."

1352. Nevins, Allan. Henry White: Thirty Years of American
Diplomacy. New York: Harper and Brothers, 1930. The
Venezuelan Boundary dispute from the perspective of an
American diplomat in London.

1353. Mowat, Robert B. Life of Lord Pauncefote, First
Ambassador to the United States. London: Constable, 1929.
The British side of the key diplomatic issues of GC's
presidency.

1354. Meyerhuber, Carl I., Jr. "Henry Lee Higginson and the New Imperialism, 1890-1900." Mid-Ameria 56 (July 1974): 182-99. Venezuelan Boundary dispute (pp. 186ff).

1355. Robertson, William Spence. "Hispanic American Appreciations of the Monroe Doctrine." Hispanic American Historical Review 3 (February 1920): 1-16. Latin American countries supported GC's use of the Monroe Doctrine in the Venezuelan Boundary dispute.

1356. Rippy, J. Fred. The United States and Mexico. New York: F. S. Crofts, 1931. Mexico gave GC's Venezuelan message "a carefully qualified approval." (p. 325)

1357. ___. "Some Contemporary Mexican Reactions to Cleveland's Venezuelan Message." Political Science Quarterly 39 (June 1924): 280-92. Mexicans read into GC's pronouncement what they wanted to hear and then praised him for it.

1358. Hill, Lawrence F. Diplomatic Relations Between the United States and Brazil. Durham: Duke University Press, 1932. GC's arbitration of the Missiones boundary caused his Venezuelan Boundary message to be well received in Brazil. (pp. 282-83)

1359. Angus, Henry F. (ed.) Canada and Her Great Neighbor. Sociological Surveys of Opinions and Attitudes in Canada Concerning the United States. Toronto: Ryerson Press, 1938. The Canadian perspective on the Venezuelan Boundary dispute. (chap. 2, part 3) Canadian newspaper comments on the Alaskan Boundary controversy. (chap. 2, part 4)

1360. Creighton, Donald. Canada's First Century, 1867-1967. Toronto: Macmillan of Canada, 1970. Canadians feared Great Britain's uncertain support should the U.S. be emboldened by its Venezuelan Boundary victory to pressure Canada. (pp. 88-89)

1361. Preston, Richard A. The Defence of the Undefended Border, Planning for War in North America, 1867-1939. Montreal: McGill-Queen's University Press, 1977. The Venezuelan Boundary dispute caused Canadians to worry that the U.S. would invade Canada.

1362. Stacey, Charles P. "Twenty-One Years of
Canadian-American Military Co-Operation, 1940-1961." In
Deener, David R. Canada-United States Treaty Relations.
Durham: Duke University Press, 1963. The Christmas 1895
crisis over the Venezuelan Boundary dispute was the last
time Canada prepared for a possible U.S. attack. (p. 103)

1363. Wade, Mason. The French Canadians, 1760-1945. New
York: Macmillan, 1955. Joseph Chamberlain's use of the
Venezuelan Boundary dispute to solidify Canadian loyalty to
Great Britain. (p. 471) Reciprocity controversy of GC's
first term. (p. 467)

1364. Kirkland, Edward Chase. Charles Francis Adams, Jr.,
1835-1915: The Patrician at Bay. Cambridge: Harvard
University Press, 1965. Adams supported GC in 1892 (p. 165)
but was shocked by GC's strong Venezuelan Boundary dispute
statement. (pp. 183-4)

1365. Wall, Joseph F. Andrew Carnegie. New York: Oxford
University Press, 1970. Carnegie worried about GC's health
and Venezuelan policy but generally liked GC's other
policies.

1366. Armstrong, William M. E. L. Godkin: A Biography.
Albany: State University of New York Press, 1978. GC's
strong relationship with this important journalist and how
they finally broke over the Venezuelan Boundary dispute.

1367. ___ . E. L. Godkin and American Foreign Policy:
1865-1900. New York: Bookman Associates, 1957. Godkin's
general support of GC and his criticism of GC's Venezuelan
Boundary position.

1368. Lodge, Henry Cabot. One Hundred Years of Peace. New
York: Macmillan, 1913. Lodge defends GC's Venezuelan
Boundary position. (pp. 122-9)

1369. Garraty, John A. Henry Cabot Lodge: A Biography.
New York: Knopf, 1965. Though he supported GC in the
Venezuelan Boundary dispute, Lodge opposed GC on almost
everything else.

1370. White, Andrew D. Autobiography of Andrew D. White. 2
vols. New York: Century, 1905. White's membership on the
Venezuelan Boundary Commission. (vol. II, chap. 39)

1371. ___. The Diaries of Andrew D. White. Edited by
Robert M. Ogden. Ithaca: Cornell University Press, 1959.
Work with GC on Venezuelan Boundary Commission. Includes GC
quotes. (pp. 334-5)

1372. Schoenrich, Otto. "The Venezuelan-British Guiana
Boundary Dispute." American Journal of International Law 43
(July 1949): 523-30. Severo Mallet-Prevost, the last
surviving arbitration attorney, and his description of how
the arbitration decision was made to benefit Great Britain
at Venezuela's expense.

1373. Child, Clifton J. "The Venezuelan-British Guiana
Boundary Arbitration of 1899." American Journal of
International Law 44 (October 1950): 682-93. Counters the
Mallet-Prevost version presented in the July 1949, issue of
the same journal.

1374. Dennis, William C. "The Venezuelan-British Guiana
Boundary Arbitration of 1899." American Journal of
International Law 44 (October 1950): 720-27. Agrees with
the Mallet-Prevost statement in the July 1949, issue of the
same journal that diplomatic compromise, not arbitration,
settled the Venezuelan Boundary dispute.

1375. Linderman, Gerald F. The Mirror of War: American
Society and the Spanish-American War. Ann Arbor:
University of Michigan Press, 1974. GC's 1897 comment on
McKinley (p. 21), and GC and the Venezuelan Boundary
dispute.

1376. Collin, Richard H. Theodore Roosevelt, Diplomacy, and
Expansion: A New View of American Imperialism. Baton
Rouge: Louisiana State University, 1985. In the Venezuelan
Boundary dispute, GC, like Theodore Roosevelt, wanted U.S.
to hold its own in world affairs. (chap. 6)

1377. Beth, Loren P. The Development of the American
Constitution, 1877-1917. New York: Harper and Row, 1971.
GC's Venezuelan Boundary policy helped strengthen the
presidency's role in foreign affairs.

MISCELLANEOUS ISSUES

1378. "Last Official Acts." Outlook 55 (March 13, 1897):
721-2. GC's veto of an illiterate immigrant restriction
bill.

1379. Schlup, Leonard. "Presidential Disability: The Case
of Cleveland and Stevenson." Presidential Studies Quarterly
9 (Fall 1979): 303-10. GC-Stevenson relationship as a test
case for lack of adequate emergency procedure.

1380. Pollard, James E. The Presidents and the Press. New
York: Macmillan, 1947. GC's bad relations with the press.
(pp. 499-537)

1381. Brayman, Harold. The President Speaks Off-The-Record.
Princeton: Dow Jones Books, 1976. GC's critical view of
the Gridiron Club. (pp. 25-37)

1382. Juergens, George. Joseph Pulitzer and the New York
World. Princeton: Princeton University Press, 1966.
Despite GC's general disdain for the press, he had good
relations with the World. See p. 104n for a GC letter on
this topic.

1383. Burg, David F. Chicago's White City of 1893.
Lexington: University Press of Kentucky, 1976. GC's visit
and speech at the 1893 World's Fair. (pp. 109-11)

1384. DeConde, Alexander. Half Bitter, Half Sweet: An
Excursion into Italian-American History. New York: Charles
Scribner's Sons, 1971. GC vetoed the 1897 Immigration
Literacy Test Act stating that the new immigrants were not
"undesirable." (p. 100)

1385. Prucha, Francis Paul. The Churches and the Indian
Schools, 1888-1912. Lincoln: University of Nebraska Press,
1979. Catholic happiness at GC's 1892 victory and their
desire to have a Catholic appointed Indian Commissioner.
(pp. 25, 26, 30)

EVALUATIONS

1386. Parker, George F. "Cleveland's Second Administration as President." Saturday Evening Post 195 (June 9, 1923): 40-50. GC's successful second term.

1387. Hollingsworth, J. Rogers. The Whirligig of Politics: The Democracy of Cleveland and Bryan. Chicago: University of Chicago Press, 1963. The struggle between the Bryan and Cleveland wings of the Democratic party from the beginning of GC's second term through the 1904 election.

1388. Williams, R. Hal. Years of Decision: American Politics in the 1890s. New York: John Wiley and Sons, 1978. GC's politically disasterous inability to handle successfully the challenges of the new industrial-urban society.

1389. Faulkner, Harold U. Politics, Reform, and Expansion 1890-1900. New American Nation Series. New York: Harper and Row, 1959. GC's conservative positions, especially on monetary matters and annexation.

1390. Parker, George F. "Cleveland's Venezuelan Message." McClure's 33 (July 1909): 314-23. This article discusses more than Venezuela: it contains letters and comments on such second term matters as GC's judicial appointments, Chief Justice Fuller, civil service, GC's opinion of Charles G. Folger, GC's biographies, and the 1904 campaign.

1391. Dunn, Arthur W. From Harrison to Harding. 2 vols. New York: G. P. Putnam's Sons, 1922. Chapters 9-16 of this personal account cover the election of 1892 and the second GC term.

1392. Binkley, Wilfred E. The Man in the White House: His Powers and Duties. Rev. ed. New York: Harper and Row, 1964. GC later paid for his hardheaded stance on veterans' issues, tariff, and Hawaii. (pp. 70-2)

1393. Jensen, Richard J. The Winning of the Midwest:
Social and Political Conflict, 1888-1896. Chicago:
University of Chicago Press, 1971. This ethno-religious
interpretation of Gilded Age politics includes critical
commentary on GC's policies.

1394. Bailey, Thomas A. Probing America's Past: A Critical
Examination of Major Myths and Misconceptions. Lexington,
MA: Heath, 1973. Hawaii, Pullman Strike, Venezuelan
Boundary, and GC's courageous but unconstructive presidency.
(vol. II, chap. 23)

1395. "Press Comment on the Message." Public Opinion 16
(December 7, 14, 1893): 238-40, 261-2. Press reaction to
GC's first annual message.

1396. "Mr. Cleveland's Message." Saturday Review 76
(December 9, 1893): 641-2. Calls 1893 annual message "a
well worded statement of policy supported by good
arguments."

1397. "An Independent." "Mr. Cleveland's Failure?" Forum
17 (April 1894): 129-38. GC must maintain enthusiastic
leadership to preserve his achievements.

1398. Snyder, Carl. "The First Year of the Administration."
American Journal of Politics 4 (May 1894): 505-14. During
the first year of the second term, GC went from "blunder to
blunder, from mistake to mistake . . . to the wreck and ruin
of the country." (p. 514)

1399. Mowry, Duane. "The First Year of the Administration:
A Reply." American Journal of Politics 5 (September 1894):
271-7. A detailed reply to Snyder's attack in the May
issue.

1400. Lodge, Henry Cabot. "Results of Democratic Victory."
North American Review 159 (September 1894): 268-77. This
leading Republican Senator blames all the nation's
corruption, its economic and foreign policy problems on GC
and Democratic party incompetence.

1401. "A Third Term for Mr. Cleveland." Public Opinion 19
(October 10, 1895): 455-6. Press reaction.

1402. "The Message." Nation 63 (December 10, 1896):   432-3.
Press reaction to GC's annual message.

1403. "Public Service of Grover Cleveland." Independent 49
(February 25, 1897):   244.   Editorial praise for GC and his
presidency.

1404. Clark, Edward P. "Mr. Cleveland." National Review 29
(March 1897): 84-98. A New York Evening Post editorial
writer's favorable evaluation.

1405. "President Cleveland." Outlook 55 (March 6, 1897):
634-6. A mixed evaluation of GC's presidency which
concludes that his Venezuelan Boundary Arbitration Treaty
"will make Mr. Cleveland's name illustrious." (p. 636)

1406. "The Record of Administration." Public Opinion 22
(March 11, 1897): 298-9. Editorials from Des Moines and
Cleveland newspapers and the NY Herald on GC's second term.

1407. "The President's Message." Outlook 54 (December 19,
1896): 1074. Condensation of GC's annual message which the
magazine says is so long and detailed that no one will read
it.

1408. Jones, Stanley L. The Presidential Election of 1896.
Madison: University of Wisconsin Press, 1964. The impact
of GC's second term on the election of 1896.

1409. Fite, Gilbert C. "The Election of 1896." in Crucial
American Elections: Symposium . . . November 10, 1972.
Philadelphia: American Philosophical Society, 1973. The
impact on the 1896 election of GC's inability to deal with
second term problems.

1410. Glad, Paul W. McKinley, Bryan and the People.
Critical Periods of History. Philadelphia: Lippincott,
1968. Several chapters detail the events of GC's second
term which influenced the 1896 election.

1411. Hollingsworth, J. Rogers. "The Historian,
Presidential Elections, and 1896." Mid-America 45 (July
1963): 185-92. GC's failure to deal with the Panic of 1893
lost the Democrats votes long before the 1896 Bryan
campaign.

1412. Kleppner, Paul J. "The Politics of Change in the
Midwest: The 1890s in Historical and Behavioral
Perspective." Ph.D. diss., University of Pittsburgh, 1967.
Analyzes the 1896 election within the context of the 1890s,
including the GC presidency.

1413. Coletta, Paolo E. "Bryan, Cleveland, and the
Disrupted Democracy, 1890-1896." Nebraska History 41 (March
1960): 1-27. Bryan as a "symbol of reform" (p. 27)
unsuccessfully battled GC's philosophy of "impossible rugged
individualism." (p. 26)

1414. ___. Williams Jennings Bryan. 3 vols. Lincoln:
University of Nebraska Press, 1964-69. GC's second term and
his refusal to support Bryan in later elections.

1415. Green, George W. "Mr. Cleveland's Second
Administration." Forum 21 (July 1896): 540-57. History
will not consider GC brilliant but determined, principled,
and courageous.

1416. "Historic Figure of Grover Cleveland." Review of
Reviews 14 (December 1896): 650-2. Overview of main issues
of second term and GC's refusal to run for re-election.

1417. "Cleveland's Last Message." Gunton's Magazine 12
(January 1897): 1-10. Despite all his mistakes, GC leaves
office as "an unrepentant blunderer."

1418. Wheeler, Everett P. "The Cleveland Administrations."
Independent 49 (February 25, 1897): 235-7. A Civil Service
reformer concludes that GC's second term "will rank with the
most glorious in American history." (p. 237)

1419. "Mr. Cleveland's Presidency." Nation 64 (March 4,
1897): 156-7. Despite some foreign policy gaffes, GC's
second term was positive.

1420. Nelson, Henry L. "Public Services of President Cleveland." Harper's Weekly 41 (March 6, 1897): 227, 230-1. Favorable overview of GC's presidency.

1421. "The Retiring President." Frank Leslie's Weekly 84 (March 11, 1897): 150. GC was ignorant, but his courage had to be admired.

1422. "Outgoing President." Century 53 (n.s. 31) (March 1897): 790-1. Complimentary overview of GC's presidency.

1423. Schouler, James. "Mr. Cleveland and the Senate." Forum 23 (March 1897): 65-74. GC was a great statesman but not a great politician.

1424. Franklin, Fabian. "Importance of Cleveland's Work." In People and Problems; A Collection of Addresses and Editorials. New York: Henry Holt, 1908, pp. 111-22. The editor of the Baltimore News in this March 3, 1897, article presents a complimentary evalution of GC's two terms.

1425. Schurz, Carl. "Grover Cleveland's Second Administration." McClure's 9 (May 1897): 635-44, and Review of Reviews 15 (May 1897): 589. Despite GC's weaknesses, he will be included among the "front rank of American Presidents." (p. 644)

1426. Biery, James S. King Grover. Chronicles of His Reign, According to Simonides, the Scribe of the Tribe of Lechay. First Book. Allentown, PA.: By author, 1894. A contemporary attack, written in Biblical form, on GC and his policies.

1427. The Fat Knight. His Complete Career with Conquest and Collapse and Final Victory, Marvelous Triumph. Written in the Light of Current History and State Papers on File in Various Castles in Columbia. His Aides and His Actions and the Magic Soup. In Three Cantos. n.p.: n.p., 1896. Anti-GC satire.

1428. Durden, Robert F. The Climax of Populism. The
Election of 1896. Lexington: University of Kentucky Press,
1965. In his second term, GC was "stubbornly conservative,
deflationary, pro-business, and party splitting." (p. 6)

1429. Cannon, Joseph G., and Busbey, L. White. Uncle Joe
Cannon. New York: Henry Holt, 1926. A Republican and
later Speaker of the House critically evaluates GC. (pp.
315-6)

1430. Clark, Champ. My Quarter-Century of American
Politics. 2 vols. New York: Harper and Brothers, 1920.
This veteran congressman, first elected in 1892, discusses
GC and his second term. (vol.I, pp. 254ff)

1431. George, Henry, Jr. Life of Henry George. New York:
Doubleday and McClure, 1900. Numerous references to GC and
his policies --- all negative.

1432. Glad, Paul W. The Trumpet Soundeth: Williams
Jennings Bryan and His Democracy. Lincoln: University of
Nebraska Press, 1960. GC, his second term, and his possible
1904 candidacy from the negative perspective of his major
Democratic party opponent.

1433. Harrison, Carter H. Stormy Years, The Autobiography
of Carter H. Harrison, Five Times Mayor of Chicago.
Indianapolis: Bobbs-Merrill, 1935. GC and the second term.

1434. Haynes, Frederick E. James Baird Weaver. Iowa City:
The State Historical Society of Iowa, 1919. GC is mentioned
negatively throughout this biography of the Populist Party
presidential candidate.

1435. Lodge, Henry Cabot and Redmond, Charles F. (eds.)
Selections from the Correspondence of Theodore Roosevelt and
Henry Cabot Lodge, 1884-1918. 2 vols. New York: Da Capo
Press, 1971. GC appears in a number of these letters,
usually negatively.

1436. Mandel, Bernard. Samuel Gompers: A Biography.
Yellow Springs: Antioch Press, 1963. Briefly mentions
Governor GC signing a favorable labor law; the Pullman
Strike; GC's veto of the Lodge immigration literacy test;

Hawaii;   Venezuelan Boundary dispute;   and GC in the
Anti-Imperialist League.

1437. McCall, Samuel W.   The Life of Thomas Brackett Reed.
Boston: Houghton Mifflin, 1914.   The Republican Speaker of
the House, GC, and the major second term issues.

1438. Strauss, Oscar.   Under Four Administrations: From
Cleveland to Taft.   Boston: Houghton Mifflin, 1922.   First
hand favorable recollections by this GC campaign worker and
three time minister to Turkey.   Some GC letters.

1439. ____ "Under Four Presidents;   The Autobiography of
Oscar Strauss."   Outlook 132 (September 6 - December 6,
1922):   20-4, 73-7, 113-17, 151-5, 195-9, 238-42, 296-9,
334-8, 382-6, 430-5, 478-83, 514-9, 569-73, 613-7.   Synopsis
of his book mentioned above.

1440. Watterson, Henry.   Marse Henry.   2 vols.   New York:
George H. Doran, 1919.   Critical observations by this famous
newsman on GC's personal and political life.   (chaps. 18-20,
26)

1441. Krock, Arthur.   The Editorials of Henry Watterson.
New York: George H. Doran, 1923.   Several editorials in
opposition to GC.

1442. Wall, Joseph F.   Henry Watterson, Reconstructed Rebel.
New York: Oxford University Press, 1956.   The tumultuous
relationship between GC and this famous newsman.   (chaps.
10, 14)

1443. Welch, Richard E., Jr.   George Frisbie Hoar and the
Half Breed Republicans.   Cambridge: Harvard University
Press, 1971.   GC and this powerful Republican during GC's
second term.   (chap. 6)

1444. Wise, John S.   Recollections of Thirteen Presidents.
New York: Doubleday, 1906.   This former congressman
favorably and personally discusses GC and his presidency.
(pp. 171-94)

1445. Wheeler, Everett P. Sixty Years of American Life. New York: E. P. Dutton, 1917. The "Presidents I have Known" chapter is a detailed favorable evaluation of GC.

1446. Depew, Chauncey M. My Memories of Eighty Years. New York: Charles Scribner's Sons, 1924. This longtime NY Republican senator provides a generally favorable evaluation of GC. (pp. 124-8)

1447. ___. "Leaves From My Autobiography." Scribner's 70 (November, December 1921): 515-30, 664-76. Favorably discusses GC and his political career. (pp. 673-5)

1448. Woodward, C. Vann. Tom Watson. New York: Macmillan, 1938. Numerous references to GC by this Georgia agrarian who considered GC honorable but a threat to everything agrarian.

1449. Morgan, H. Wayne. William McKinley and His America. Syracuse: Syracuse University Press, 1963. McKinley's bitter-sweet inauguration day call on GC whom he found still working. (pp. 270-1)

1450. "An Era of Good Feeling." Review of Reviews 15 (April 1897): 387-9. Contrast between GC and McKinley, their inaugurations, and cabinets.

14
Administration Associates

1451. Abraham, Henry. Justices and Presidents: A Political History of Appointments to the Supreme Court. New York: Oxford University Press, 1974. GC's Supreme Court appointees. (pp. 130-6)

1452. Anderson, David L. Imperalism and Idealism: American Diplomats in China, 1861-1898. Bloomington: Indiana University Press, 1985. Includes information on diplomats who served during GC's presidency.

1453. Babst, Earl D., and Vander Velde, Lewis G. (eds.) Michigan and the Cleveland Era: Sketches of University of Michigan Staff Members and Alumni Who Served the Cleveland Administrations, 1885-1889, 1893-1897. Ann Arbor: University of Michigan Press, 1948. Articles on Henry C. Adams, James B. Angell, Thomas M. Cooley, Donald M. Dickinson, Lawrence Maxwell, J. Sterling Morton, Alfred Noble, Thomas W. Palmer, William E. Quinby, John M. B. Sill, Henry T. Thurber, Edwin F. Uhl, and Edwin Willets.

1454. Barnes, William; Barnes, Morgan; and Heath, John. The Foreign Service of the United States. Origins, Development, and Function. Washington: Department of State, 1961. GC's foreign service appointees (pp. 140-2); his 1895 consular reform order. (pp. 148-50)

1455. "The Cabinet." Harper's Weekly 37 (March 4, 1893):
198-9. A brief biographical note on each member of GC's
second cabinet.

1456. Chase, Harold; Krislov, Samuel; Boyum, Keith O.;
and Clark, Jerry N. (comps.) Biographical Dictionary of the
Federal Judiciary. Detroit: Gale, 1976. Brief sketches of
Supreme Court justices during GC's time.

1457. Dougall, Richardson, and Chapman, Mary P. United
States Chiefs of Mission, 1778-1973. Washington:
Department of State, 1973. Includes American diplomats and
their diplomatic posts during GC's presidency.

1458. Finding, John E. Dictionary of American Diplomatic
History. Westport, CT: Greenwood, 1980. Brief
biographical sketches of and sources on leading American
diplomats and diplomatic events.

1459. Friedman, Leon, and Israel, Fred L. (eds.) The
Justices of the United States Supreme Court 1789-1969:
Their Lives and Major Opinions. 4 vols. New York: Chelsea
House, 1969. Vols II and III contain biographical sketches
and representative opinions of justices who served during
GC's presidency.

1460. Garraty, John A. Encyclopedia of American Biography.
New York: Harper and Row, 1974. Modern, concise
biographical sketches of GC and the major figures of his
age.

1461. Johnson, Rossiter. (ed.) The Twentieth Century
Biographical Dictionary of Notable Americans. Boston: The
Biographical Society, 1904. Extended sketches of GC and
leading figures in his two terms still living at that time.

1462. Kennon, Donald R. The Speakers of the U.S. House of
Representatives, A Bibliography, 1789-1984. Baltimore:
Johns Hopkins Press, 1985.

1463. Kvasnicka, Robert M., and Viola, Herman J. (eds.) The
Commissioners of Indian Affairs, 1824-1977. Lincoln:
University of Nebraska Press, 1979. GC's commissioners are
represented here: Gregory C. Thompson is author of the

essay on "John D. C. Atkins, 1885-1888"; Floyd O'Neil on
"John H. Oberly 1888-1889"; William T. Hagan on "Daniel M.
Browning 1893-1897."

1464. Martin, Michael and Gelber, Leonard. Dictionary of
American History. Rev. ed. Totowa, NJ: Rowman and
Littlefield, 1978. Includes major personalities and issues
of the GC presidency.

1465. Morris, Dan, and Morris, Inez. (ed.) Who Was Who in
American Politics. A Biographical Dictionary of Over 4,000
Men and Women . . . . New York: Hawthorn Books, 1974.
Brief biographical sketches of GC and the major figures of
his presidency.

1466. The National Cyclopaedia of American Biography. New
York: James T. White, 1892-1897. Contemporary sketches of
GC and the major figures associated with his presidency.

1467. Parker, George F. "Cleveland, The Man." McClure's 32
(February-April 1909): 337-46, 457-72, 569-81. Parts I and
II discuss GC's two terms, and Part III presents GC's
opinions of contemporaries: Thomas F. Bayard, James J.
Hill, George Gray, Patrick A. Collins, Joseph B. Foraker,
and Theodore Roosevelt.

1468. ___ . "Cleveland's Estimate of His Contemporaries."
McClure's 33 (May 1909): 24-34. GC's comments on Chester
A. Arthur, James G. Blaine, William Jennings Bryan, George
B. Cortelyou, Benjamin Harrison, David B. Hill, William
McKinley, John E. Russell, and the election of 1908.

1469. Roos, Charles A. "Physicians to the Presidents and
Their Patients, A Biobibliography." Medical Library
Association Bulletin 49 (July 1961): 291-360. Short
sketches of GC's physicians. (pp. 339-40)

1470. Sobel, Robert. (ed.) Biographical Directory of the
United States Executive Branch, 1774-1977. Westport, CT:
Greenwood, 1977. Brief sketches of GC, his vice presidents,
and all his cabinet members.

1471. Stuart, Paul. The Indian Office: Growth and
Development of an American Institution, 1865-1900. Studies
in American History and Culture, No. 12. Ann Arbor: UMI
Research, 1979. Includes brief accounts of GC's Indian
School Superintendent appointees.

1472. U.S. Congress. Biographical Directory of the American
Congress, 1774-1971. Rev. ed. Washington: Government
Printing Office.

1473. ___. Congressional Directory. Washington:
Government Printing Office, 1809 to present. Published
yearly, it includes short biographical sketches of
congressmen, their committee assignments, and other
pertinent data on Congress for the year.

1474. Vexler, Robert I. (ed.) The Vice Presidents and
Cabinet Members: Biographies Arranged Chronologically by
Administration. 2 vols. Dobbs Ferry, NY: Oceana, 1975.
Brief sketches of GC's vice presidents and cabinets with an
inadequate bibliography after each sketch. (vol. I, pp.
339-58, 374-91)

1475. Who Was Who in America, Volume One, 1897-1942: A
Companion Volume of Who's Who in American History. Chicago:
Marquis, 1943. Short biographical sketches of GC and major
figures of his presidency.

1476. Wilson, James Grant, and Fiske, John. (ed.)
Appleton's Cyclopaedia of American Biography. 6 vols. New
York: D. Appleton, 1901. Biographical sketches of GC and
major figures of his presidency.

VICE PRESIDENTS: THOMAS A. HENDRICKS AND ADLAI E. STEVENSON

1477. Barzman, Sol. Madmen and Geniuses: The Vice
Presidents of the United States. Chicago: Follett, 1974.

1478. Bell, Christopher. (comp.) Vice Presidents of the
United States, 1789-1961. Washington: Library of Congress,
Legislative Reference Service, 1962.

1479. Curtis, Richard, and Wells, Maggie. Not Exactly A
Crime: Our Vice Presidents From Adams to Agnew. New York:
Dial Press, 1972. Brief satirical accounts. (pp. 108-11,
116-19)

1480. Harwood, Michael. In the Shadow of Presidents: The
American Vice-Presidency and Succession System.
Philadelphia: Lippincott, 1966. Brief biographical
sketches.

1481. Hatch, Louis Clinton. A History of the
Vice-Presidency of the United States. Revised and edited by
Earl L. Shoup. New York: American Historical Society,
1934. GC's vice presidents and his 1888 running mate, Allen
G. Thurman. (chap. 17)

1482. Healy, Diana Dixon. America's Vice-Presidents: Our
First Forty-Three Vice Presidents and How They Got to be
Number Two. New York: Atheneum, 1984. Brief sketches and
photos. (pp. 112-16, 122-6)

1483. Laird, Archibald. The Near Great --- Chronicle of the
Vice Presidents. North Quincy, MA: Christopher, 1980. A
photo of the tombstones of GC's vice presidents and their
chronology. (pp. 203-8, 221-8)

1484. Waugh, Edgar W. Second Consul, The Vice Presidency:
Our Greatest Political Problem. Indianapolis:
Bobbs-Merrill, 1956. Brief sketches. (pp. 223-4)

1485. Williams, Irving G. The Rise of the Vice Presidency.
Washington: Public Affairs, 1956. Brief sketches. (pp.
67-9)

1486. Young, Klyde H., and Middleton, Lamar. Heirs
Apparent: The Vice Presidents of the United States. New
York: Prentice-Hall, 1948.

1487. Stathis, Stephen W., and Moe, Ronald C. "America's
Other Inaugurations." Presidential Studies Quarterly 10
(Fall 1980): 550-70. The inaugurations of GC's two vice
presidents. (p. 562)

THOMAS A. HENDRICKS, VICE PRESIDENT

1488. Woodburn, James A. "Hendricks, Thomas A." Dictionary
of American Biography. Edited by Dumas Malone. New York:
Charles Scribner's Sons, 1932. (vol. VIII, pp.534-5)

1489. Holcombe, John W. and Skinner, Hubert M. Life and
Public Services of Thomas A. Hendricks. Indianapolis:
Carlon and Hollenbach, 1886. Texts of speeches, the 1884
campaign, and the early days of the first term before
Hendricks' sudden death. (chaps. 19, 20)

ADLAI E. STEVENSON, VICE PRESIDENT

1490. Hicks, John D. "Stevenson, Adlai Ewing." Dictionary
of American Biography. Edited by Dumas Malone. New York:
Charles Scribner's Sons, 1935. (vol. XVII, pp. 629-30)

1491. Ewing, James S. "Mr. Stevenson, the Democratic
Candidate for Vice President." Review of Reviews 22
(October 1900): 420-4. An overview of his life and
political career.

1492. Cook, John W. "The Life and Labors of Hon. Adlai Ewing
Stevenson." Journal of the Illinois State Historical
Society 8 (July 1915): 209-31. An eulogistic biographical
sketch.

1493. Schlup, Leonard. "Democratic Talleyrand: Adlai E.
Stevenson and Politics in the Gilded Age and Progressive
Era." South Atlantic Quarterly 78 (Spring 1979): 182-94.
Overview of Stevenson's political career. GC is often
mentioned in his vice president's letters excerpted in this
article.

1494. ___. "Adlai E. Stevenson and the Presidential
Election of 1896." Social Science Journal 14 (April 1977):
117-28. Stevenson's unifying role, particularly on silver.

1495. ___. "Adlai E. Stevenson and the Presidential
Campaign of 1900." Filson Club History Quarterly 53 (April
1979): 192-208. Stevenson was acceptable as vice
presidential candidate because he had been GC's vice
president and he was a moderate on silver.

1496. ___. "Vice President Stevenson and the Politics of
Accommodation." Journal of Political Science 7 (Fall
1979): 30-9. Stevenson was a reconciler of political
differences in the Democratic party and founded a political
dynasty.

1497. ___. "Reluctant Expansionist: Adlai E. Stevenson and
the Campaign Against Imperialism in 1900." Indiana Social
Studies Quarterly 29 (Spring 1976): 39-42. The foreign
policy positions of the Democratic nominees of 1900.

1498. Stevenson, Adlai E. Something of Men I have Known.
Chicago: A. C. McClurg, 1909. Chapter 18, "Cleveland As I
Knew Him."

1499. Martin, John Bartlow. Adlai Stevenson of Illinois:
The Life of Adlai E. Stevenson. Garden City, NY:
Anchor/Doubleday, 1977. Chapter 1 includes information on
Grandfather Adlai, GC's vice president.

1500. Davis, Kenneth, S. The Politics of Honor, A Biography
of Adlai E. Stevenson. New York: G. P. Putnam, 1967.
Chapter 1 includes information on Grandfather Adlai, GC's
vice president.

1501. Gianakos, Perry E., and Karson, Albert. (eds.)
American Diplomacy and the Sense of Destiny: Events and
Attitudes. 4 vols. Vol. I: The Initial Thrust, 1885-1900.
Belmont, California: Wadsworth, 1966. Includes excerpt of
Stevenson's Republic or Empire: The Philippine Question
(1899).

THOMAS F. BAYARD, SECRETARY OF STATE

1502. Tansill, Charles C. The Congressional Career of
Thomas Francis Bayard. Washington: Georgetown University
Press, 1946. GC's 1884 nomination. (chap. 12)

1503. ___. The Foreign Policy of Thomas F. Bayard:
1885-1897. New York: Fordham University Press, 1940.

1504. Robinson, William A. "Bayard, Thomas Francis."
Dictionary of American Biography. Edited by Allen Johnson.
New York: Charles Scribner's Sons, 1929. (vol. II, pp.
70-2)

1505. Shippee, Lester B. "Thomas Francis Bayard." The
American Secretaries of State and Their Diplomacy. Edited
by Samuel Flagg Bemis. New York: Pageant, 1958. GC's
first term foreign policy. (vol. VIII, pp. 47-108)

1506. Guida, Anthony J. "Thomas F. Bayard and the Abortive
Chinese Immigration Treaty of 1888." Ph.D. diss.,
Georgetown University, 1962. In depth account of a
diplomatic event of GC's first term.

JOHN G. CARLISLE, SECRETARY OF THE TREASURY

1507. Barnes, James A. John G. Carlisle: Financial
Statesman. New York: Dodd, Mead, 1931. Biography.

1508. Coulter, E. Merton. "Carlisle, John Griffin."
Dictionary of American Biography. Edited by Allen Johnson.
New York: Charles Scribner's Sons, 1929. (vol. III, pp.
494-6)

NORMAN J. COLMAN, SECRETARY OF AGRICULTURE

1509. Lemmer, George F. Norman J. Colman and Colman's Rural
World. Columbia: University of Missouri Press, 1953.

1510. Swanson, Frederick C. "Colman, Norman J." Dictionary
of American Biography. Edited by Allen Johnson and Dumas
Malone. New York: Charles Scribner's Sons, 1930. (vol.
IV, p. 314)

GEORGE B. CORTELYOU, PRIVATE SECRETARY

1511. Ford, Benjamin T. "A Duty to Serve: The Government
Career of George Bruce Cortelyou." Ph.D. diss., Columbia
University, 1963. GC's secretary would later play more
important roles in the Theodore Roosevelt and William Howard
Taft administrations.

1512. Chandler, Albert D. "Cortelyou, George Bruce."
Dictionary of American Biography. Edited by Robert
Livingston Schuyler and Edward T. James. New York: Charles
Scribner's Sons, 1958. (vol. XXII (supplement 2), pp.
122-3)

DONALD M. DICKINSON, POSTMASTER GENERAL

1513. Bolt, Robert. "A Biography of Donald M. Dickinson."
Ph.D. diss., Michigan State University, 1963. GC's trusted
advisor ruined his own political career supporting GC on the
silver issue.

1514. ___. "Donald Dickinson and the Second Election of
Grover Cleveland, 1892." Michigan History 49 (March 1965):
28-39. His major role in GC's re-election.

1515. ___. Brown, Everett S. "Dickinson, Donald McDonald."
Dictionary of American Biography. Edited by Allen Johnson
and Dumas Malone. New York: Charles Scribner's Sons, 1930.
(vol. V, pp. 295-7)

WILLIAM C. ENDICOTT, SECRETARY OF WAR

1516. Fuess, Claude M. "Endicott, William Crowningshield."
Dictionary of American Biography. Edited by Allen Johnson
and Dumas Malone. New York: Charles Scribner's Sons, 1931.
(vol. VI, pp. 158-9)

1517. Adams, Charles Francis. Memoir of W. C. Endicott,
LL.D. Cambridge: John Wilson, 1902. An old biographical
sketch.

CHARLES S. FAIRCHILD, SECRETARY OF THE TREASURY

1518. Paxson, Frederick L. "Fairchild, Charles Stebbins."
Dictionary of American Biography. Edited by Allen Johnson
and Dumas Malone. New York: Charles Scribner's Sons, 1931.
(vol. VI, pp. 251-2)

DAVID R. FRANCIS, SECRETARY OF THE INTERIOR

1519. Pusateri, Cosmo J. "A Businessman in Politics: David
R. Francis, Missouri Democrat." Ph.D. diss., St. Louis
University, 1965. Supported GC until GC's anti-silver stand
made Francis a Democratic outcast.

1520. Pusateri, C. Joseph. "Rural-Urban Tensions and the
Bourbon Democrat: The Missouri Case." Missouri Historical
Review 69 (April 1975): 181-98. GC's conservatism,
particularly on silver, made Governor Francis's support in
Missouri a politically difficult position.

1521. Shaw, William B. "Francis, David Rowland."
Dictionary of American Biography. Edited by Allen Johnson
and Dumas Malone. New York: Charles Scribner's Sons, 1931.
(vol. VI, pp. 577-8)

AUGUSTUS H. GARLAND, ATTORNEY GENERAL

1522. Watkins, Beverly N. "Augustus Hill Garland,
1832-1899: Arkansas Lawyer to United States
Attorney-General." Ph.D. diss., Auburn University, 1985.
Biography.

1523. Schlup, Leonard. "Augustus Hill Garland: Gilded Age
Democrat." Arkansas Historical Quarterly 40 (Winter 1981):
338-46. Seven 1884-1888 letters to GC, a brief overview of
Garland's career, and his relationship to GC.

1524. Thomas, David Y. "Garland, Augustus Hill."
Dictionary of American Biography. Edited by Allen Johnson
and Dumas Malone. New York: Charles Scribner's Sons, 1931.
(vol. VII, pp. 150-1)

WALTER Q. GRESHAM, SECRETARY OF STATE

1525. Calhoun, Charles W. Gilded Age Cato, The Life of
Walter Q. Gresham. Lexington: University of Kentucky
Press, 1988. Argues that Gresham was not an expansionist.
His traditionalist viewpoint "foreshadowed the
anti-imperialist movement." (p. 6)

1526. Gresham, Matilda. Life of Walter Quintin Gresham. 2
vols. Chicago: Rand McNally, 1919. Volume 2 of this
biography discusses the early years of GC's second term in
detail.

1527. Schuyler, Montgomery. "Walter Quintin Gresham." In
The American Secretaries of State and Their Diplomacy.
Edited by Samuel Flagg Bemis. New York: Pageant, 1958.
Foreign policy of the first two years of GC's second term.
(vol. VIII, pp. 227-72)

1528. Wright, Herbert F. "Gresham, Walter Quintin."
Dictionary of American Biography. Edited by Allen Johnson
and Dumas Malone. New York: Charles Scribner's Sons, 1931.
(vol. VII, pp. 607-9)

1529. Dorwart, Jeffrey M. "Walter Quintin Gresham and East
Asia, 1894-1895: A Reappraisal." Asian Forum V
(January-March 1973): 55-63. GC ignored Asia, but Gresham
conducted a realistic policy toward belligerents in the
Korean Rebellion and the Sino-Japanese War.

RICHARD W. GILDER, FRIEND

1530. Gilder, Rosamond. (ed.) The Letters of Richard Watson
Gilder. Boston: Houghton, 1916. Includes letters of this
close GC friend about various aspects of GC's political and
personal life. A few GC letters.

1531. Gilder, Richard W. Grover Cleveland: A Record of
Friendship. New York: Century, 1910. The two men were
friends beginning in 1887.

1532. ___. "Grover Cleveland: A Record of Friendship."
Century 78, 79 (August, October, November 1909): 483-503,
687-705, 846-80, 24-31. Excerpts from the book cited above.

1533. ___. "Cleveland." Putnam's 6 (June 1909): 318-9. A
poem praising GC.

1534. ___. "Birds of Westland (Princeton, June 1908)"
Century 76 (October 1908): 924. A poem about birds at GC's
home.

1535. Tomsich, John A. Genteel Endeavor: American Culture
and Politics in the Gilded Age. Stanford: Stanford
University Press, 1971. GC's friendship with Gilder. (p.
80)

1536. John, Arthur. The Best Years of the Century: Richard
Watson Gilder, Scribner's Monthly, and the Century Magazine,
1870-1909. Urbana: University of Illinois Press, 1981.
His journalistic career.

1537. Fitzpatrick, Sister Martha Ann. "Richard Watson
Gilder, Genteel Reformer." Ph.D. diss., Catholic
University, 1966. Served as an intermediary between GC and
civil service reformers.

1538. Kammen, Michael G. "Richard Watson Gilder and the New
York Tenement House Commission of 1894." Bulletin of the
New York Public Library 66 (June 1962): 364-82. Reform in
New York City housing.

JUDSON HARMON, ATTORNEY GENERAL

1539. Burke, James L. "The Public Career of Judson Harmon."
Ph.D. diss., Ohio University, 1969. As GC's attorney
general (1895-1897), he successfully prosecuted three key
anti-trust suits which set precedents for Theodore
Roosevelt's later successful anti-trust activity.

1540. Cole, Arthur C. "Harmon, Judson." Dictionary of
American Biography. Edited by Dumas Malone. New York:
Charles Scribner's Sons, 1932. (vol. VIII, pp. 276-8)

HILARY A. HERBERT, SECRETARY OF THE NAVY

1541. Hammett, Hugh B. "Hilary Abner Herbert: A Southerner
Returns to the Union." Ph.D. diss, University of Virginia,
1969. Biography.

1542. Davis, Hugh C. "Hilary A. Herbert: Bourbon
Apologist." Alabama Review 20 (July 1967): 216-25. His
writings reflected his philosophy of the "old ways" of
"constitutionalism, sectionalism tempered with
reconciliation, and race paternalism." (p. 225)

1543. Farmer, Hallie. "Herbert, Hilary Abner." Dictionary
of American Biography. Edited by Dumas Malone. New York:
Charles Scribner's Sons, 1932. (vol. VIII, pp. 572-3)

1544. Herbert, Hilary A. "Grover Cleveland and His Cabinet at Work." Century 85 (March 1913): 740-4. GC's personality and his handling of his cabinet.

1545. ___. Why the Solid South ? or, Reconstruction and Its Results. Baltimore: R. H. Woodward, 1890. Written in response to the 1890 Lodge Election Bill of 1890.

1546. ___. The Abolition Crusade and Its Consequences. New York: Charles Scribners Sons, 1912. Critical view of abolitionists because of their perceived assault on the Constitution.

DAVID B. HILL, U.S. SENATOR FROM NEW YORK

1547. Bass, Herbert J. "I am a Democrat": The Political Career of David Bennett Hill. Syracuse: Syracuse University Press, 1961. His stormy relationship with GC throughout GC's political career.

1548. Carman, Harry J. "Hill, David B." Dictionary of American Biography. Edited by Dumas Malone. New York: Charles Scribner's Sons, 1932. (vol. IX, pp. 28-9)

JOSEPH JEFFERSON, FRIEND

1549. Wilson, Francis. Joseph Jefferson, Reminiscences of a Fellow Player. New York: Charles Scribner's Sons, 1907. Information on GC as a fisherman and a friend; a 1905 GC letter regarding one of their fishing adventures. (pp. 54-60, 178-9)

1550. Eaton, Walter P. "Jefferson, Joseph." Dictionary of American Biography. Edited by Dumas Malone. New York: Charles Scribner's Sons, 1933. (vol. X, pp. 15-17)

L. Q. C. LAMAR, SECRETARY OF THE INTERIOR/SUPREME COURT
JUSTICE

1551. Mayes, Edward. Lucius Q. C. Lamar: His Life, Times,
and Speeches, 1825-1893. Nashville: Publishing House of
the Methodist Episcopal Church, 1896. Biography, including
GC letters.

1552. Cate, Wirt A. Lucius Q. C. Lamar, Secession and
Reunion. New York: Russell and Russell, 1935. Biography
which cites closeness of GC and Lamar.

1553. Murphy, James B. L. Q. C. Lamar: Pragmatic Patriot.
Baton Rouge: Louisiana State University Press, 1973. Lamar
pursued a national program of economic development and local
control over social and racial matters.

1554. Pearce, Haywood J., Jr. "Lamar, Lucius Quintus
Cincinnatus." Dictionary of American Biography. Edited by
Dumas Malone. New York: Charles Scribner's Sons. 1933.
(vol. X, pp. 551-3)

1555. Stone, James H. (ed.) "L. Q. C. Lamar's Letters to
Edward Donaldson Clark, 1868-1885." Journal of Mississippi
History 35 (February 1973): 65-73; 37 (May 1975):
189-201; 43 (May 1981): 135-64. Clark was Lamar's junior
law partner from 1868-1873. These letters contain comments
on Mississippi and U.S. politics.

DANIEL S. LAMONT, PRIVATE SECRETARY/SECRETARY OF WAR

1556. Medved, Michael. The Shadow Presidents. The Secret
History of the Chief Executives and Their Top Aides. New
York: Times Books, 1979. Includes GC's relationship with
Lamont "The Assistant President." (pp. 75-87)

1557. Fitzsimmons, Sister Anne Marie. "The Political Career
of Daniel S. Lamont, 1870-1897." Ph.D. diss., Catholic
University, 1965. Lamont was a major advisor to GC as
long-time private secretary and then cabinet member.

1558. Paxson, Frederic L. "Lamont, David Scott."
Dictionary of American Biography. Edited by Dumas Malone.
New York: Charles Scribner's Sons, 1933. (vol. X, pp.
563-4)

DANIEL MANNING, SECRETARY OF THE TREASURY

1559. Carman, Harry J. "Manning, Daniel." Dictionary of
American Biography. Edited by Dumas Malone. New York:
Charles Scribner's Sons, 1933. (vol. XII, pp. 248-9)

J. STERLING MORTON, SECRETARY OF AGRICULTURE

1560. Olson, James C. J. Sterling Morton. Lincoln:
University of Nebraska, 1942. Morton's unfavorable opinion
of GC and his presidency.

1561. Hicks, John D. "Morton, Julius Sterling." Dictionary
of American Biography. Edited by Dumas Malone. New York:
Charles Scribner's Sons, 1934. (vol. XIII, pp. 257-8)

ROBERT L. O'BRIEN, PRIVATE SECRETARY

1562. O'Brien, Robert Lincoln. "Grover Cleveland as Seen by
His Stenographer, July, 1892 - November, 1895." Proceedings
of the Massachusetts Historical Society 70 (1957): 128-43.
This paper, delivered in 1951, praises GC, his personality,
and his second term.

1563. ___. "The Personality of a Presidential Candidate."
Proceedings of the Massachusetts Historical Society 57
(1924): 282-91. In 1892, GC ignored his campaign manager,
W. C. Whitney, and stayed away from the campaign.

RICHARD OLNEY, ATTORNEY GENERAL/SECRETARY OF STATE

1564. Eggert, Gerald G. Richard Olney: Evolution of a
Statesman. University Park: Pennsylvania State University
Press, 1974. A biography which shows how closely GC and
Olney worked together.

1565. Schuyler, Montgomery. "Richard Olney." The American
Secretaries of State amd Their Diplomacy. Edited by Samuel
Flagg Bemis. New York: Pageant, 1958, VIII. The foreign
policy of the last two years of GC's second term. (vol.
VIII, pp. 273-325)

1566. James, Henry. Richard Olney and His Public Service.
Boston: Houghton Mifflin, 1923. Biography.

1567. Carson, Donald K. "Richard Olney, Secretary of State,
1895-1897." Ph.D. diss., University of Kentucky, 1969.

1568. Fuller, Joseph V. "Olney, Richard." Dictionary of
American Biography. Edited by Dumas Malone. New York:
Charles Scribner's Sons, 1934. (vol. XIV, pp. 32-3)

1569. Olney, Richard. "Growth of Our Foreign Policy."
Atlantic Monthly 85 (March 1900): 289-301. U. S. foreign
policy moved from historic isolationism to the
internationalism of the Spanish-American War years.

1570. Eggert, Gerald G. (ed.) "Richard Olney: Summation
for the Defense." American Journal of Legal History 13
(January 1969): 68-84. Transcript of 1875 Olney murder
trial defense summation.

GEORGE F. PARKER, BIOGRAPHER

1571. Moon, Gordon A., II. "George F. Parker: A 'Near
Miss' as First White House Press Chief." Journalism
Quarterly 41 (No. 2, 1964): 183-90. GC's personal press
adviser (1889-1892) but he did not become GC's press
secretary.

WILLIAM E. RUSSELL, FRIEND

1572. Norton, Charles Eliot. "The Public Life and Services
of William Eustis Russell." Harvard Graduates' Magazine 5
(December 1896): 177-98. Sketch and photograph.

1573. Russell, William E. "Grover Cleveland." The
Presidents of the United States 1789-1894. New York: D.
Appleton, 1894. A sketch of GC's life to his 1892 election
written by a leading Democratic politician and friend.
Includes many excerpts from his speeches.

HOKE SMITH, SECRETARY OF THE INTERIOR

1574. Grantham, Dewey W.,Jr. Hoke Smith and the Politics of
the New South. Baton Rouge: Louisiana State University
Press, 1958. GC's cabinet member who resigned over GC's
position on silver.

1575. Vinson, J. Charles. "Hoke Smith and the 'Battle of
the Standards' in Georgia, 1895-1896." Georgia Historical
Quarterly 36 (September 1952): 201-19. His resignation
from GC's cabinet over silver revealed a split in the
Democratic party.

1576. Brooks, Robert P. "Smith, Hoke." Dictionary of
American Biography. Edited by Dumas Malone. New York:
Charles Scribner's Sons, 1935. (vol. XVII,   pp. 280-2)

SAMUEL J. TILDEN, DEMOCRATIC PARTY ELDER

1577. Tilden, Samuel J. Letters and Literary Materials. 2
vols. Edited by John Bigelow. New York: Harper and
Brothers, 1908. Two GC letters to GC are included in volume
2.

1578. Kelley, Robert. "The Thought and Character of Samuel
J. Tilden: The Democrat as Inheritor." Historian 26
(February 1964): 176-205. Tilden's attitude and ideas when
GC entered New York political life in the late 1870s and
early 1880s.

1579. Flick, Alexander C. "Tilden, Samuel Jones."
Dictionary of American Biography. Edited by Dumas Malone.
New York: Charles Scribner's Sons, 1936. (vol. XVIII, pp.
537-41)

WILLIAM F. VILAS, POSTMASTER GENERAL/SECRETARY OF THE
INTERIOR

1580. Merrill, Horace Samuel. William Freeman Vilas,
Doctrinaire Democrat. Madison: State Historical Society of
Wisconsin, 1954. GC and Vilas were very close.

1581. Paxson, Frederic L. "Vilas, William Freeman."
Dictionary of American Biography. Edited by Dumas Malone.
New York: Charles Scribner's Sons, 1936. (vol. XIX, pp.
270-1)

1582. Schlup, Leonard S. "Vilas, Stevenson, and Democratic
Politics." North Dakota Quarterly 44 (Winter 1976): 44-52.
Political activities of these two GC loyalists.

WILLIAM C. WHITNEY, CAMPAIGN MANAGER/SECRETARY OF THE NAVY

1583. Hirsch, Mark C. William C. Whitney: Modern Warwick.
New York: Dodd, Mead, 1948. Much information on the
relationship of GC and Whitney.

1584. Paxson, Frederic L. "Whitney, William Collins."
Dictionary of American Biography. Edited by Dumas Malone.
New York: Charles Scribner's Sons, 1936. (vol. XX, pp.
165-6)

WILLIAM L. WILSON, POSTMASTER GENERAL

1585. Summers, Festus P. William L. Wilson and Tariff
Reform. New Brunswick: Rutgers University Press, 1953. GC
is prominently mentioned in this biography.

1586. Wilson, William L. The Cabinet Diary of William L.
Wilson, 1896-1897. Edited by Festus P. Summers. Chapel
Hill: University of North Carolina Press, 1957.

1587. Durden, Robert F. "Grover Cleveland and the Bourbon
Democracy." South Atlantic Quarterly 57 (Summer 1958):
333-8. GC's defense of the status quo and Wilson's charming
ability to chronicle it in his diary.

1588. Nevins, Allan. "Wilson, William Lyne." Dictionary of
American Biography. Edited by Dumas Malone. New York:
Charles Scribner's Sons, 1936. (vol. XX, pp. 351-2)

1589. Craighill, W. P. "Funeral of William L. Wilson,
Postmaster General at Charleston, W. Va." Jefferson County
Historical Society Magazine 18 (1952): 33-4. A letter to
the writer's daughter concerning GC's reception in
Charlestown.

15
Post-Presidential Career

1590. Williams, Jesse Lynch. Mr. Cleveland: A Personal Impression. New York: Dodd, Mead, and Company, 1909. Many anecdotes about GC's life and character in the years after his presidency.

1591. Finley, James H. "Ex-President." Century 73 (March 1907): 682-7. A New York Times' reporter's favorable evaluation of GC's post-presidential years.

1592. ___. "Cleveland - Gentle But Inexorable." Scribner's 81 (April 1927): 340-4. GC's retirement years.

1593. Parker, George F. "Grover Cleveland's Life in Princeton, 1897-1908." Saturday Evening Post 197 (November 10, 1923): 40-8. Detailed account.

1594. West, Andrew F. "Grover Cleveland: A Princeton Memory." Century 77 (January 1909): 323-37. GC's friend, the Graduate Dean, discusses GC's relationship with Princeton in the post-presidential years.

1595. Van Dyke, Paul. "My Neighbor: Grover Cleveland." Scribners 81 (April 1927): 349-53. Princeton History professor discusses GC's retirement years and his character.

1596. ___. "Cleveland at Princeton." American Monthly Review of Reviews 38 (August 1908): 185-7. Earlier version of previous article.

1597. Martin, Asa Earl. After The White House. State College, PA: Penns Valley Publishers, 1951. GC in the post-presidential years. (pp. 316-41)

1598. "The Cleveland's New Jersey Home." Leslie's Weekly 84 (March 11, 1897): 164. A picture and description of GC's Princeton home.

1599. "Future Home at Princeton." Illustrated American 20 (December 19, 1896): 807. Two photographs.

1600. Baker, Ray Stannard. Woodrow Wilson, Life and Letters. 7 vols. New York: Charles Scribner's Sons, 1946. GC and Wilson relationship at Princeton. (vols. I and II)

1601. Bragdon, Henry Wilkinson. Woodrow Wilson: The Academic Years. Cambridge: Belknap Press of Harvard University Press, 1967. GC's relationship with Princeton University during Wilson's presidency there.

1602. Link, Arthur. Wilson, The Road to the White House. Princeton: Princeton University Press, 1947. GC and Wilson at Princeton.

1603. Wilson, Woodrow, and Wilson, Ellen Axson. The Priceless Gift, The Love Letters of Woodrow Wilson and Ellen Axson Wilson. Edited by Eleanor Wilson McAdoo. New York: McGraw-Hill, 1962. Woodrow Wilson mentions GC in these letters beginning with the 1884 election and ending soon after GC's 1908 death.

1604. Wilson, Woodrow. The Papers of Woodrow Wilson. 55 vols. Edited by Arthur S. Link. Princeton: Princeton University Press, 1966-1986. There are references even after GC's death to a wide variety of subjects concerning GC.

1605. White, William Allen. Woodrow Wilson. The Man, His
Times, and His Task. Boston: Houghton Mifflin, 1924. GC's
role in the 1909 contest between Wilson and Dean Andrew F.
West over the Princeton graduate school.

1606. Saunders, Frances Wright. First Lady Between Two
Worlds: Ellen Axson Saunders. Chapel Hill: University of
North Carolina Press, 1985. The acquaintanceship between
the Wilsons and the GCs in Princeton.

1607. Norris, Edwin M. The Story of Princeton. Boston:
Little Brown, 1917. GC speaks at Woodrow Wilson's Princeton
inauguration. (p. 237-8) GC Memorial Monument built in
1911 at Princeton. (p. 257)

1608. Houston, David. Eight Years With Wilson's Cabinet. 2
vols. Garden City: Doubleday, Page, 1926. Woodrow Wilson
called GC a very practical man who became a party leader.
(vol. II, pp. 171, 212-3)

1609. McClellan, George B. Jr. The Gentleman and the Tiger.
The Autobiography of George B. McClellan, Jr. Edited by
Harold C. Syrett. New York: Lippincott, 1956. The
important NY political son of the famous general discusses
GC, his life at Princeton, and Theodore Roosevelt's bad
manners at GC's funeral.

POLITICS

1610. Rhodes, James Ford. The McKinley and Roosevelt
Administrations, 1897-1909. New York: Macmillan, 1927.
Presidential transition from GC to McKinley; GC letter to
Theodore Roosevelt re: 1902 anthracite coal strike; and
1904 GC presidential boom.

1611. Koenig, Louis W. Bryan, A Political Biography. New
York: Putnam, 1971. GC's antagonistic attitude toward
Bryan from the 1896 to the 1908 elections.

1612. "Fateful Antipathy of Cleveland and Bryan." Current
Literature 45 (August 1908): 155-9. GC-Bryan political
feud and their personal similarities and differences.

1613. Winkler, John K. Hearst, An American Phenomenon. New York: Simon and Schuster, 1928. GC refused to serve on a U.S. battleship Maine memorial committee because he considered it a newspaper circulation gimmick.

1614. Roosevelt, Theodore. "Cleveland and the Coal Strike." Outlook 89 (August 22, 1908): 881-4. GC letters and TR commentary about TR's offer and GC's acceptance to be a member of a Coal Strike Commission.

1615. Sageser, A. Bower. "Ex-President Cleveland Invited to Head the Counsel for the Venezuelan Arbitration." American Historical Review 39 (October 1933): 78-81. GC and Richard Olney's post-presidential connection with the Venezuelan Boundary issue. Includes GC and Olney letters.

1616. "Mr. Cleveland in New Jersey." Nation 75 (November 6, 1902): 356. Praises GC's one campaign speech in New Jersey's 5th Congressional district.

1617. Tarbell, Ida M. All In The Day's Work: An Autobiography. New York: Macmillan, 1939. Her literary relationship with GC and the 1904 possibility of her ghost writing GC's reminiscences. Includes excerpts of GC letters. (pp. 268-72)

1618. Merrill, Horace Samuel and Merrill, Marion Galbraith. The Republican Command, 1897-1913. Lexington: University Press of Kentucky, 1971. 1904 GC nomination boom and comparison of GC and Taft.

1619. "Comment." Harper's Weekly 47 (October 31, 1903): 1428-9. The ulterior motives of some politicians supporting GC for the presidency in 1904.

1620. "Democrats and the Presidency." Independent 56 (May 12, 1904): 1061-4. GC and Richard Olney as possible Democratic presidential nominees in 1904. Political cartoons included.

1621. "Grover Cleveland's Message to the American People."
Outlook 90 (September 12, 1908):   49-51.   GC's alleged
posthumous political statement published in the August 30,
1908 New York Times supporting Taft for president and
criticizing Bryan.

1622. "Alleged Last Message of Grover Cleveland."   Current
Literature 45 (November 1908):   485-7.   GC's alleged
posthumous support for Taft over Bryan.

1623. Hornig, Edgar Albert.   "Cleveland's Ghost in the
Taft-Bryan Duel, 1908."   Mid-America 51 (July 1969):
205-16.   Analysis of the controversy over GC's alleged
statement of support for Taft over Bryan in 1908
presidential contest.

1624. Wreszin, Michael.   Oswald Garrison Villard: Pacifist
at War.   Bloomington: Indiana University Press, 1965.   The
reformer looked to GC as the model for the person he hoped
to be able to support in the 1912 presidential election.
(pp. 26-7)

1625. Munsey, Frank A.   "Grover Cleveland Twice President of
the United States."   Munsey 34 (March 1906): 756-8.   A call
for the nation to make better use of ex-presidents like GC.

INSURANCE INDUSTRY

1626. Parker, George F.   "Cleveland and the Insurance
Crisis."   McClure's 33 (June 1909):   184-91.   GC and his
1905-1908 directorship of the Equitable Life Assurance
Society.   Includes several letters.

1627.   "Grover Cleveland's One Business Venture."   Saturday
Evening Post 196 (March 29, 1924):   36-9, 46-54.   GC's
post-presidential insurance career.   Includes several
letters.

1628. Morton, Paul, and Finley, John, et.al.   "Cleveland
Memorial Meeting."   The Association of Life Insurance
Presidents' Proceedings 2 (December 4, 1908):   9-31.
Eulogies of GC emphasizing his post-presidential association

with the insurance industry and letters about GC from
several former Cabinet members.

DEATH

1629. "Grover Cleveland." Outlook 89 (July 4, 1908):
493-4. GC's illness, death, and funeral.

1630. Laird, Archibald. Monuments Marking the Graves of the
Presidents. Quincy, MA: Christopher Publishing House,
1971. A picture of GC's simple monument in Princeton, NJ.
(pp. 154-5)

1631. Wills of the U. S. Presidents. New York:
Communication Channels, 1976. GC's will, some editorial
comments on it, a sketch of his life; and pictures of his
wedding cake box, his trout fly case and flies, and his
spectacles and case. (pp. 141-5)

1632. "Grover Cleveland." New York Times, June 25-27, 1908.
Obituary and allied articles.

1633. Abbott, Lyman. "Grover Cleveland." New York
Genealogical and Biological Record. 39 (October 1908):
237-41. Eulogy which praises GC for his integrity and
courage.

1634. Benton, Joel. "Grover Cleveland: Poem." Independent
65 (July 2, 1908): 11. Eulogistic poem.

1635. Brown, William G. "Cleveland; Poem." Nation 87
(July 2, 1908): 9 Eulogistic poem.

1636. "Grover Cleveland." Harper's Weekly 52 (July 4,
1908): 4, 6, 9. Eulogy; GC's attitude toward Bryan and
Theodore Roosevelt; funeral; March 14, 1908, GC letter.

1637. "Grover Cleveland." Independent 65 (July 2, 1908):
47-8. GC had his weaknesses, but "he would allow no taint
to attach to his service of the State." (p. 48)

1638. "Grover Cleveland." Outlook 89 (July 4, 1908):   503-5.
Eulogistic overview of GC's life.

1639. Harvey, George. "Grover Cleveland." North American
Review 188 (July 1908):   131-6. Eulogy.

1640. McClellan, George B., Jr. "Grover Cleveland."
Outlook 89 (August 22, 1908):   912-9. Eulogy.

1641. Farquhar, Arthur B. "Recollections of Grover
Cleveland." Harper's Weekly 52 (August 1, 1908):   15.   An
intimate's eulogistic recollections of GC.

1642. McKelway, St. Clair. "Grover Cleveland as a Public
Man." American Monthly Review of Reviews 38 (August 1908):
188-90. Eulogy.

1643. "Mr. Cleveland." Nation 87 (July 2, 1908):   4.
Eulogy.

1644. Nelson, Henry Loomis. Revised by Daniel S. Lamont.
"Grover Cleveland." North American Review 188 (August
1908):   161-87. Eulogy arguing that GC was not responsible
for the break-up of the Democratic party.

1645. Peck, Harry Thurston. "Grover Cleveland - Some
Comments and Conclusions." Forum 40 (August 1908):   187-91.
GC alienated many people, but he was great because of his
"high courage and singleness of purpose." (p. 191)

1646. Benton, Joel. "Retrospective Glimpses of Cleveland."
Forum 40 (August 1908):   191-6. Stories about GC's
political independence and courage. A February 3, 1898,
letter, is included.

1647. The Grover Cleveland Memorial, The Eighteenth of
March, in the Year One Thousand Nine Hundred and Nine,
Carnegie Hall and College of the City of New York. New
York: The DeVinne Press, 1910. Memorial service --- many
anecdotes from various times of GC's life.

1648. "Cleveland Memorial Meetings." Outlook 91 (March 27, 1909): 659-60. Synopsis of the two March 18, 1909, New York City GC memorial meetings.

1649. "Cleveland Memorial." Outlook 99 (September 23, 1911): 186-7. The Cleveland Memorial Tower at Princeton University and the subscription campaign to build it.

1650. "Books and Things." New Republic 18 (March 29, 1919): 280. A synopsis of the Cleveland Memorial Meeting at the New Amsterdam Theatre, New York.

16
Personal Life

PERSONALITY TRAITS

1651. Lingley, Charles R. "Official Characteristics of President Cleveland." Political Science Quarterly 33 (June 1918): 255-65. Responsibility, attention to detail, sarcasm, coldness, obstinancy, sternness, courageousness, honesty.

1652. Williams, Jesse Lynch. "Grover Cleveland, Stories By Him, Stories About Him." American Magazine 67 (April 1909): 533-41. GC anecdotes showing his personal side.

1653. Wise, John S. "Man Who Never Talked Politics." Current Literature 45 (September 1908): 350-3. The human side of GC while he was president.

1654. Holt, Henry. Garrulities of an Octogenarian Editor. Boston: Houghton Mifflin, 1923. A GC friend provides some information on GC, e.g., his avoidance of coarseness in telling a story. (p. 224)

1655. Bishop, Joseph B. Notes and Anecdotes of Many Years. New York: Charles Scribner's, 1925. GC's unwavering frankness in all human relations. (pp. 182-6)

1656. Tumulty, Joseph P. Woodrow Wilson As I Know Him. Garden City: Doubleday, Page, 1921. GC's calmness during every one of his election eves. (pp. 223-4)

1657. Pettigrew, Richard F.　Imperial Washington, The Story of American Public Life from 1870-1920.　Chicago:　Charles H. Kerr, 1922.　Reprinted by Arno Press, 1970.　The former South Dakota U.S. Senator says GC had "a naturally perverse disposition" (p. 218) and was a drunk. (p. 220)

1658. Child, Richard W.　"Sh - They Say the President ---." Colliers 79 (February 12, 1927):　8-9, 42.　GC and the false rumor that he drank excessively.

1659. Fuller, Edmund, and Green, David E.　God in the White House:　The Faiths of American Presidents.　New York: Crown, 1968.　GC and religion.　(pp. 148-52)

1660. Thompson, Slason.　Life of Eugene Field, the Poet of Childhood.　New York:　Appleton, 1927.　Several humorous poems about GC, his politics, and his marriage.　(chap. 12)

1661. Hoover, Irwin H. ("Ike").　"Presidents Are People." Saturday Evening Post 206 (March 3, 1934):　16-17, 81-2.　GC told 5 year old FDR not to become president and told Harrison in 1893 he wished Harrison were staying in office. (p. 82)

1662. Taylor, John M.　From the White House Inkwell: American Presidential Autographs.　Rutland, Vermont:　C. E. Tuttle, 1968.　Examples and analysis of GC's handwriting. (pp. 89-92)

HUNTING AND FISHING

1663. Lindop, Edmund.　White House Sportsmen.　Boston: Houghton Mifflin, 1964.　GC, the sportsman.　(pp. 58-61, 75-8)

1664. Jefferson, Eugenie P.　"Biography of a Fishing Reel." Outing 53 (March 1909):　737-46.　GC inherited a friend's fishing reel.　Several GC letters.

1665. Nelson, Henry L. "Days at Gray Gables." Harper's Weekly 36 (July 23, 1892): 697, 700. GC's life and fishing at his Buzzard's Bay summer home.

1666. Putnam, Nina W. "The Day I Went Fishing with Grover Cleveland." Reader's Digest 68 (February 1956): 109-12. A young girl's fishing experience with GC after he talked her out of running away from home.

1667. Sanders, C. W. "Grover Cleveland Goes A-Fishing." Outing 42 (September 1903): 686-90. GC's love of fishing.

1668. Wilson, Calvin Dill. "Our Presidents Out of Doors." Century 77 (March 1909): 699-713. GC's love for fishing. (pp. 709-11).

FAVORITE FOODS

1669. Klapthor, Margaret Brown. The First Ladies' Cook Book: Favorite Recipes of All the Presidents of the United States. New York: Parents' Magazine Press, 1975. GC's favorite foods and social habits. Recipes include "Turban of Chicken Cleveland Style" and "White Cake." Photo of state china from the GC years. (pp. 146-51)

1670. Rysavy, Francois with Frances S. Leighton. A Treasury of White House Cooking. New York: G. P. Putnam, 1972. GC's frequent breakfast menu (p. 75), GC's wedding lunch, and Mr. and Mrs. GC's wedding supper. (pp. 310-1)

1671. Jones, Robert. (comp.) The President's Own White House Cookbook. Chicago: Culinary Arts Institute, 1973. Recipes for GC's braised duck (p. 49) and a cake. (p. 87)

CANCER SURGERY AND HEALTH

1672. Keen, William W. "The Surgical Operations on President Cleveland in 1893." Saturday Evening Post 190 (September 22, 1917): 24-5, 53-5. GC's physician first tells about the cancer surgery on GC during his second term.

1673. ___. The Surgical Operations on President Cleveland in 1893. Philadelphia: Jacobs, 1917. Republication of the magazine article.

1674. ___. "President's Operation; Oral Surgery for Cancer Performed on G. Cleveland." Saturday Evening Post 249 (July/August/September 1977): 106-9. Synopsis of 1917 magazine article.

1675. Dale, Philip M. Medical Biographies: The Ailments of Thirty-Three Famous Persons. Norman: University of Oklahoma Press, 1952. GC's health, particularly his cancer surgery. (pp. 219-26)

1676. Cross, Wilbur, and Moses, John B. "'My God, sir, I think the President is Doomed.'" American History Illustrated 17 (November 1982): 40-5. GC's cancer surgery.

1677. Martin, John Stuart. "When the President Disappeared." American Heritage 8 (October 1957): 10-13, 102-3. GC's 1893 cancer surgery.

1678. Marx, Rudolph. The Health of the Presidents. New York: Putnam, 1961. GC's cancer surgery and minor ailments. (pp. 253-67)

1679. Tobey, James A. "Two American Presidents Who Had Cancer." Hygeia 11 (June 1933): 520-2. GC quickly sought medical advice and lived; Grant did not and died.

1680. Peattie, Donald C. "Grover Cleveland's Heroic Secret." Reader's Digest 71 (October 1957): 129-32. A popular account of GC's cancer surgery.

1681. "Suffering in Silence; Past Leaders Hid Illnesses." Time 126 (July 22, 1985): 27. GC's cancer surgery is briefly synopsized.

1682. Brooks, John; Enterline, Horatio; Apontent, Gonzalo. "The Final Diagnosis of President Cleveland's Lesion." In

_Transactions and Studies of the College of Physicians of
Philadelphia_ 2 (March 1980): 1-25. No trace of syphilis.

1683. "Cancer and the Stock Market." _Survey_ 66 (August 15,
1931): 457. The New Haven Department of Health's retelling
of the GC cancer incident and how secrecy about it prevented
a national financial crisis.

1684. Butler, Francelia. "President Cleveland Scoops the
Press." _American Mercury_ 78 (January 1954): 79-82. The
successful secrecy surrounding GC's 1893 cancer surgery.

1685. Hansen, Richard H. _The Year We Had No President._
Lincoln: University of Nebraska Press, 1962. GC's cancer
surgery. (pp. 46-9, 126)

1686. Wold, Karl C. _Mr President --- How is Your Health?_
St. Paul, MN: Bruce, 1948. GC's cancer surgery, his
rheumatism, and his stomach and heart problems. (chap. 22)

WEDDING

1687. Williams, Francis Howard. _The Bride of the White
House._ Philadelphia: Bradley, 1886. Thirty five page
contemporary account of GC's wedding.

1688. Smith, Marie, and Durbin, Louise. _White House Brides._
Washington: Acropolis Books, 1966. A photograph of Mrs. GC
and reproductions of contemporary press accounts and
sketches. (pp. 104-17)

1689. "The Wedding at the White House." _Public Opinion_ 1
(June 5, 1886): 141-4. Newspaper comments.

1690. Jeffries, Ona Griffin. _In and Out of the White House,
From Washington to the Eisenhowers: An Intimate Glimpse
Into the Social and Domestic Aspects of the Presidential
Life._ New York: W. Funk, 1960. Chap. 22, "Wedding in the
White House," is a brief, excellently illustrated account of
GC's wedding and married life.

1691. "1886 One Hundred Years Ago." American Heritage 37 (June/July 1986): 109-10. Brief account of GC's wedding.

1692. Fairbank, John. China Perceived: Images and Policies in Chinese-American Relations. New York: Alfred A. Knopf, 1974. A photograph of GC's wedding with Chinese commentary about the shocking public appearance of Mrs. GC and other bare necked women.

1693. "Journalism." Public Opinion 1 (June 12, 1886): 173-5. Press reaction to reporters' hounding Mr. and Mrs. GC on their honeymoon.

FRANCES FOLSOM CLEVELAND

1694. Strong, Dennis F. "Frances Folsom Cleveland." In James, Edward T.; James, Janet Wilson; Boyer, Paul S. (eds.) Notable American Women, 1607-1950: A Biographical Dictionary. 3 vols. Cambridge, MA.: Belknap Press of Harvard University, 1971. Excellent biographical sketch.

1695. Caroli, Betty Boyd. First Ladies. New York: Oxford University Press, 1987. Frances Cleveland, one of the 19th century's most popular first ladies, "was the model of simplicity and maturity." (p. 106) This book also includes information on GC's first official hostess, his sister, Rose. (pp. 102-3)

1696. Boller, Paul F., Jr. Presidential Wives. New York: Oxford University Press, 1988. Includes a chapter comprising a biographical sketch and anecdotes about Mrs. GC.

1697. Barzman, Sol. The First Ladies. New York: Cowles, 1970. Biographical sketch. (pp. 198-207)

1698. Bassett, Margaret Byrd. Profiles and Portraits of American Presidents and Their Wives. Introduction by Henry F. Graff. Freeport, ME: B. Wheelwright, 1969. Mrs. GC as a political wife. (pp. 206-18)

1699. Gordon, Lydia L. From First Lady Washington to Mrs. Cleveland. Boston: Lee and Shephard, 1889. Mrs. GC's life to 1889. (pp. 431-48)

1700. Klapthor, Margaret Brown. The First Ladies. Washington: White House Historical Association, 1975. Portraits of Mrs. GC and Rose Cleveland, GC's first White House hostess. (pp. 52-3)

1701. Brown, Margaret W. The Dresses of the First Ladies of the White House. Washington: Smithsonian Institution, 1952. Photos of Mrs. GC and of mannequin wearing her dress. (pp. 102-5)

1702. National Museum of History and Technology. The First Ladies' Hall. Washington: Smithsonian Institution Press, 1973. Photo of dress Mrs. GC wore to GC's second inaugural ball.

1703. Truett, Randle B. First Ladies in Fashion. New York: Hastings House, 1965. Photos and description of a second term Mrs. GC gown. (pp. 54-5)

1704. Lampton, William James. "Mrs. Grover Cleveland as a College Girl." Ladies Home Journal 21 (March 1904): 12. An October 23, 1884, letter talks about GC courting college girl, Frances Folsom.

1705. Frank, Jerome P. "Mrs. Cleveland's White House Autographs Preserved." Publisher's Weekly 220 (July 3, 1981): 128. Autograph book, gift of noted authors, for her support of 1888 copyright law.

1706. "Anecdotal Side of Mrs. Cleveland." Ladies Home Journal 15 (June 1898): 1, and Review of Reviews 17 (June 1898): 745. Several stores about Mrs. GC's concern for average people and about Princeton being a good place to marry off her daughters.

1707. Thomas, Katherine E. "Day in the Life of Mrs. Grover Cleveland." Harper's Bazaar 29 (May 9, 1896): 402, 414-5. Life in the White House. Includes photo of Mrs. GC and baby.

1708. Hoover, Irwin H. ("Ike") "Mrs. Cleveland Weeps." Edited by W. Stout. Saturday Evening Post 206 (March 10, 1934): 16-17, 46, 50. Life in the White House. She cried on leaving in 1897.

1709. Crook, W. H. Memories of the White House. Compiled and edited by Henry Rood. Boston: Little Brown, 1911. GC's family life in the White House with special emphasis on Mrs. GC. (chap. 6)

1710. Lucas, Mildred K. "Among Those Present; First Congress of Mothers." PTA Magazine 57 (February 1963): 17. Mrs. GC hosted a February 1897 meeting of the forerunner of the modern Parents-Teachers Association.

1711. "Mrs. Cleveland's Inherent Courtesy." Ladies Home Journal 20 (March 1903): 6. Mrs. GC saved a reporter's job by giving her an interview.

1712. Gerlinger, Irene. Mistresses of the White House: Narrator's Tale of a Pageant of First Ladies. New York: French, 1950. Sentimental biographical sketch. (pp. 70-3)

1713. Hendrick, Burton J. The Life of Andrew Carnegie. 2 vols. Garden City, NY: Doubleday, Doran, 1922. GC would not accept Carnegie's offer of financial support in the post-presidential years, but Carnegie did remember Mrs. GC in his will.

1714. U.S. Congress. Senate Committee on Pensions. 61st Congress, 2nd Session. . . . Frances F. Cleveland and Mary Lord Harrison . . . Report No. 506 [To Accompany S. 124]. Washington: Government Printing Office, 1910. Majority and minority opinions, both favorable, on the bill to grant pensions to GC's and Benjamin Harrison's widows.

1715. "Mrs. Grover Cleveland." American Magazine 69 (November 1909): 64-9. Mrs. GC one year after GC's death.

1716. Selden, Charles A. "Six White House Wives and Widows." Ladies Home Journal 44 (June 1927): 18-19. GC as a father and husband and his widow's life after his death.

1717. "Preston, Frances Folsom Cleveland." Obituary. New York _Times,_ October 30, 1947, p. 25, col. 1. She remarried after GC's 1908 death.

FAMILY

1718. Tucker, Robert W. _The Descendants of the Presidents._ Charlotte, NC: Delmar, 1975. GC's descendants to the fifth generation. (pp. 131-2)

1719. Quinn, Sandra L., and Kanter, Sanford. _America's Royalty: All the President's Children._ Westport, CT: Greenwood, 1983. Brief sketches of each of GC's five children and one illegitimate child. (chap.18)

1720. Sadler, Christine. _Children in the White House._ New York: Putnam, 1967. GC's wedding, his children, and their later lives. (pp. 203-11)

1721. Perling, Joseph J. _President's Sons: The Prestige of Names in a Democracy._ New York: Odyssey, 1947. Richard and Francis Cleveland. (chap. 14)

SOCIAL LIFE

1722. Smith, Marie D. _Entertaining in the White House._ Rev. ed. New York: Macfadden-Bartell, 1970. Social life of Mr. and Mrs. GC in the White House. (chap. 14)

1723. Buel, Charles Clough. "Our Fellow-Citizen of the White House." _Century_ 53 (n.s. 31) (March 1897): 642-64. GC as the prime example of late 19th century presidents' lives in the White House.

1724. Carpenter, Frances. (ed.) Carp's Washington.   New York: McGraw-Hill, 1960. Columns from the 1882-1888 Cleveland Leader including "The Clevelands in the White House."

1725. Furman, Bess. White House Profile: A Social History of the White House, Its Occupants and Its Festivities. Indianapolis: Bobbs-Merrill, 1951. GC is discussed in chapters 12 and 13.

1726. Kirk, Elise K. Music at the White House: A History of the American Spirit. Urbana: University of Illinois Press, 1986. Mrs. GC played a particularly important role in supporting music in the GC White House. (pp. 138-46)

1727. Nelson, Henry L. "Grover Cleveland at Home." Harper's Weekly 36 (July 2, 1892): 625, 630. A disappointingly general account.

1728. Colman, Edna M. White House Gossip From Andrew Johnson to Calvin Coolidge. Garden City: Doubleday Page, 1927. A sketchy account of GC's personal and social life. (chaps. 7, 9)

1729. "Anecdotes of President Cleveland." Century 85 (March 1913): 800. GC and visitors, his cabinet, his wife and children.

HOMES

1730. "Mr. Cleveland's Private Residence in Washington." Harper's Weekly 37 (March 4, 1893): 208-9. Photos and descriptions of the White House interior and GC's private residence three blocks away.

1731. Harlow, Louis K. At Gray Gables and Walk Along the Shore of Buzzard's Bay . . . . New York: Turk, 1895. Color paintings and description of the area where GC had a summer home.

1732. Christie, Trevor L. "Cleveland on the Cape."
Saturday Review 52 (March 8, 1969): 56, 58. GC at his
summer home at Buzzard's Bay, Cape Cod.

1733. Lewis, Henry H. "Visit to the Home of Ex-President
Cleveland." Woman's Home Companion 31 (September 1904):
12-3, 47. Anecdotes about GC at home and description of
"Westland," his Princeton retirement home.

1734. "Mr. Cleveland's Future Home." Harper's Weekly 40
(December 12, 1896): 1226-7. GC's Princeton home.

HISTORICAL SITES

1735. Eastman, John. Who Lived Where: A Biographical Guide
to Homes and Museums. New York: Facts on File, 1983.
Lists all GC's residences from birth to death including the
Cleveland Birthplace State Historic Site, 207 Bloomfield
Avenue, Caldwell, New Jersey.

17
Historiographical Materials

1736. Blodgett, Geoffrey. "The Political Leadership of Grover Cleveland." South Atlantic Quarterly 82 (Summer 1983): 288-99. "Cleveland's constant search for ways of asserting his personal and public integrity (often at direct cost to the fortunes of the Democratic party) was what enabled him to leave the presidency a more powerful office in 1897 than he found it in 1885." (p. 291)

1737. Bradford, Gamaliel. "Grover Cleveland." Atlantic Monthly 126 (November 1920): 654-64. GC could say no, but he left no enduring positive achievements.

1738. American Portraits 1875-1900. Boston: Houghton Mifflin, 1922. Chapter 6 concludes that "it was as a suberb negative force acting for a great positive purpose [that] Grover Cleveland did his work in the world." (p. 170)

1739. DeSantis, Vincent P. "Grover Cleveland--Another Look." Hayes Historical Journal 3 (Spring-Fall 1980): 41-50. GC is still rated a great president not for his accomplishments, but for his "independence and courage." (p. 49)

1740. ___. "Grover Cleveland." In Morton Borden. (ed.) America's Ten Greatest Presidents. Chicago: Rand McNally, 1961; Reprint in 1971 as America's Eleven Greatest Presidents. GC had definite weaknesses, but he was the best of the Gilded Age politicians.

1741. Eggert, Gerald G. "I Have Tried So Hard to Do Right."
American History Illustrated 12 (January 1978):   10-23.
GC's dying words exemplified his life.

1742. Kelley, Robert. "Presbyterianism, Jacksonianism and
Grover Cleveland." American Quarterly 18 (Winter 1966):
615-36. GC's "career embodied the paradoxes not only of
Presbyterianism, but of the Jacksonian world view." He
devoted himself "to only a few large and essentially
negative goals." (p. 635)

1743. ___. The Transatlantic Persuasion: The
Liberal-Democratic Mind in the Age of Gladstone. New York:
Alfred A. Knopf, 1969. Chapter 8, "Grover Cleveland: The
Democrat As Social Moralist," argues that GC shared
international classic Liberal-Democratic principles with
Gladstone and other British Empire politicians.

1744. Kent, Frank R. The Democratic Party, A History. New
York: Century, 1928. GC is praised in this dated book.
(chaps. 20-3)

1745. Masters, Edgar Lee. "Grover Cleveland." American
Mercury 8 (August 1926): 385-97. This famous American
writer calls GC "one of the first and perhaps the most
notable character of modern American statesmanship." (p.
385)

1746. Nevins, Allan. "Grover Cleveland: An Ill-Appreciated
Personality." American Scholar 3 (Spring 1934): 133-43.
GC's "unyielding moral courage" that "made him great was the
result of "his fine conscientiousness, his warm sensibility,
and his innate religious feeling." (p. 143)

1747. Northrup, Cyrus. "Three Great Presidents." In
Addresses, Educational and Patriotic. Minneapolis: H. W.
Wilson, 1909, 321-45. The former President of the
University of Minnesota compares GC to Lincoln and Theodore
Roosevelt because of his integrity and steadfastness.

1748. Parker, George F. "Grover Cleveland: Estimate of His
Character and Work." Saturday Evening Post 197 (October 25,
1924): 112-22. Highly favorable analysis, for example

calling the 1887 tariff message "the most influential declaration ever made in time of peace by any man in our history." (p. 122)

1749. Rhodes, James Ford. "Cleveland's Administrations." Scribner's Monthly 50 (October, November 1911): 496-504, 602-12. GC was a great president.

1750. Robertson, Pearl L. "Grover Cleveland As a Political Leader." Ph.D. diss., University of Chicago, 1937. An early "psycho-history" which concludes that despite his weaknesses he achieved "a height of pragmatic success that few American political leaders have achieved." (p. 288)

1751. Ross, Earle D. "Grover Cleveland and the Beginning of an Era of Reform." South Atlantic Quarterly 18 (April 1919): 156-66. GC's main contribution was his inauguration of an era of reform after years of political corruption.

1752. Rutland, Robert A. The Democrats From Jefferson to Carter. Baton Rouge: Louisiana State University Press, 1979. "Cleveland: Honest and Lucky." (chap. 6)

1753. Sater, Lowry F. Grover Cleveland; A Paper Read Before the Kit-Kat Club on February 28, 1922. Columbus: Warner P. Simpson, 1924. GC had courage and integrity and convinced people that the election of a Democrat did not endanger the results of the Civil War.

1754. Sievers, Harry J. (ed.) Six Presidents from the Empire State. Tarrytown, NY: Sleepy Hollow Restorations, 1974. Vincent P. DeSantis praises GC for strengthening the presidency through his negative actions. Mark Hirsch agrees.

1755. Smith, Rembert. "If Cleveland Came Back Now." National Republic 24 (October 1936): 12, 18. GC was correct when he said that "It is not the duty of the government to support the people, but the duty of the people to support the government."

1756. White, William Allen. "Cleveland." McClure's 18
(February 1902): 322-30. This famous newsman says GC was
colorless, but he will remain "the symbol of a national
aspiration toward public virtue." (p. 330)

1757. ___. Masks In A Pageant. New York: Macmillan, 1928.
In chapters 9-12, the author argues that "From 1885 to 1889
Cleveland was an obstructionist; from 1893 to 1897 he was a
militant obstructionist. . . ." (p. 133)

1758. Wilson, Woodrow. "Mr. Cleveland as President."
Atlantic Monthly 79 (March 1897): 289-300, and Review of
Reviews 15 (March 1897): 327. A future president calls GC
"the greatest personality" in American politics since
Abraham Lincoln. (p. 300)

1759. Workmaster, Wallace F. "Grover Cleveland: American
Victorian." Historian 22 (February 1960): 185-96. GC
displayed "stubborn adherence" to the Victorian virtues of
"principle, individual example, family, public morality,
religion, and humanitarianism." (p. 196)

BRIEF EVALUATIONS

1760. Angoff, Charles. "Review of Letters of Grover
Cleveland. Edited by A. Nevins." American Mercury 31
(March 1934): 374-6. This is actually a critical
evaluation of GC.

1761. Bailey, Thomas A. Presidential Greatness: The Image
and the Man from George Washington to the Present. New
York: Appleton-Century-Crofts, 1966. If GC "was the ablest
President between Lincoln and Theodore Roosevelt, the others
must have been an indifferent lot indeed." (pp. 300-2)

1762. ___. Presidential Saints and Sinners. New York:
Free Press, 1981. GC was straightforwardly honest even when
it served him politically ill. (chaps. 21, 23)

1763. ___. The Pugnacious Presidents: White House Warriors on Parade. New York: Free Press, 1980. Chapters 22 and 24 discuss GC's combativeness, ranking him "as one of the most combative of the Presidents." (p. 297)

1764. Balch, Thomas W. "The Trend Toward Centralization." American Antiquarian Society Proceedings n.s. 35 (Part 2, 1926): 253-71. Praises GC for his hard money and decentralized government philosophy. (pp. 261-7)

1765. Barney, William L. The Passage of the Republic, An Interdisciplinary History of Nineteenth-Century America. Lexington, MA.: D. C. Heath, 1987. GC was an inept stubborn defender of the status quo during a period of rapid social, economic, and political change.

1766. "Centenary." Nation 144 (March 20, 1937): 311. Urges Democrats to celebrate the 100th anniversay of GC's birth because he was a "curious blend of courageous reformer and the diehard conservative."

1767. DeSantis, Vincent P. The Shaping of Modern America: 1877-1916. Boston: Allyn and Bacon, 1973. GC was less a reformer and more an unimaginative conservative.

1768. Dobson, John M. Politics in the Gilded Age: A New Perspective on Reform. New York: Praeger, 1972. Emphasizes GC's major role in reform.

1769. Goldman, Eric. Rendezvous with Destiny. New York: Knopf, 1952. There were limits to GC's liberalism. (pp. 39-40)

1770. Green, Thomas M., and Pederson, William D. "The Behavior of Lawyer-Presidents: A 'Barberian' Link." Presidential Studies Quarterly 15 (Spring 1985): 343-52. GC was an "active-passive" president, his lawyer background being one reason for this trait. (pp. 348-9)

1771. Hofstadter, Richard. The American Political Tradition and the Men Who Made It. New York: Knopf, 1948. GC was an honest man "who gave to the interests what many a lesser politician might have sold them for a price." (p. 182)

1772. McGerr, Michael E. The Decline of Popular Politics:
The American North, 1865-1928. New York: Oxford University
Press, 1986. GC's political career meshed with the appeal
to anti-party politics which helped kill the popular
partisan politics of the 19th century.

1773. Mencken, H. L. "A Good Man in a Bad Trade: Book
Review of Grover Cleveland, A Study in Courage by Allan
Nevins." American Mercury 28 (January 1933): 125-7. This
leading American cynic positively evaluates GC and this book
about him.

1774. Milton, George Fort. The Use of Presidential Power,
1789-1943. Boston: Little Brown, 1944. GC's use of
presidential powers was "the starting point for much of the
authority exerted by Presidents since." (p. 172)

1775. Rhodes, James Ford. "Presidential Office."
Scribner's 33 (February 1903): 157-73. GC made an
important stamp on the presidency despite his failure as a
party leader. (pp. 165-7)

1776. Tugwell, Rexford G. The Enlargement of the
Presidency. Garden City: Doubleday, 1960. GC "was a
strong man as he was also a strong President." (p. 251)

1777. Williams, R. Hal. "'Dry Bones and Dead Language':
The Democratic Party." In H. Wayne Morgan. (ed.) The Gilded
Age: An Age in Need of Reinterpretation. Rev. ed.
Syracuse: Syracuse University Press, 1970, 129-48. GC
reflected the "sterility of the Democratic ideal of negative
government." (p. 147)

PRESIDENTIAL RATINGS

1778. Schlesinger, Arthur M. "Historians Rate United States
Presidents." Life 25 (November 25, 1948): 65-8, 73-4. The
most famous rating of American presidents ranked GC number
8, among the "Near Great."

1779. ___. "Our Presidents: A Rating by Seventy-Five Historians." New York Times Magazine (July 29, 1962): 12-13, 40-3. GC is ranked number 11, among the "Near Great," in this updating of the author's 1948 poll.

1780. Rossiter, Clinton. "The Presidents and the Presidency." American Heritage 7 (April 1956): 28-33, 94-5. GC is ranked number 8, at the top of the "Near Great."

1781. Sokolsky, Eric. Our Seven Greatest Presidents. New York: Exposition, 1964. GC is ranked "Very Good (Near Great)."

1782. Bailey, Thomas A. Presidential Greatness. New York: Appleton-Century, 1966. GC is ranked number 15, "Average."

1783. Kynerd, Tom. "An Analysis of Presidential Greatness and 'President Rating.'" Southern Quarterly 9 (April 1971): 309-29. An analysis of previous presidential evaluation polls. GC does well in each.

1784. Maranell, Gary M. "The Evaluation of Presidents: An Extension of the Schlesinger Polls." Journal of American History 57 (June 1970): 104-13. GC continued to be ranked in the upper third.

1785. Murray, Robert, and Blessing, Tim. "The Presidential Performance Study: A Progress Report." Journal of American History 70 (December 1983): 535-55. The most recent presidential poll lists GC as an "above average" president, a drop from earlier evaluations.

BIBLIOGRAPHIES

1786. Goehlert, Robert U., and Martin, Fenton S. (eds.) The Presidency, A Research Guide. Santa Barbara: ABC-Clio Information Services, 1985. Helpful for locating information on GC and his era.

1787. Davison, Kenneth E. The American Presidency: A Guide to Information Sources. Volume 11 in the American Studies Information Guide Series. Detroit: Gale, 1983. Includes four pages on GC.

1788. U.S. Library of Congress. General Reference and Bibliography Division. The Presidents of the U.S., 1789-1962: A Selected List of References. Compiled by Donald H. Mugridge. Washington: Government Printing Office, 1963. A dated short list of references on GC. (pp. 105-7)

1789. Miles, William. The Image Makers: A Bibliography of American Presidential Campaign Biographies. Metuchen, NJ: Scarecrow, 1979. Includes GC biographies.

1790. An Index to the Presidential Election Campaign Biographies, 1824-1972. Ann Arbor: University Microfilms International, 1981. Includes GC biographies. (pp. 58-9)

1791. Vexler, Robert I. (ed.) Grover Cleveland, 1837-1908: Chronology - Documents - Bibliographical Aids. Presidential Chronologies Series. Dobbs Ferry, NY: Oceana Publications, 1968. A collection of documents with a brief bibliography section.

1792. DeSantis, Vincent P. "The Political Life of the Gilded Age: A Review of Recent Literature." History Teacher 9 (November 1975): 73-86. GC's reputation has gone from the favorable one of Nevins to the critical one of Merrill. (pp. 85-6)

1793. Freitag, Ruth S. Presidential Inaugurations: A Selected List of References. Third rev. ed. Washington: Government Printing Office, 1969. Available sources on GC's inaugurations. (pp. 117-21)

1794. Benjamin, Mary A. The Presidents: A Survey of Autograph Values, 1965. New York: W. R. Benjamin, 1965. GC letters are fairly common, and there is little demand for them. (pp. 24-5)

INDEXES AND GUIDES

1795. Ames, John Griffith. Comprehensive Index to the
Publications of the United States Government, 1881-1893.   2
vols. Washington: Government Printing Office, 1905.
Includes information on government documents from GC's first
term.

1796. Blandford, Linda A. and Evans, Patricia Russell (eds.)
Supreme Court of the United States, 1789-1980: An Index to
Opinions Arranged by Justice. 2 vols. Millwood, NY:
Kraus, 1983.

1797. CIS U.S. Congressional Committee Hearings Index.
Washington: Congressional Information Service, 1985.

1798. CIS U.S. Congressional Committee Prints Index.
Washington: Congressional Information Service, 1980.

1799. Jacob, Kathryn A., and Hornyak Elizabeth A. Guide to
Research Collections of Former United States Senators,
1789-1982. Washington: Historical Office, United States
Senate, 1983.

1800. Kavas, Igor I., and Michael, Mark A. (comps.) United
States Treaties and Other International Agreements,
Cumulative Index, 1776-1949. Buffalo: William S. Stein,
1975.

1801. Lester, Daniel, and Faull, Sandra. (comps.)
Cumulative Title Index to United States Public Documents,
1789-1976. Arlington, Virginia: United States Historical
Documents Institute, 1978.

1802. Kanley, Edna A. (ed.) Cumulative Subject Index to the
Monthly Catalog of U. S. Government Publications, 1895-1899.
2 vols. Arlington, VA: Carrollton Press, 1978.

1803. Lord, Clifford, L. (ed.) List and Index of
Presidential Executive Orders, Unnumbered Series. Newark:
Historical Records Survey, 1943.

1804. McClendon, Walter H., and Gilbert, Wilfred C. (comps.) Index to the Federal Statutes, 1874-1931. Washington: Government Printing Office, 1933.

1805. Slocum, Robert B. Biographical Dictionaries and Related Works: An International Bibliography of Collective Biographies, Bio-Bibliographies, Collections of Epitaphs, Selected Genealogical Works, Dictionaries, Biographical Materials in Government Manuals, Bibliographies of Biography, Biographical Indexes, and Selected Portrait Catalogs. Detroit: Gale Research Company, 1967. Includes GC and other leading personalities of his time.

1806. Checklist of United States Public Documents, 1789-1945. Arlington, VA: United States Historical Documents Institute, 1978. The most comprehensive bibliography of government documents.

1807. U.S. Superintendent of Documents. Monthly Catalogue of United States Publications. Washington: Government Printing Office, 1895 to present.

HISTORIC SITE

1808. Cleveland Birthplace State Historic Site. 207 Bloomfield Avenue, Caldwell, New Jersey.

18
Iconography of Grover Cleveland

Because photography was well advanced by the time of his presidency, there are many photographs available of Grover Cleveland. Both the Library of Congress and the Princeton University Library, for example, have significant collections of Cleveland likenesses. Almost every book and article written by or directly about Cleveland contains photographs. [1809.] William Coolidge Lane and Nina E. Browne (eds.), A.L.A. Portrait Index Washington: Government Printing Office, 1906, contains a listing of some of the Cleveland likenesses appearing in books and articles. The following is a suggestive list of more recent sources for photographs of Cleveland and Frances Folsom Cleveland, his wife.

1810. American Heritage Pictorial History of the Presidents of the United States. New York: Simon and Schuster, 1968. Photographs, cartoons, and basic facts about GC. (pp. 552-75)

1811. Barclay, Barbara. Lamps to Light the Way: Our Presidents. Presidential Portraits by Celeste Swayne-Courtney. Glendale, CA: Bowmar, 1970. Collection of photographs and sketches of GC and his presidency. (pp. 227-35)

1812. Bassett, Margaret Boyd. Profiles and Portraits of American Presidents and Their Wives. Introduction by Henry F. Graff. New York: McKay, 1976. A brief sketch of GC's life and a David Bacharach photograph of him. (pp. 58-60)

1813. "Builders of America; Picture: Grover Cleveland."
Scholastic 46 (April 9, 1945): 23. A five panel cartoon
view of the GC presidency.

1814. "Cleveland in His Hours of Ease." Harper's Weekly 51
(June 8, 1907): 842-3. Two pages of photographs of GC, his
family, and his Princeton home.

1815. "Ex-President Grover Cleveland." World's Work 5
(December 1902): opposite p. 2813. A photograph of GC in
academic cap and gown.

1816. Ferris, Robert G. (ed.) The Presidents . . . Historic
Places Commemorating the Chief Executives of the United
States. Washington: U.S. Department of the Interior,
National Park Service, 1977. Includes portrait of GC and
photographs of his second inaugural and his young family.
(pp. 473-5)

1817. Grosvenor, Charles H. The Book of the Presidents.
Washington: Continental Press, 1902. A Sarony of New York
photograph and a biographical sketch of GC. (pp. 96-102)

1818. "Grover Cleveland." Engraving by Henry B. Hall, Jr.
In Hayward and Blanche Cirker (eds.) Dictionary of American
Portraits. New York: Dover, 1967. (no. 120)

1819. Isely, Bliss. The Presidents: Men of Faith. Boston:
W. A. Wilde Co., 1953. Includes an Eastman Johnson portrait
and a brief chronology of GC. (pp. 170-7)

1820. Jensen, Amy LaFollette. The White House and Its
Thirty-Five Families. Rev. ed. New York: McGraw-Hill,
1971. Photographs of GC, his wife, and scenes from the
White House of that period.

1821. Jones, Cranston. Homes of the American Presidents.
New York: McGraw-Hill, 1962. Photographs of several of
GC's homes, his family and a sketch of his post-presidential
life. (pp. 144-7)

1822. Lockwood, Wilton. "Portrait." International Studio
31 (June 1907): Sup. 111; 32 (October 1907): Sup. 268.
The same portrait of GC appears in both issues.

1823. Madigan, Thomas F. A. A Catalogue of Autographs. New
York: T. F. Madigan, n.d. A list and brief description of
GC and Mrs. GC letters and portraits for sale. (pp. 16-17)

1824. Milhollen, Hirst D., and Kaplan, Milton. Presidents
on Parade. New York: Macmillan, 1948. A series of
photographs and drawings of and about GC including a
striking one in a hunting camp.

1825. Miller, Lillian B.; Cox, Beverly J.; Voss, Frederick
S.; Hussey, Jeanette M.; and King, Judith S. "If Elected
. . .": Unsuccessful Candidates for the Presidency
1796-1968. Washington: Smithsonian Institution Press,
1972. Catalogue for National Portrait Gallery exhibit which
includes a portrait of GC and some campaign memorabilia.
(pp. 264-7)

1826. Patrick, Sam J. The Presidents: Washington to
Reagan. New York: Greenwich House, 1984. A true to life
illustration of GC is located on p. 53.

1827. "Portrait." Harper's Monthly 125 (October 1912):
772. Photograph of Mrs. GC which she presented to the
family of Mark Twain.

1828. Post, Robert C. (ed.) Every Four Years. Washington:
Smithsonian Exposition Books, 1980. A color portrait of GC
and other illustrations.

1829. White House Gallery of Official Portraits of the
Presidents. New York: The Gravure Company of America,
1907. An April 1891 E. Johnson portrait of GC.

1830. Whitney, David C. The Graphic Story of the American
Presidents. Edited by Thomas C. Jones. Chicago: J. G.
Ferguson, 1975. A collection of photographs and sketches
from the GC presidency. Particularly interesting are
photographs of Mrs. GC and cabinet wives and Mrs. GC and
sculptor Augustus Saint-Gaudens.

1831. Willard, Frances. A Woman of the Century. Buffalo:
Charles Wells Moulton, 1893. Includes photographs of GC's
sister, Rose, and Mrs. GC.

1832. Zorn, Anders L. "Portrait." International Studio 12
(November 1900): Sup 3, 5. Etchings of GC and Mrs. GC.

1833. ___. "Portrait." Mentor 16 (October 1928): 48. A
full length portrait of Mrs. Thomas J. Preston, Jr., the
former Mrs. GC.

Periodicals

Alabama Review
Americana
Americas
American Bar Association Journal
American Heritage
American Historical Review
American History Illustrated
American Journal of International Law
American Journal of Legal History
American Journal of Politics
American Magazine
American Mercury
American Monthly Review of Reviews
American Neptune
American Quarterly
American Scholar
American Antiquarian Society Proceedings
Arena
Arkansas Historical Quarterly
Asian Forum
Atlantic Monthly

Bay State Monthly
Bookman
Buffalo Historical Society Publications
Business History Review

Canadian Historical Review
Century
Charities
Chronicles of Oklahoma
Church History
Colby Library Quarterly

Colliers
Congressional Studies
Connecticut Historical Society Bulletin
Contemporary Review
Cosmopolitan
Country Calendar
Critic
Current History
Current Literature

Duquesne Review

Eclectic Magazine
Essex Institute Historical Collections

Filson Club History Quarterly
Fortnightly Review
Forum

Georgia Historical Quarterly
Gunton's Magazine

Harper's Weekly
Harper's Monthly
Harvard Graduates' Magazine
Hayes Historical Journal
Hispanic American Historical Review
Historian
Historical Reflections
History Teacher
History Today
Hygeia

Illustrated American
Independent
Indiana Social Studies Quarterly
International Studio

Jefferson County West Virginia Historical Society Magazine
Journal of American Culture
Journal of American History
Journal of Church and State
Journal of Economic History
Journal of Education
Journal of Forest History

Journal of the Illinois State Historical Society
Journal of Mississippi History
Journal of Political Economy
Journal of Political Science
Journal of Politics
Journal of Popular Culture
Journal of Social History
Journalism Quarterly

Labor History
Labor Law Journal
Ladies Home Journal
Leslie's Weekly
Life
Lippincott

Macmillan
Massachusetts Historical Society Proceedings
McClure's
Medical Library Association Bulletin
Mentor
Michigan History
Mid-America
Military Affairs
Mississippi Quarterly
Mississippi Valley Historical Review
Missouri Historical Review
Missouri Historical Society Bulletin
Montreal University Magazine
Munsey

Nation
National Monthly
National Republic
National Review
Nebraska History
New England Historical and Genealogical Register
New Republic
New York Genealogical and Biological Record
New York Historical Society Quarterly
New York History
New York Public Library Bulletin
New York Times Magazine
Niagara Frontier
Nineteenth Century
North American Review
North Carolina Historical Review
North Dakota Quarterly
Northwest Ohio Quarterly

Outing
Outlook

Pacific Historical Review
Pacific Monthly
Pacific Northwest Quarterly
Political Science Quarterly
Presidential Studies Quarterly
Princeton Alumni Weekly
Princeton University Library Chronicle
PTA Magazine
Public Opinion
Publishers Weekly
Putnams

Quarterly Review of Historical Studies [India]

Readers' Digest
Register of the Kentucky Historical Society
Review of Politics
Review of Reviews

Saturday Evening Post
Saturday Review
Scholastic
Science & Society
Scribner's
Smithsonian
Social Economist
Social Science Journal
South Atlantic Quarterly
Southern Quarterly
Spectator
State Service
Studies in History and Society
Survey

Time
Transactions and Studies of the College of Physicians of
    Philadelphia

Virginia Magazine of History and Biography

Wall Street Journal

West Georgia College Studies in the Social Studies
West Virginia History
Western Political Quarterly
Wisconsin Magazine of History
Woman's Home Companion
World's Work

Yankee
Youth's Companion

Index to Authors

Index to Subjects

Abbott, Lawrence F., 941
Abolitionism, 1546
Adams, Charles Francis, 1102
Adams, Charles Francis, Jr., 1364
Adams, Henry, 872
Adams, Henry C., 1453
Africa, 764, 982
Alabama, 1093, 1157
Alaska, 985
Alaskan Boundary Dispute, 992-93, 1002, 1359
Albany (NY) Argus, 437
Albany (NY) Evening Journal, 438
Aldrich, Nelson W., 1015
Altgeld, John Peter, 134-42, 1186-90
Angell, James B., 1453
Anglophobia, 676, 973
Anti-imperialism, 127, 1243-44, 1247, 1273-1314, 1335, 1389,
    1436, 1497, 1525
Apgar, E. K., 649
Argentina, 780-81, 1262
Armenians, 1270
Army, 1183, 1198-1202
Arthur, Chester A., 963, 965
Astrology, 1119
Atkins, John D. C., 1463
Atlanta Constitution, 439
Atlanta Exposition (1895), 1230-33
Attorney General, 728
Australia, 980, 1268

Baltimore American, 440
Baltimore News, 123
Baltimore Sun, 441
Bank directors, GC on, 579